FEAST WITHOUT FUSS

PAMELA HARLECH

FEAST
WITHOUT
FUSS

New York

ATHENEUM

1977

Library of Congress Cataloging in Publication Data

Harlech, Pamela.
  Feast without fuss.
  Includes index.
  1. Cookery. I. Title.
TX652.H37 1977   641.5   77-3559
ISBN 0-689-10787-0

Designed by Kathleen Carey
First Edition

To David, and the two Virginias

———————————

To order dinner is a matter of invention and combination. It involves novelty, simplicity and taste; whereas, in the generality of dinners, there is no character but that of routine according to the season.

Original, by Mr. WALTERS

ACKNOWLEDGMENTS

I would like to thank my mother, who, although she does not cook herself, knows about the chemistry of food and in whose house I learned to appreciate good food; my father, who taught me about wine; my husband, who shares my love of food and who has been a patient and appreciative guinea pig; all my friends who have encouraged my gastronomic experiments and thus this book; Mrs. Sylvia Guirey and Comtesse Sheila de Rochambeau, both of whom helped teach me to cook many years ago, and all the kind people who have allowed me to publish their recipes.

Special thanks must go to Beatrix Miller and Barbara Tims of British *Vogue*, both of whom read the typescript and suggested alterations; to Philien Mantel, who typed and typed through all the material; to Fiona Charlton-Dewar for helping with the timing and experimentation, and to Judith Kern, who gave me valuable editorial help.

The following recipes are reproduced by kind permission of Condé Nast Publications Ltd.—Miss Fleur Cowles's Jerusalem artichoke soup; Mrs. John Hay Whitney's oyster stew; Madame Jacques de

Beaumarchais's *oeufs chimay;* the Earl of Gowrie's *oeufs en cocotte* with duck jelly; Mrs. Anthony Lund's *taramasalata;* Mrs. Rory McEwen's avocado and caviar mousse; Peter Coats's Mr. Briggs's avocado ramekin; Baroness Dacre's curried melon and shrimp; Mrs. Arthur Schlesinger's spinach quiche; Lady Elizabeth von Hofmannsthal's poached bass; Fiona Charlton-Dewar's *kedgeree;* the Honorable Mrs. James Ogilvy's deviled pheasant; Anthony West's good chicken recipe; Mrs. Jeanette de Rothschild's special stuffing; the Earl of Gowrie's cold steak au poivre; Derek Hart's stew; Mrs. Ralph F. Colin's baked Virginia ham; Mrs. Anthony Lewis's veal goulash; Anthony West's veal roast; Anthony West's kidneys in cream and Calvados; Madame Sergio Corrêa da Costa's pistachio soufflé; Mrs. Anthony Lewis's ginger soufflé; Madame Sergio Corrêa da Costa's crêpes Copacabana; Lady Victoria Waymouth's burnt ice cream; Mrs. Jeanette de Rothschild's melon and blackberries; Mrs. Ralph F. Colin's lemon meringue pie; the Countess of Drogheda's eggplant with crab meat; Mrs. Mark Littman's ham jambalaya; Lady Victoria Waymouth's cheese pudding; Derek Hart's salad; Mrs. Gordon Douglas III's apricot nut bread; Mrs. Ralph F. Colin's chocolate cake; Fiona Charlton-Dewar's mocha cake; Mrs. Mark Mainwaring's gingerbread; Mrs. Anthony Hambro's Creole jam; Mrs. Anthony Hambro's three-fruits jam; Mrs. Anthony Hambro's liqueur à l'orange.

CONTENTS

THE RECIPES

FEAST
WITHOUT
FUSS

INTRODUCTION

In 1884 Mrs. Henderson wrote *Practical Cooking and Dinner Giving*. Many instructions in her good book might be thought old-fashioned and out of date today, but two pieces of advice are eternal —these I pass on to the reader.

1. Never attempt a new dish with company—one that you are not entirely sure of having cooked in the very best manner.

2. Care must be taken about selecting a company for a dinner party, for upon this depends the success of the entertainment. Always put the question to yourself when making up a dinner party. Why do I ask him or her? And unless the answer be satisfactory, leave him or her out. Invite them on some other occasion. If they are not sensible, sociable, unaffected and clever people, they will not only not contribute to the agreeability of the dinner, but will positively be a serious impediment to conversational inspiration and the general feeling of ease. Consequently, one may consider it a compliment to be invited to a dinner party.

The first point speaks for itself. I never make a new dish for friends unless I have made it first for my husband and myself. Although a recipe may be well written, tried and tested, nothing is foolproof, and one must take into account the cook's individuality. I often find that I prefer more herbs and seasoning, for example, than specified. But the best reason for trying it first is that almost any recipe takes longer the first time you make it. Thus you can get into an awful panic if time is suddenly running out, and the meal hasn't been finished: chaos and a badly cooked meal result, just what this book is meant to help the reader to avoid.

The second point is simple sense. In these days when everything is so expensive and we have less and less time to relax, it seems to me that time should be spent with those whom one likes and with whom one enjoys a good meal and good talk. Certainly some people must entertain for business reasons, but thankfully economic reasons have made this less prevalent. Happily, I have had to do it rarely: we only have people to lunch, dinner or for the weekend with whom we enjoy being—to talk, to laugh. And we take great pains to invite people who will enjoy one another's company—if they have never met but would be interested in each other, that is an added pleasure.

There are those who think that good cooking necessitates extravagance. Often bad planning is the real extravagance—the haphazard choosing of food, and the waste of it in cooking. The basis of good cooking is *good* material. One economy is to eat only what is in season. To wait is to increase your pleasure as well as to spare your purse. June strawberries will have lost a great deal of their delight if you have anticipated them with their expensive imported or hothouse forerunners.

The use of good butter or good oil often makes the chief difference between dull and delicious cooking. Economize on something else. In any case, at the moment of writing, margarine is as expensive if not more expensive than butter. Cream, too, is often avoided on the grounds of economy, yet even a tablespoonful will give a specially delicate quality to many dishes. As to wine, little more than a glass is needed to enhance a sauce or a dish. These things need not even be used every day, but they will add to a meal as a tribute to friendship and help it to linger pleasantly in the memory.

Mrs. Henderson also wrote, "One of the worst diseases that can

fall upon a man is the disease of worrying about his food and drink."
Where dieting is made a fetish, bad or at best dull cookery is com-
mon—a not unnatural reaction of the cook in the faddist's household.
Undoubtedly dieting is necessary for certain people: for the too fat,
for the too thin and for those who are ill. These people, however,
have no right to dissuade others more fortunate than themselves from
enjoying anything that is good to eat. Nothing is more depressing for
hostess or guests than to have taken a great deal of trouble and time
in preparing food only to see people take a token helping and pick
at it. The joy of a good meal is lessened for everyone. I always try to
keep a record of foods to which my friends are allergic, such as shellfish, oysters, strawberries, and so on. Then, if we are having any of
those foods, I have something else already prepared for them so there
is no sudden embarrassment. In fact, I prepare more than enough so
that there is plenty if an unknown guest is also allergic. I also keep
a list of people on specific diets.

Conscientious vegetarianism, although it may be a bore to those
immediately concerned, must be tolerated, all the more as it offers
some scope for ingenuity. I have had a great deal of practice in this
because three of my stepchildren have been vegetarians at some point
in their lives.

As a general rule, people digest better and thrive better when they
eat what they like and like what they eat. Also, to be temperate in
food is far wiser and more practicable than to be scientific. Too much
knowledge of proteins and vitamins has a tendency to kill joy in
eating.

The most delightful and remembered meals are those imbued with
a sense of the individuality of the house—meals obviously planned
for the delight of the guest and to suit his tastes. Even if a high level
of excellence cannot be kept up, some *spécialité de la maison* can be
used often. If there is some dish that has been a particular success,
don't be afraid of serving it again. Most people are pleased that you
remembered it was a favorite of theirs.

Among other simple but distinguishing specialities over which
too much trouble cannot be taken are delicious, strong coffee, good
bread (homemade is the ideal), perfect butter, excellent cheese in
its best season and the best tea. If possible, good wine (it need not be
expensive) or a good brew of beer or cider should be served. Many a

guest will remember that he has drunk good wine or beer at a certain house when he has forgotten whether the food was fine or ordinary.

If a hostess makes a determined effort to select good fresh materials and decent drinks; if she can depend on good roast meats, poultry and game, well-cooked vegetables and fish, and half a dozen dishes that are peculiarly her own specialities, she will gain much credit among and give great pleasure to her friends.

The three most important things about which to think when planning a meal are color, texture and taste. There is nothing so off-putting as an all-white meal—nothing so distasteful as three dishes, all lavishly laced with cream. Equally, to plan a meal in which the first course and main dish both have a heavy taste of garlic or curry is madness. Variety in all three cases makes a meal exciting and enticing.

Another rule that ought to be followed faithfully is that no dish can be served too hot, and in summer a cold soup *must* be well chilled, as must some desserts. The plates for a hot course should be well heated—nothing is more useless than serving a dish about which great trouble has been taken on cold plates. It is ruined—and heating plates takes no time or effort.

Planning one meal takes some time. If you have guests for the weekend, the planning time multiplies but is essentially the same. But there variety takes on a greater importance, and more care must be taken to avoid duplication of taste, texture and color. At weekends I usually prepare the more elaborate dishes for dinner, with light lunches—maybe a cold soup or egg dish to start, followed by a casserole, salad and cheese or fresh fruit. If lunch is too heavy, sleep seems to descend on people and the afternoon is gone. We tend to drink hard cider, beer or apple juice at lunch, sometimes wine—but it too leads to sleep. When planning weekend meals, write them out on one large sheet of paper so that you can see *all* the menus at a glance and avoid duplication, so that you don't start every meal with a soup and end it with a mousse, or serve fish at two consecutive dinners. Also, then you can organize the meals, to serve a main course such as Virginia ham one evening, so that the leftovers may be used the following day in a first course like the ham and cream cheese dish.

In the summer one should try to use fresh fruit for dessert, from the garden if one is lucky enough to have one, otherwise from the market. Summer pudding is very good, as it is both sweet and tart, and not heavy. There are about two to three weeks when many different berries are in season: raspberries, loganberries, red currants and black currants. Chilled and tossed with sugar, these make a perfect end to a heavy meal. Their marvelous fresh taste rounds the whole meal off.

Planning meals can show off the cook's creativity—and a well-planned menu is a joy to the palate.

THE
IMPORTANCE
OF BEING
ORGANIZED

For the past twenty-five years cooking has played a large part in my life, partly because I love to eat and partly because the whole business of cooking fascinates me.

Unable to paint, sculpt or compose, I like to work with my hands, and all the senses have assumed tremendous importance in my life. Cooking is creative, relaxing (if done in a reasonable manner) and informative (I am continually learning something new: new combinations of tastes or new methods, and trying the new equipment that keeps on appearing). Turn me loose in a catering-equipment shop and I go mad. Frequently the basic equipment that has served professional cooks through the years turns out to be the best and truest, but, like an artist in an art-supply shop, I tend to think a new brush will work miracles and add new dimensions. Reading cookbooks is a favorite pastime. To me, they are as fascinating as any novel. The same recipes may reappear, but often with a new spice or herb, or new cooking method.

Personally, I don't like communal cooking with everyone helping. I don't even particularly like people talking to me while I cook. If you take cooking fairly seriously, concentration is important—not holy, but important. People wouldn't think of chatting to a pianist while he is playing or a painter while he is painting. Also, cooking is quicker and easier if you are not continually explaining the method or chatting about someone's love life or babies.

The whole secret is organization. Most important is the organization of the kitchen itself and next the organization and planning of the meal, whether it is for two people or twenty; for, much as you may like cooking, the kitchen is not the place to spend your life, particularly if you have a husband or guests.

When I was younger I used to think "organization" and "efficiency" were dirty words. When I was accused of them lame protestations of denial would rush from my mouth. "No, I am really not organized, it just happens that way" or "I am not efficient, I just cannot sit still." As I grew up, went to college, worked in various jobs from bookshops to publishing houses, ran a small business of my own and finally became an editor for *Vogue,* I found that organization and efficiency were not such bad things, that if I wished to have any social life after the working day was over, the only way was to plan it so that I could enjoy it. Now that I am married and have a fairly large family of children, some inherited, some of my own, plus a variety of jobs, *organization and efficiency are absolutely essential.*

I do all the cooking in our country and London homes, although sometimes, if we have a lot of guests, a woman comes in to help me. But there have been many times, such as Christmas, when for ten days there have been twelve to fourteen people at every meal and only me in the kitchen. The freezer is the greatest help: many of the desserts come out of it, made by me a few months ahead. Mousses and crêpes always come in handy, as do pâtés and even stews, when I am suddenly faced with an unexpected drove of people, although if possible I prefer to make everything fresh. I think it tastes better and the creativity of it pleases me. But vegetables out of the garden, even frozen, are delicious, and it does mean one less thing to do at the last minute.

I plan menus so that either the first course or the desserts can be made in advance, and sometimes both, or sometimes the main course. The disastrous plan is to have three courses that have to be made at the same time, plus vegetables. This means utter panic and chaos.

It is essential to read each recipe all the way through before beginning to cook so that there are no ugly surprises halfway through, such as ingredients lacking or length of time needed to marinate or bake or simmer. For this reason I have listed all the ingredients, given the preheated oven temperature and a guide for preparation and cooking time, although these are approximate because everyone has his or her own method and speed of cooking. Thus you can choose one course that takes a long time to cook and two quicker ones. When making a recipe for the first time, allow 50 percent more time than that stated, as you will have to keep referring to the recipe. Afterwards it is a good idea to make a note of your own cooking times in the margin.

Always check the ingredients for preparation, *i.e.,* what has to be done to them before "entering the pot": whether they have to be peeled, seeded, skinned, ground, chopped and so on. If all this is done in advance, the actual cooking becomes easy. It irritates me, watching cooking programs on television, to see it made to look so easy because all the ingredients sit in pretty little bowls, already prepared in the right quantities and the right consistencies. The cook just dumps ingredients into pots and pans with a breezy air of simplicity. One forgets that he or she has already spent some time peeling, slicing and chopping, and that this boring and extremely important part of cooking must be taken into account when planning a menu. The other check is to see that the right pots, pans and other utensils are available and clean. It is essential always to clean pots and pans as you use them, partly because they are much easier to clean if washed at once before food has had time to harden and stick, and partly so that you won't have to face a lot of dirty pots to wash at the end.

I have included quite a few main dishes that require marinating, sometimes overnight, sometimes for an hour or two. If well planned, the rest of the meal may be prepared while the main course is marinating. I like to marinate. The combination of liquids and highly flavored herbs and spices in which meat, game or fish is left to soak not only gives an added flavor but also tenderizes it. The marinade may be cooked or uncooked, and there are a variety of marinade combinations.

I find that people tend to be frightened of garlic and onions. Admittedly, when used indiscriminately in a dish, both become overwhelming, but when used with care and restraint they add a subtle taste that often brings out the flavor of other ingredients. Ginger is included in many recipes in this book. It, too, when used sparingly, gives a new dimension to dishes. Even if you do not like the taste of pure ginger, it takes on a subtlety when mixed with other herbs such as coriander and cumin. The use of herbs in all cooking is very important; I can think of very few dishes whose taste they do not improve when used with restraint. It is easy to grow parsley, chives, tarragon, basil and mint in pots or window boxes.

Where butter is included in the recipes, I often say "butter or margarine." I always use unsalted butter so that I can gauge the amount of salt in a dish accurately. I also use all-vegetable margarine for cooking but never for putting on vegetables or even to top meat or fish. Butter is best for that. Sometimes I use margarine for sautéing, but I prefer peanut or olive oil, or a mixture of half butter and half oil to prevent burning. This can be expensive, but if one is going to the trouble of preparing a delicious meal, two ounces of margarine instead of butter won't save much money and might change the taste. I would rather economize by planning a less expensive but equally delicious meal. I also prefer to make fresh stocks once a week. However, this is not always possible because time is short, and in recipes where chicken, beef or fish stock is called for, a bouillon cube may be substituted, or, for fish stock, a can of clam juice, which can be found in most supermarkets. If you are doing a large batch of cooking, over Christmas for example, you will save time by keeping a small pitcher of freshly squeezed lemon juice ready—you won't have to keep stopping to squeeze small amounts.

Most of the recipes in this book are ones I have collected and used and sometimes improved upon over the years. Others were given to me by friends and acquaintances, some of whom I met while writing a cooking column for *Vogue*. I have used them all myself. They are delicious, they work and I hope the readers of this book will find them equally delicious and a help in planning their culinary lives.

Planning the Kitchen

If the kitchen has been well planned and the right tools are in the right places, a good deal of the work has already been done. A big kitchen is nice but not necessary. And good cooks know that the number of utensils is not as important as their size and shape.

I am a great believer in putting the ugliest and largest utensils, such as roasting and baking pans and soufflé dishes, in cupboards, and hanging everything else on the walls or putting them in baskets and bowls on top of the working surfaces so they are handy and also make the kitchen look cozy.

A very good and very cheap way of conserving space is to hang pegboard on the walls on either side of the stove. Then saucepans, frying pans, colanders, strainers, cooking forks, spatulas and the like can be hung from hooks attached to it. More expensive, but good-looking, is a French copper half-moon saucepan-holder to hang on the wall. This will take three or four frying pans, three saucepans and two or three strainers. If the ceiling is high enough, a butcher's iron bar hung from it, in a square with crossbars over the table, means that almost all necessary implements can be suspended from it.

A large, strong, magnetic knife-holder is essential. You can put scissors as well as knives on it, and other small metal objects. A lot of time can be saved if knives are kept sharp; corks on the tips will keep them that way. Another necessity is a wall-holder for your cooking spoon, fish slicer, slotted spoon, ladle and two-pronged fork. Wooden spoons and the even more useful wooden spatula can be kept in a jug or something similar on top of the working counter near the stove. I prefer to keep vegetables—potatoes, onions, garlic— and lemons, oranges and so on in baskets, not in the refrigerator.

Using Herbs and Spices Intelligently

Herbs and spices are an integral part of my cooking and I like to have them near the stove or where I mix things. If you are lucky enough to be able to grow your own, a good trick for drying them is to hang them on a string—again you might use pegboard. If you buy dried and ground herbs, the hanging shelves especially designed for herb bottles are useful, or if, like me, you buy them in bulk because it is cheaper, you can put them in large glass jars.

These are the herbs and spices I consider essential—and their uses.

ALLSPICE: use in the preparation of beef, pork and game; for flavoring slices of lemon for tea, for fruitcake, spinach and carrots.

FRESH BASIL: sweet, delicate and pungent. Annual. Increases in flavor when cooked. Add to egg, cheese and fish dishes. Particularly good with tomato. Use in French dressing, spaghetti sauce, sausages and stuffings. Rub on poultry before cooking. Add to asparagus, eggplant, broccoli, cabbage, carrots and spinach.

BAY LEAF: use with tomato juice, beef, lamb and veal stews, chicken casserole, tomato sauce, poached fish, chicken and vegetable soups.

CAPERS: use with fish, seafood, tête de veau, vitello tonnato, steak tartare, cold meats with vinaigrette dressing, eggplant.

CARAWAY: use with fish, shellfish, sauerkraut, Irish stew, choucroute, Hungarian goulash, Muenster cheese.

CARDAMOM: said to neutralize the smell of garlic if chewed. Use in gingerbread, spice bread and curries, with game, and as flavoring for coffee and tea.

CAYENNE PEPPER: use with crayfish, crab salad, fish soups, risotto, paella, chicken casserole, white sauce, omelettes, cauliflower au gratin, baked cheese dishes and the smallest amount with fried bananas.

CELERY: seed, powder or salt. Use with tomato juice, baked fish, cheese soufflé, cauliflower au gratin and artichokes.

CHERVIL: slightly sweet flavor; useful as an alternative flavoring to parsley. Necessary for béarnaise sauce and important in wine and vinaigrette sauces. Add to salads, raw vegetables and vegetable soups.

CHILI PEPPERS: use whole with jambalaya, chicken casserole, with shrimp in oil and garlic.

CHIVES: use in salads, sauces, omelettes.

CINNAMON: ground and stick. Use in couscous, mussel soup, roast pork, duck with cherries, pasta e fagioli (Italian thick bean soup), Ceylonese curry. Also Christmas pudding and sangria.

CLOVES: whole and ground. Whole cloves can be stuck in an onion and added to bread sauce, chicken in the pot, pot-au-feu, or used with restraint in tomato soup. A clove of garlic can be studded with cloves and put in the knuckle of a leg of lamb. Add to apple sauce and apple pies. Also mulled wine. Ground cloves sometimes used in gingerbread, certain cheeses, Irish stew.

CORIANDER: seed used mainly to add to taste of artichokes, mushrooms à la Grecque and sauerkraut. Pulverized it can be dusted lightly on roasted meats to be eaten cold. Use in marinades, with game and curry.

CUMIN: seed or ground. Used in bread, curry and Greek dishes.

DILL: the seed is sharper than the herb and should be used for soups, lamb stew, grilled or boiled fish and rice dishes. Use the herb for salads, delicate vegetables, cucumber soup and pickling cucumbers.

GINGER: whole, ground and crystallized. Add to gingerbread, chicken stew, chicken curry, Cantonese pork, most Oriental dishes, plum puddings. May be used as a salt substitute in strict diets.

MACE: use with lemon and honey cakes, milk shakes, fruit tarts, stuffed eggs, omelettes, soufflés, cheese soufflé, Welsh rarebit, béchamel sauce. Add a blade to the stock pot.

SWEET MARJORAM: a strong herb, so use sparingly. Rub on strong meats, add to potato dishes and stuffed vegetables.

MINT: good with melon, fruit juice, iced tea, cream cheese, lamb, pea soup, carrots, peas, summer fruit drinks.

MIXED SPICE: use for gingerbread and other spiced breads.

NUTMEG: use with egg and cheese dishes.

OREGANO: also known as wild marjoram, especially good with tomatoes, egg and cheese dishes.

PAPRIKA: use with meat soups, veal, chicken, fish stews, lobster, risotto, cheese.

WHOLE BLACK OR WHITE PEPPERCORNS: use for poivrade sauce, steak au poivre, piperade, goulashes.

ROSEMARY: must be dried carefully, stored and used with discretion, otherwise it takes on a musty flavor. Use for sage and onion stuffing, with pork, duck, lamb, liver, fish, cottage and cream cheese. Also summer fruit drinks.

SAFFRON: add to rice, cream cheese, chicken, duck, turkey, fish and shrimp dishes.

TARRAGON: a strong aromatic herb and a good salt substitute in strict diets. French tarragon is better than the Russian variety. Use as a base for béarnaise, hollandaise and mousseline sauces. Chopped leaves delicious in French dressing and green salads. Use in herb bouquets and fines herbes mixtures; in marinades for meat, omelettes, eggs, chicken, veal, fish, spinach, zucchini, asparagus, artichokes.

THYME: very strong and pungent, must be used with discretion. Add to stews, or thick soups such as split pea and bean soup. Rub on lamb, fat pork and veal. Use with beans, beets, carrots, potatoes, mushrooms, tomato and herb sauces. Makes a good infusion for sore throats, and, when cold, an astringent for the face.

TURMERIC: use with curry, céleri rémoulade, crab pilaf, Oriental fish soup. Can be used as a coloring substitute in place of saffron.

ESSENTIAL
UTENSILS

CASSEROLES : either heavy cast-iron enameled, or enameled steel. Good for any stove and easy to clean and can be used in the oven or on top of the stove. I like 2 round and 2 oval-round: 3 pint, 5¼ pint; oval: 7 pint and 10 pint.

DOUBLE BOILER : aluminum, 2 pint. For delicate sauces.

FISH KETTLE : the largest that will fit on your stove.

FRYING PANS : heavy steel with sloping sides, long handles—
7-inch diameter,
10-inch diameter,
12-inch diameter,
Enameled steel with white inside, black heatproof plastic handles for cooking egg yolks or white wine, as nonstaining material. Heavy enough for all types of stoves—
8-inch diameter,

10-inch diameter.

Oval cast iron for sautéeing fish. An oval nonstick gratin dish can be used for fish as well.

KNIVES: the most important item to keep in good repair. They must always be kept sharply honed with a butcher's steel. Carbon steel knives are best but stainless steel are less expensive.

Bread knife, stainless steel, serrated edge
Carving knife and fork
Chinese cleaver for chopping mushrooms, parsley and so on
Cook's knife, 10¼ inches; 3 wedge-shaped, 8 inches; 3 chopping and paring
Filleting knife, 6 inches
Frozen-food knife, 10¼ inches, stainless steel, or hacksaw
Grapefruit knife (optional)
Ham knife
Meat cleaver
Palette knife
Sharpening steel
Slicing knife, 10¼ inches, curved blade
Vegetable knife, 4 inches

LARGE ALUMINUM COLANDER with tripod base, 8½-inch diameter.

LARGE JAMMING PAN.

ROASTING PANS: aluminum with a rack fitting into it to lift roasts out of the juices. Flameproof dishes, 2 inches deep, are also good for baking, roasting and gratinéing.

SAUCEPANS: I prefer the French chef strong aluminum with pouring rim and well-fitting lid—
4½-inch diameter for sauces,
7-inch diameter,
8¼-inch diameter,
Enameled steel or heavy cast-iron enameled saucepans with long wooden handles or heatproof plastic handles.
Milk saucepan (no lid)—5½-inch diameter.

Medium with lid—6¼-inch diameter.
Large with lid—13½-inch diameter.
Oval chicken roaster with lid—13½-inch diameter.
Deep fryer (with spare basket for blanching).

SAVARIN MOLD : for savory mousses and rum babas.

SOUP KETTLE : or preserving kettle, thus doubling for jams and so on: 8 quart, 18 quart.

Miscellaneous

Apple corer
Baking pans:
  2 baking sheets
  two 7-inch cake pans
  1 loaf pan 8 to 9 inches
  1 muffin pan
  2 pie pans
  one 8-inch plain flan ring
  1 wire cooling rack
  1 Yorkshire pudding pan
Candy thermometer: can also be used for deep-fat frying.
Can opener
Cheese grater
Citrus zester
Corkscrew with bottle and can opener
Folding salad basket or spin-dryer salad basket that folds flat.
Food processor: Cuisinart or other, for quick chopping, mixing, blending, including pastry dough.
Garlic press
Hand-held electric beaters: for whipping egg whites and cream.
Individual ramekins: 3 fluid ounces, for baked eggs, mousse, crème brûlée.
Kitchen shears
Kitchen utensil set: two-pronged fork, ladle, slotted spoon, fish slicer, shallow strainer, spatula.
Larding needle

Mandoline for slicing potatoes and vegetables, particularly cucumbers.

Measuring cup

Measuring spoons

Meat thermometer

Metal tongs

Mixing bowls: 2 large, 1 medium, 2 small

Mouli légumes for puréing vegetables and fruits. With 3 blades for mashing and grating.

Mouli parsmint

Nutmeg grater

Pastry brushes: one to be used for pastry, the other for meat and barbeques.

Pastry or chopping board: ideally two separate ones so that the smell of onions and garlic on one are not incorporated in the other. The larger the better.

Pie pans and funnel

Porcelain mortar and pestle: for pounding herbs and spices.

Potato baller, also useful for melons.

Potato peeler

Rolling pin

Round bread board

Scales

Skewers

Small bowl: stainless steel or unlined copper for whipping egg whites.

Soufflé dishes: 8½ inch, 7 inch, 5¼ inch and 4½ inch.

Strainers: stainless steel, 2¼ inch and 7 inch.

Trussing needles

Wire whisks: small and large.

Wooden salt and pepper mills

Wooden spoons: 4 or 5—I find the bowlless wooden ones most efficient for stirring or scraping, and a flat wooden spatula. It is a good idea to mark 1 spoon and use it for curry only.

ESSENTIALS FOR YOUR STORE CUPBOARD

For organized cooking, it is important to have certain staples so you can always make a dish more interesting. These are the things I like to have in the house:

Active dry yeast
Almonds: whole blanched and extract
Anchovy essence‡
Anchovy paste‡
Baking powder
Baking soda
Bouillon cubes, chicken and beef

‡ Can be bought at most specialty food shops or ordered from Maison Glass, 52 East 58 Street, New York, New York 10022.

Bread crumbs, homemade, white and toasted, in separate screw-top
   jars, in freezer
Capers
Chocolate, dark unsweetened
Chutneys
Commercial poultry seasoning
Curry powder
Dried milk (for emergencies)
Flour, all-purpose and self-raising
Grated Parmesan cheese
Hazelnuts
HP sauce
Honey, clear
Horseradish sauce
Lemons, whole, in cold water in a bowl in a cool place (changing
   the water twice a week)
Maple syrup
Mayonnaise, Hellman's
Meat glaze‡
Mushroom ketchup‡
Mustard, English, Dijon, moutarde de Meaux
Oil: olive, peanut, safflower, sesame
Peppercorns, whole green, canned or bottled
Pine nuts
Pistachio extract
Pulses: black-eyed, butter and kidney beans, lentils, chickpeas
Raisins, seedless
Rice, long-grain
Sea salt
Soy sauce
Spaghetti
Sugar: confectioners', granulated, superfine, brown
Sultanas
Tabasco sauce
Tomato ketchup and paste
Vanilla beans and extract
Vinegar: red wine, white wine, herb and cider
Walnuts

Worcestershire sauce

Cans: anchovies, shrimp, sardines, tomatoes, mince (for emergencies or sauces), tomato soup, Crosse & Blackwell clear consommé madrilène and beef consommé, whole red peppers

Jams and jellies: red-currant jelly, cranberry jelly, apricot jam (for chicken recipes and glazing pastry)

Note on Symbols

An asterisk (*) next to a recipe means that the dish is suitable for freezing.

A dagger (†) indicates the degree of difficulty, 1 being the easiest, 3 being the most difficult.

SOUPS

---

†*ALMOND AND WATERCRESS SOUP

SERVES 4 TO 5

¼ cup onion, diced
¼ cup celery, diced
2 tablespoons sweet butter or margarine
3 cups watercress leaves, chopped
2 tablespoons ground blanched almonds
2 tablespoons flour

3 cups chicken stock or broth
1 bay leaf
1½ cups milk
Salt and pepper to taste
Sour cream
Chopped toasted almonds
Sprigs of watercress

In a saucepan sauté the onion and celery in the butter or margarine for 5 minutes or until the vegetables are tender. Add the watercress and cook over moderate heat, stirring, for 10 minutes. Stir in ground almonds and flour and continue to cook, always stirring, for about 3 minutes. Stir in the chicken stock and the bay leaf, and bring the mixture to the boil. Reduce the heat and simmer the soup, stirring occasionally, for 10 minutes. Remove from the heat and discard the bay leaf. In a blender purée the mixture, in 2 batches, and return it to a saucepan. Stir in the milk, heat the soup and season it with salt and pepper to taste. Pour the soup into bowls and top each serving with sour cream, and sprinkle with chopped toasted almonds and a sprig of watercress.

Preparation and cooking time: approximately 1 hour.

††*MISS FLEUR COWLES'S JERUSALEM ARTICHOKE SOUP

SERVES 6
Also good served cold.

2 pounds Jerusalem artichokes	Salt
Iced water	¾ cup milk, combined with
2 large onions, minced fine	¾ cup light cream
2 tablespoons butter	Fresh-ground black pepper

Scrape and peel the artichokes. Put them aside (whole) in iced water for ½ hour before needed. Sauté the onions gently in the butter in a large iron frying pan. Dry the artichokes thoroughly with a towel, then slice as transparently thin as possible. Add them gradually to the onions and cook over moderate heat until they are soft, and add salt to taste. When all are done, make into a fine purée in the blender or food processor. Put back on the heat and gradually add slightly warmed milk-and-cream mixture until the desired consistency is reached. As the soup goes to the table, grind fresh black pepper over it and mix. This soup should be served either hot or cold, always with very tiny, very crisp, very hot croutons.

Preparation and cooking time: approximately 1 hour 30 minutes.

††THIN CHESTNUT SOUP

SERVES 6

2 tablespoons butter or margarine
1½ pounds chestnuts, shelled and peeled
  (see page 137)
3 stalks celery, sliced thin
2 onions, sliced thin

2 leeks, sliced thin
Garlic clove, sliced thin
Water
Salt and pepper
1 cup chicken stock

In a deep saucepan melt the butter or margarine and add the chestnuts, celery, onions, leeks and garlic clove. Cook the vegetables over low heat until they are lightly browned. Add warm water to cover, season with salt and pepper to taste, and simmer over low heat until the vegetables are tender. Remove any whole chestnuts and reserve them. Force the rest of the mixture through a fine sieve or purée it in a blender. Add the chicken stock to the purée and the reserved chestnuts. Reheat the soup gently and serve.

Preparation time: 45 minutes. Cooking time: 1 hour 30 minutes.

†CHICKPEA AND SPINACH SOUP

SERVES 12

1 pound dried chickpeas
2½ quarts water
2 bay leaves
2 small dried chili peppers
¾ teaspoon thyme
1 large onion, minced
2 tablespoons olive oil or vegetable oil

4 tomatoes, peeled, seeded and
  chopped
1 pound fresh spinach, washed,
  trimmed and chopped or one
  8-ounce package unthawed
  frozen spinach
Parsley, chopped fine
Hard-boiled egg, chopped fine

Put dried chickpeas in a bowl, cover them with water and allow them to soak overnight. In a kettle combine 2½ quarts of water, bay leaves, chili peppers, thyme and chickpeas, drained. Bring to the boil, covered, and simmer for 30 minutes. In a frying pan sauté the onion in the oil until soft. Add the tomatoes and cook for 3 minutes more. Add the tomato mixture to the chickpea mixture and simmer the soup for 20 to 30 minutes, or until the chickpeas are tender but not mushy. Bring the soup to the boil and add the spinach. Cook the soup, covered, for 6 to 8 minutes, or until the spinach is cooked. Before serving, sprinkle parsley and hard-boiled egg over the top.

Preparation time: 24 hours. Cooking time: approximately 1 hour 45 minutes.

††FENNEL, EGG AND LEMON SOUP

SERVES 6

10 cups water
1 pound veal shoulder, cubed
2 bunches fennel, stalks and leaves removed and reserved
3 carrots, peeled and sliced
2 tablespoons salt
2 onions, unpeeled

1 garlic clove, unpeeled
Bouquet garni (6 sprigs parsley, 1 bay leaf, 1 large strip lemon rind, few peppercorns)
5 egg yolks
1 teaspoon lemon juice
Salt and lemon juice to taste

In a large saucepan bring the water to the boil and add the cubed veal, fennel stalks, carrots, salt, onions, garlic and bouquet garni. Cook, skimming the froth as it rises to the surface, for 5 minutes. Reduce the heat and barely simmer, half covered, for 1 hour. Strain the broth into a bowl, pressing the solids with the back of a wooden spoon to squeeze out all the liquid. Measure the liquid, pour it into another saucepan and reduce it over high heat to 7½ cups. In a bowl beat the egg yolks with 1 teaspoon of lemon juice and slowly stir the mixture into the hot broth. Cook the soup over low heat until it thickens slightly, but do not allow it to boil. Season with salt and additional lemon juice to taste and sprinkle it with the reserved fennel leaves, snipped fine.

Preparation and cooking time: approximately 2 hours.

†QUICK GREEK LEMON SOUP

SERVES 4

2 cans chicken with rice soup	Juice of 2 lemons
2 eggs, separated	Grated rind of lemon

Pour chicken with rice soup into a good-sized saucepan. Stir with a wire whisk to separate the rice. Bring to the boil. In a bowl combine the egg yolks with the lemon juice and the grated lemon rind. Gradually stir a little of the hot soup into the egg-yolk mixture and then pour it slowly back into the soup, stirring constantly. Beat the egg whites until they hold definite peaks and fold them into the hot soup. Allow it to stand for 3 minutes before serving.

Preparation and cooking time: approximately 30 minutes.

†GREEN-BEAN SOUP

SERVES 4

1½ pounds green beans	Salt and fresh-ground black
1½ cups béchamel sauce (see	pepper
page 278)	Parsley, chopped fine
2½ cups heavy cream	Chives, snipped fine
2 tablespoons Cognac	

In a heavy saucepan cook the beans in boiling salted water for 10 minutes and drain. Add to the béchamel sauce and simmer gently, being careful that the sauce does not scorch, for about 15 minutes or until the beans are just tender. Purée the mixture in a blender or food processor. Combine the purée with the cream and heat it just to the boiling point. Add the Cognac, salt and pepper to taste. Bring the soup back to the boiling point and serve it in heated bowls with parsley and chives sprinkled on top.

Preparation and cooking time: approximately 45 minutes, plus 45 minutes for making the béchamel sauce.

††LENTIL SOUP

SERVES 6

6 tablespoons butter
1 cup onion, chopped fine
½ cup carrots, chopped fine
½ cup celery, chopped fine
1 garlic clove, minced
¼ pound bacon, diced
1½ cups lentils

6 cups game stock (see page 280), or brown stock (see page 279) if game stock is not available
Bouquet garni (6 sprigs parsley, 1 bay leaf, ½ teaspoon thyme)
¼ pound garlic sausage, optional
Salt and pepper
Lemon juice to taste
2 tablespoons chopped parsley

In a frying pan melt 3 tablespoons of the butter and add the onion, carrots, celery, garlic and bacon. Cover the pan with a sheet of waxed paper, greased with 1 tablespoon of butter, and the lid and cook slowly for 10 minutes. Put the lentils and game or brown stock into a deep saucepan and bring to the boil, skimming the surface carefully. Add the vegetable mixture and the bouquet garni and simmer for 1 hour. Add the garlic sausage and simmer for another 30 minutes. Discard the bouquet garni. Take out the garlic sausage, slice it and reserve it. Put the soup through a blender or food processor. Return it to the saucepan, add salt, pepper and lemon juice, and cook until heated through. Just before serving swirl in 2 tablespoons of butter cut into tiny pieces. Top the soup with the garlic sausage slices and chopped parsley.

Preparation and cooking time: approximately 3 hours.

†MUSHROOM CONSOMMÉ

SERVES 6 TO 8

2 tablespoons dried mushrooms or cèpes
½ pound fresh mushrooms
6 cups beef consommé
·Salt and cayenne pepper

Dry sherry
Slices fresh raw mushrooms

Soak the dried mushrooms or cèpes in enough hot water to cover for at least 3 hours. Chop the fresh mushrooms, and put in a saucepan with the beef consommé. Drain and reserve the liquid from the dried mushrooms. Discard the mushrooms, and add the liquid to the soup. Simmer for 10 minutes, strain, season with salt and cayenne to taste. Pour the soup into individual cups, adding 1 to 2 tablespoons of sherry to each, and top with a few slices of fresh raw mushrooms.

Preparation time: 3 hours. Cooking time: approximately 30 minutes.

†ONION SOUP

SERVES 8

8 small onions, sliced thin
2 tablespoons butter
2 tablespoons oil
2 teaspoons flour
8 cups beef consommé

Salt and pepper to taste
Eight 1-inch-thick slices French bread, toasted
8 tablespoons grated Parmesan cheese

In a large saucepan sauté the onions in the butter and oil until they are golden and soft, stirring from time to time. Sprinkle the onions with flour and cook, stirring, for 1 to 2 minutes. Add the beef consommé and salt and pepper to taste. Simmer the soup for 15 minutes. Arrange the slices of toast in the bottoms of 8 small flameproof casseroles. Pour the soup over the toast and sprinkle the surface generously with the cheese. Put the bowls under the broiler to brown the cheese. Serve immediately.

Preparation and cooking time: approximately 45 minutes.

†*SPINACH SOUP

SERVES 6
Also good served cold.

2 tablespoons butter
1 large onion, chopped fine
2 tablespoons flour
5 cups chicken stock, or the equivalent amount of broth made from bouillon cubes
1 teaspoon salt
½ teaspoon black pepper
½ teaspoon paprika
½ teaspoon nutmeg
2 tablespoons lemon juice
1½ pounds spinach, trimmed, washed and coarse-chopped
⅓ cup sour cream
6 slices lean bacon, cooked until crisp and coarse-chopped

In a large, heavy saucepan melt the butter over moderate heat. When the foam subsides add the onion and cook, stirring occasionally, for 5 to 7 minutes, or until it is soft and translucent but not brown. Remove the pan from the heat. With a wooden spoon, stir in the flour to make a smooth paste. Gradually stir in the chicken stock, being careful to avoid lumps. Stir in the salt, pepper, paprika, nutmeg, lemon juice and spinach. Return the pan to the heat and bring to the boil, stirring constantly. Reduce the heat to low, cover the pan and simmer for 20 to 25 minutes or until the spinach is very tender. Remove the pan from the heat, ladle the soup into a blender or food processor, a little at a time, and blend until it is smooth and creamy.

Return the blended soup to the saucepan, place over moderate heat and, stirring occasionally, bring back to the boil. Taste and add more seasoning if necessary. Remove the pan from the heat and spoon the soup into individual bowls. Add a tablespoon of sour cream to each serving and sprinkle bacon on top. Serve. If serving cold, allow to cool, then put in the refrigerator to chill, and add the sour cream and bacon just before serving.

Preparation and cooking time: approximately 30 minutes. Chilling time: 3 hours.

†VEGETABLE SOUP WITH GARLIC

SERVES 6

1½ cups onion, chopped

3 garlic cloves, minced

2 tablespoons olive oil

3 cups shredded cabbage

1 cup tomatoes, peeled, seeded and chopped

⅔ cup parsley, chopped

6 cups boiling water

2 large potatoes, cut into 1-inch cubes

1½ cups cauliflower flowerets

1 cup peas

Salt and pepper

1½ cups frozen (and thawed) or canned artichoke hearts

6 thin slices of slightly stale whole-wheat bread

Olive oil

Pimento strips

In a large saucepan sauté the onions and garlic in oil until the onion is softened. Stir in the cabbage, tomatoes and parsley and cook for 5 minutes. Add the boiling water, potatoes, cauliflower, peas and salt and pepper to taste. Simmer for 40 minutes, or until the vegetables are almost tender. Add the artichoke hearts and cook for 5 minutes longer. Transfer the soup to a large bowl. Put the slices of bread in a saucepan and sprinkle them lightly with olive oil. Add the soup and heat for 3 minutes. Spoon the bread and soup into warm bowls and top each serving with pimento strips.

Preparation and cooking time: approximately 1 hour 30 minutes.

††CRAB SOUP

SERVES 6

Three 10-ounce cans clear chicken broth
1 teaspoon saffron
¼ pound butter
2 leeks, diced
1 cup celery, diced
1 cup carrots, diced
4 shallots, chopped fine
3 large green peppers, seeded and diced

3 tomatoes, skinned and diced
Three 6½-ounce cans crab meat
2 teaspoons Worcestershire sauce
Salt and fresh-ground black pepper
¼ cup parsley, chopped
1½ cups long-grain rice

Heat the chicken broth with the saffron, first skimming off any fat in the broth. Melt the butter, add the celery, leeks, carrots and shallots and cook, covered, for about 10 minutes. Add the peppers and continue cooking for approximately 5 minutes longer without allowing the vegetables to brown, and stirring once in a while. Add the tomatoes and continue cooking until soft, adding a little more butter if necessary. Remove any hard particles from the crab, and shred the meat at the same time. Add to the vegetables, together with the Worcestershire sauce, and cook for 5 minutes, stirring. Add the vegetable-and-crab mixture to the saffroned broth, along with salt and pepper to taste. Simmer for a few minutes and reheat at serving time. Cook the rice so that it is a little underdone and serve in a heated dish. Pour the hot crab soup into a heated tureen and sprinkle with parsley. Put a generous spoonful of rice into each heated soup plate and pour the soup over the rice.

Both the soup and the rice can be prepared in advance.
Preparation and cooking time: approximately 1 hour 45 minutes.

††CASTILIAN MUSSEL SOUP

SERVES 6 TO 8

1 cup onion, chopped
2 garlic cloves, chopped
2 cups spinach, blanched and
  chopped
½ teaspoon rosemary
1 tomato, peeled, seeded and
  chopped
½ cup olive oil
Salt to taste

½ teaspoon fresh-ground
  pepper
½ teaspoon ground coriander
2 quarts mussels, washed,
  scrubbed and bearded
  (see note below)
6 cups fish stock (see page 276)
⅓ cup Cognac
parsley, chopped fine

In a heavy frying pan sauté the onion, garlic, spinach, rosemary and tomato in oil until the onion is soft. Add salt to taste and the fresh-ground pepper and coriander. Put the mussels into a heavy braising pan with the fish stock and steam them over moderate heat for 12 to 15 minutes. Remove the opened mussels and steam those still shut for 5 minutes more. Discard any mussels that still have not opened. Remove the open mussels from their shells. Strain the broth through a triple thickness of cheesecloth or a linen napkin. Then add the Cognac. Combine the mussels, the sautéed vegetables and the broth and bring to the boil. Reduce the heat and simmer for 5 minutes. Correct the seasoning and force the mixture through a food mill, or purée it in a blender or food processor. Reheat the soup, sprinkle parsley on top and serve.

NOTE: To clean mussels, put 2 tablespoons natural oatmeal into the cold water in which the mussels are soaking. Leave to soak at least 2 hours, ideally 4 to 6 hours.

Preparation time for scrubbing and bearding mussels: approximately 30 minutes. Cooking time: approximately 1 hour 30 minutes.

††DUBLIN MUSSEL SOUP

SERVES 4

36 mussels, washed, scrubbed
and bearded (see note
page 34)
½ cup hard cider
1 onion, chopped
1 sprig parsley
2 leeks, chopped fine
1 stalk celery, chopped fine

2 tablespoons butter
¼ cup flour
1 quart scalded milk
2 teaspoons salt
½ teaspoon fresh-ground pepper
½ teaspoon grated nutmeg
2 tablespoons heavy cream

Put the mussels in a large kettle with the cider, onion and parsley. Cover the pan and steam the mussels, shaking the pan frequently, until they open. Discard any that do not open. Strain the mixture into a bowl through several layers of cheesecloth and reserve the liquid. Remove mussels from their shells and reserve. In a large saucepan sauté the leeks and celery in butter for 3 minutes. Add the flour and cook, stirring constantly, for 2 minutes. Gradually stir in the scalded milk, add the salt, pepper and nutmeg and simmer for 20 minutes. Pour the soup through a fine sieve, add the reserved liquid, heavy cream and the mussels and heat slowly.

Preparation time for scrubbing and bearding mussels: approximately 30 minutes. Cooking time: approximately 1 hour.

†MRS. JOHN HAY WHITNEY'S OYSTER STEW

SERVES 10 TO 12

4 dozen shelled oysters, with the juice
2 tablespoons butter
1 large onion, chopped fine
2 large leeks, diced fine
1 medium potato, diced fine

1 tablespoon flour
Salt and pepper to taste
1 cup heavy cream
Fresh-chopped parsley

Bring the shelled oysters to the boil in their own juice, then set aside. In another saucepan melt the butter and sauté the onion, leeks and potato until soft; then add the flour, salt and pepper and oyster juice, without the oysters. Cook until the vegetables are tender, then add the oysters with the cream and bring the mixture once more to the boil and skim. Add chopped parsley and serve.

Preparation time for opening the oysters: approximately 45 minutes. Cooking time: approximately 45 minutes.

†SHRIMP SOUP

SERVES 4 TO 6

1½ pounds raw shrimp	½ teaspoon thyme
4 cups fish stock (see page 276)	½ teaspoon fresh-ground pepper
1 cup heavy cream	1 garlic clove, chopped fine
¼ cup chopped onions	1 cup cream whipped with a pinch of salt
3 tablespoons dry sherry	Grated lemon rind

Boil the shrimp in the fish stock for 3 minutes. Shell the shrimp and return the shells to the broth. Combine the shrimp with the heavy cream in a blender or food processor and purée. Add the onions, sherry, thyme, pepper and garlic to the broth. Bring the mixture to the boil and cook for 10 minutes. Strain the broth and combine it well with the shrimp purée. Correct the seasoning and pour the soup into bowls. Top each serving with salted whipped cream and sprinkle it with grated lemon rind.

Preparation and cooking time: approximately 30 minutes.

†SHRIMP AND CORN CHOWDER

SERVES 6

2½ cups fresh corn cut off the cob or frozen corn kernels

2½ cups scalded milk

2 slices onion

2½ cups thin white sauce (see page 278)

2 egg yolks

½ cup light cream or milk

1 cup shrimp, chopped

2 tablespoons butter

Salt and pepper

Grated nutmeg

In the top of a double boiler combine the corn (canned or frozen may be used if fresh corn is not in season), scalded milk and onion. Cook over boiling water for 20 minutes. Remove the onion, if desired, and put the mixture through a blender or food processor. Add the purée to the white sauce and bring to the boil. Beat the egg yolks and cream or milk together and stir into the soup. Sauté the shrimp in butter for a few minutes and stir into the chowder. Season with salt, pepper and grated nutmeg to taste.

Preparation and cooking time: approximately 1 hour.

†CREAMED GAME SOUP

SERVES 6

4½ cups game stock (see page 280)

Meat used in making game stock

1 egg yolk

½ cup heavy cream

Watercress croutons (see page 38)

Heat ½ cup of the stock. Combine it with the meat in a food processor and purée. In a kettle heat the remaining game stock, add the puréed mixture, and simmer the soup for 10 minutes. Beat the egg yolk with the cream and add ½ cup of the soup, stirring. Add the mixture to the kettle, stirring. Heat the soup without allowing it to boil. Serve with watercress croutons.

Preparation and cooking time: approximately 30 minutes.

†WATERCRESS CROUTONS

2 cups watercress leaves
4 cups boiling water
Salt

2 to 3 tablespoons butter
24 slices white bread (approximately)

Preheat the oven to 250° F.

Blanch the watercress leaves in boiling water for 1 minute and drain thoroughly. Put the leaves through a food mill or purée them in a blender or food processor, and combine the purée with salt to taste and enough softened butter to make a pale-green mixture. Spread the mixture on small rounds of white bread, arrange them on a buttered baking sheet and bake them in the oven about 5 minutes or until they are golden.

†GAME ESSENCE SOUP

SERVES 4

Meat from 1 pheasant or 1 par-
tridge or a haunch of venison
3¾ cups hot game stock (see page
280)

½ cup red wine
1 tablespoon red-currant jelly

In a blender purée the meat that was used in making game stock—1 pheasant, partridge or haunch of venison. Transfer the purée to a soup kettle and add hot game stock, red wine and red-currant jelly. Simmer the soup until heated through.

††PHEASANT SOUP WITH PHEASANT BALLS

THE SOUP
SERVES 6

Cracked bones, scraps of meat and the skin
   from 2 roasted pheasants
Few sprigs of parsley and celery tops
Pinch of thyme
1 bay leaf
5 peppercorns
2 carrots, quartered

2 leeks, quartered
2 onions, quartered
1½ teaspoons salt
White wine, optional
Sprinkling of paprika
Heavy cream

THE PHEASANT BALLS
MAKES 3 TO 4 BALLS PER PERSON

6 tablespoons ground cooked
   pheasant meat
4 tablespoons bread crumbs

1 large or 2 medium egg yolks
Enough game stock to moisten

Place the remains of the pheasants into a large soup kettle with the parsley and celery tops, thyme, bay leaf and peppercorns. Add the carrots, leeks, onions and salt. Add cold water, or a mixture of cold water and white wine, to cover, and bring the liquid slowly to the boiling point. Lower the heat and simmer the soup, partially covered, over low heat for 2 hours. Strain the soup and allow it to cool. Skim the fat from the top, reheat and strain through a fine cloth. Bring to a rolling boil and reduce to approximately 8 cups. Serve hot, sprinkled with a little paprika.

Make little pheasant balls by combining bits of the pheasant meat with the bread crumbs, egg yolk and a little of the stock and rolling the mixture into balls. Just before serving add a little heavy cream and the pheasant balls to the soup.

Preparation and cooking time: approximately 3 hours.

††APPLE AND WINE SOUP

SERVES 6

3 cups water
½ cup sugar
Pinch of salt
6 cups green apples, peeled,
    cored and sliced
1 cinnamon stick
Rind of 1 lemon, sliced thin
6 tablespoons dry white bread
    crumbs

2 cups red wine
3 to 4 tablespoons lemon juice
3 tablespoons red-currant jelly
6 tablespoons sweetened
    whipped cream
Sprinkling of ground
    cinnamon

In a saucepan combine the water, sugar and salt and bring to the boil. Add the apples, cinnamon, lemon rind and bread crumbs, and cook, stirring occasionally, for about 10 minutes or until the apples are tender. Remove the cinnamon stick and lemon rind and force the mixture through a sieve or the fine disk of a food mill. Return to the pan and add the wine, lemon juice and red-currant jelly. Simmer, stirring, until the mixture is heated through and the jelly has dissolved. Top each serving with a dollop of sweetened whipped cream and a sprinkling of ground cinnamon.

Preparation and cooking time: approximately 1 hour.

††HOT BEER SOUP WITH SNOWBALLS

SERVES 4

4 cups dark beer
1 tablespoon butter
2 tablespoons flour
1 tablespoon sugar
6 cloves

1 cinnamon stick
Juice and rind of ½ lemon, chopped fine
2 egg yolks
2 teaspoons water

Pour the beer into a saucepan and allow it to stand at room temperature for about 3 hours, or until it is flat. In another saucepan melt the butter, stir in the flour and sugar and cook the mixture very gently, stirring, until it turns a caramel color. Do not allow it to burn. Heat the beer slowly, add it to the flour-and-sugar mixture, stirring until well blended and smooth. Add the cloves, cinnamon, lemon juice and rind and simmer the soup for 15 minutes. Discard the cinnamon and cloves. Combine the egg yolks with the water and beat in a little of the hot soup. Add the mixture to the rest of the soup and blend thoroughly. Serve in heated mugs and top with snowballs (see below), if desired.

Preparation time: 3 hours. Cooking time: approximately 45 minutes.

SNOWBALLS

2 *egg whites*
2 *tablespoons sugar*
Sprinkling of ground cinnamon

In a bowl beat the egg whites until they are stiff, then gradually beat in the sugar. Using 2 teaspoons, form the mixture into tiny balls and drop them into a saucepan of boiling water. Cover the saucepan, remove it from the heat at once and allow it to stand for 5 to 10 minutes, or until the snowballs puff up and are done. Remove the snowballs from the saucepan with a slotted spoon, and sprinkle them with a little cinnamon.

Preparation and cooking time: approximately 30 minutes.

†LEMON ALE SOUP

SERVES 6

4 cups ale	1 cinnamon stick
½ cup lemon juice	Salt
4 slices cucumber, peeled	Fresh-grated nutmeg
½ teaspoon grated lemon rind	1 teaspoon arrowroot
3 peppercorns	6 lemon slices
2 whole cloves	

In a saucepan combine all the ingredients except the arrowroot and lemon slices. Heat the soup slowly, stirring constantly, but do not allow it to boil. Thicken with arrowroot mixed to a paste with a little cold water and simmer for 5 minutes. Strain the soup through a fine sieve and reheat it. Serve topped with lemon slices in individual warmed soup plates.

Preparation and cooking time: approximately 25 minutes.

†GRUYÈRE SOUP

SERVES 6

¼ cup butter	2½ cups grated or shredded Swiss
¼ cup flour	Gruyère cheese
2 cups milk	Dash of Tabasco sauce
2 cups chicken stock (see	Salt and pepper to taste
page 276)	Toasted croutons
1 teaspoon Dijon mustard	Parsley, chopped fine

In a 2-quart saucepan melt the butter, add the flour and cook the roux over low heat, stirring, for several minutes. Stir in the milk and continue to cook, stirring, until slightly thickened. Add the chicken stock blended with 1 teaspoon Dijon mustard or more (to taste) and heat through. Very carefully stir in the cheese and a dash or two of Tabasco, just until the cheese is melted. Correct the seasoning and serve the soup in heated cups or soup plates, adding a few croutons and a bit of parsley to each serving.

Preparation and cooking time: approximately 30 minutes.

COLD SOUPS

†AVOCADO SOUP

SERVES 4

1 ripe avocado	*½ teaspoon salt*
2 cups chicken consommé	*Juice of 1 lime*
1 cup light cream	*Fresh-ground white pepper*
2 tablespoons white rum	*Chives, snipped fine*
½ teaspoon curry powder	

Place all the ingredients except the chives in the container of a blender or food processor. Blend the mixture until it is creamy and chill it thoroughly. Serve with a sprinkling of chives on top.

Preparation time: 10 minutes. Chilling time: 3 hours.

††*COLD BORSCH

SERVES 6

7½ cups strong beef stock or beef consommé
*5 uncooked medium beets, peeled and
   grated*
½ cup red wine
1 tablespoon sherry
1 tablespoon tomato paste
2 teaspoons lemon juice

4 egg whites
6 small cooked beets
Sour cream
Grated lemon rind
Salt and cayenne

In a large, deep saucepan combine the cold beef stock or consommé
with the grated uncooked beets, red wine, sherry, tomato paste and
lemon juice. Beat the egg whites until they are stiff and turn them
onto the stock. *Do not fold them in.* Bring the mixture to the boil,
whisking constantly with a wire whisk across the center of the pan.
Remove the pan from the heat and allow to stand for 10 minutes.
Line a large, fine sieve with cheesecloth wrung out in cold water.
Place the sieve over a large, deep bowl and slowly pour in the contents of the pan. Let the mixture stand until it has completely dripped
through and discard the residue in the cheesecloth. Cool the soup
and chill it. Cut the 6 cooked beets into julienne strips, divide them
among 6 chilled soup plates and add the soup. Serve with a sauceboat of sour cream seasoned with grated lemon rind and salt and
cayenne to taste.

*Preparation and cooking time: approximately 1 hour 45 minutes.
Chilling time: 3 hours.*

†*JELLIED CUCUMBER SOUP

SERVES 6

4 large cucumbers, peeled and
  cubed
1 onion, sliced
1 teaspoon mixed pickling spices
3 cans Crosse & Blackwell clear
  consommé madrilène

Salt and pepper to taste
1 tablespoon chopped parsley
Sour cream
Chopped parsley

In a large saucepan combine the cucumber with the onion, mixed pickling spices, consommé, salt and pepper to taste. Bring the mixture to the boil and simmer for 1 hour. Press the soup through a sieve and stir in the tablespoon of chopped parsley. Allow the soup to cool, pour it into a shallow pan and chill until firm. Chop it into small cubes, spoon a dollop of sour cream and a sprinkling of parsley on top of each serving.

Preparation and cooking time: approximately 1 hour 30 minutes. Chilling time: 3 hours.

†*GAZPACHO ANDALUZ

SERVES 6 TO 8

4 tomatoes, fresh or canned
1 small cucumber or ½ large cucumber
1 sweet red pepper, fresh or
  canned
1 onion
4 cloves garlic
Salt, pepper and cayenne to taste

¾ cup fine fresh bread crumbs
3 tablespoons olive oil
2 tablespoons lemon juice
½ pound ice
Croutons
Chopped cucumber
Chopped green pepper
Chopped onion

Mince the tomatoes, cucumber, red pepper and onion. Pound the garlic in a mortar, and add the salt, pepper, cayenne and bread crumbs. Mix in the oil drop by drop until a thick paste is formed. Stir the lemon juice slowly into the paste and place the mixture in a soup tureen, then mix in the tomatoes, cucumber, red pepper and onion. If the soup is too thick, add a little water. Purée all the ingredients in the blender or food processor, or, if you prefer a chunkier soup, purée only the garlic, bread crumbs, salt, pepper, oil, lemon juice and water mixture, and then add the chopped or minced vegetables. For either method, the ice should then be added and the soup chilled in the refrigerator. Serve with croutons, chopped cucumbers, green peppers and onions.

Preparation and cooking time: approximately 30 minutes. Chilling time: 2 to 3 hours.

†GARLIC SOUP

SERVES 6

4 cloves garlic
10 almonds, blanched and toasted
2 slices white bread, with crusts removed, cut into small dice
2 tablespoons olive oil
3 cups chicken stock or chicken consommé

2 tablespoons dry white wine
1 teaspoon salt
Pepper, to taste
¼ cantaloupe, cubed
6 ice cubes

In a blender pulverize the garlic and almonds, then combine with the bread. Heat the olive oil in a skillet and add the bread-and-garlic mixture. Cook, stirring, until the croutons are golden. Remove the pan from the heat and mash the mixture to a paste. Add the chicken stock, white wine, salt and pepper. Blend well, and stir in the melon cubes. Cool the soup and chill. To serve, put an ice cube in each soup bowl and ladle the soup over it.

Preparation and cooking time: approximately 45 minutes. Chilling time: 3 hours.

†*GREEN-PEPPER SOUP

SERVES 9

Also good served hot.

2 medium-sized green peppers, chopped,
reserving some for decoration

¼ cup onion, chopped

2 tablespoons butter

2 cups chicken stock (see page 276)

¼ teaspoon oregano

1 tablespoon flour

¼ teaspoon salt

1 cup milk

Sauté the green peppers and onion in half the butter until the onion is golden. Add the chicken stock and oregano and simmer for 10 minutes. Purée the soup for a few seconds in a blender or a food processor. In a saucepan melt the remaining butter and blend in the flour and salt. Cook the roux until it is bubbly and remove the pan from the heat. Gradually stir in the milk and return the pan to the heat. Cook the sauce, stirring constantly, until it is thick and smooth. Stir in the green-pepper mixture. Put in the refrigerator until cold, then serve sprinkled with the reserved chopped green pepper. This soup is also delicious served hot in the winter.

Preparation and cooking time: approximately 30 minutes. Chilling time: 3 hours.

†*COLD ORANGE AND CARROT SOUP

SERVES 6

½ cup onion, chopped

3 tablespoons butter or margarine

1½ pounds small carrots, sliced thin

2 cups water

1½ cups orange juice

Salt and pepper

1 cup light cream

Dash of nutmeg

Chives, snipped fine

Sauté the onion in the butter or margarine. Add the carrots, water, orange juice and salt and pepper. Cook the carrots until they are tender. Purée the soup in a blender or food processor. If it is still too thick, thin it with orange juice to the desired consistency. Cool the soup and chill it. Stir in the light cream and season with nutmeg. Sprinkle each serving with the snipped chives.

Preparation and cooking time: approximately 30 minutes. Chilling time: 2 hours.

†*COLD SORREL SOUP

SERVES 8

1 pound sorrel	*3 egg yolks*
2 quarts water	*2 tablespoons milk*
2 teaspoons salt	*1 cup sour cream*
2 tablespoons sugar	*Chopped cucumber*
2 tablespoons lemon juice	

Remove the heavy stems from the sorrel and discard them. Wash and drain the leaves. Shred or chop the leaves fine and put them in a heavy enamel saucepan. Add the water and salt. Bring the mixture to the boil and cook it over low heat for 30 minutes. Add the sugar and lemon juice and cook for 10 minutes longer. In a bowl beat the egg yolks with the milk. Pour 1 cup of hot soup in a stream over the yolks, stirring, and return the mixture, stirring, to the saucepan. Remove the pan from the heat and allow the soup to cool. In a bowl lighten the sour cream with ½ cup of the cooled soup and return it, stirring, to the saucepan. Chill the soup well, divide among 8 bowls and sprinkle with chopped cucumber.

Preparation and cooking time: 1 hour. Chilling time: 2 hours.

††*COLD SUMMER SOUP

SERVES 6

2½ pounds ripe tomatoes, peeled
2 ice cubes
1 tablespoon sugar
2 teaspoons salt
½ teaspoon onion juice
Juice and grated rind of ½ lemon
½ cup sour cream

8 slices cold ham, cut into ju-
    lienne strips
1 cantaloupe
1 honeydew melon
2 large cucumbers
Salt and pepper to taste
Minced parsley
Minced mint

Press the tomatoes through a sieve and chill thoroughly. When ready to serve, add ice cubes, sugar, salt, onion juice, lemon juice and the grated lemon rind. Stir well. Add the sour cream and beat until smooth. Add the julienne strips of ham. With a melon-ball cutter scoop out an equal number of balls from the cantaloupe, honeydew melon and cucumbers. Salt the melon and cucumber balls and grind a little pepper over them. Mound several seasoned melon and cucumber balls in the center of individual soup dishes and sprinkle them with minced parsley and mint. Pour the soup around the mounds.

Preparation time: approximately 30 minutes. Chilling time: 3 hours.

†*TOMATO SOUP WITH BASIL

SERVES 6

2 pounds tomatoes (about 16)
3 tablespoons butter
Salt and pepper to taste
1 teaspoon sugar
Chopped fresh basil to taste

1¼ cups light cream
½ cucumber, unpeeled
Poppadums (spicy Indian unleav-
    ened bread)

Peel the tomatoes, cut up and cook in the butter, very slowly, for approximately 10 minutes, or until soft and mushy. Add the salt and pepper and the sugar. Force the tomatoes through a sieve into a bowl. Add the basil—*do not use dried basil*—and mix in the cream and grate in the cucumber. Serve very cold, with poppadums.

Preparation time: approximately 45 minutes. Chilling time: 3 hours.

††*TOMATO AND DILL SOUP

SERVES 4
Also good served hot.

2 tablespoons vegetable oil	*1 heaping tablespoon tomato paste*
1 tablespoon butter	*1 teaspoon sugar*
1 onion, chopped fine	*2 level tablespoons potato flour*
1 clove garlic	*2½ cups water*
Salt and black pepper	*1¼ cups milk*
4 medium-sized tomatoes	*1 heaping tablespoon fresh dill*

In a heavy 1½-quart saucepan, heat the vegetable oil and butter. Add the onion, garlic, salt and pepper, and cook very slowly until soft but not browned. Slice the tomatoes with their skins on and add, cooking quickly for 3 to 4 minutes. Remove from the heat and add the tomato paste, sugar, potato flour and water. Mix well, return to the heat and stir until the soup boils. Rub through a fine sieve (or put in a blender or food processor and then through a fine strainer to separate the tomato seeds). Add the milk and dill and chill. This soup is also excellent served hot, and the consistency can be varied by adjusting the amount of flour used, and by substituting cream for the milk.

Preparation and cooking time: 1 hour. Chilling time: 3 hours.

†*COLD CURRIED CHICKEN AND APPLE SOUP

SERVES 6

2 apples, peeled, cored and sliced
2 onions, peeled and sliced
1 tablespoon butter or margarine
2 teaspoons curry powder
1 teaspoon flour
2 cups chicken stock (see page 276)

Pinch of cayenne
Salt and pepper to taste
1 cup dry white wine
1 cup light cream
½ cup white meat of
   chicken, diced fine

Sauté the apples and onions in the butter or margarine, over low heat, until the onions are translucent. Stir in the curry powder mixed with the flour, and cook for 5 minutes, stirring frequently. Add the chicken stock, cayenne, salt and pepper. Stir in the white wine and cook the soup, stirring, for 10 minutes longer. Rub through a fine sieve or put through a food processor, cool and chill the purée. Just before serving stir in the light cream and diced chicken.

Preparation and cooking time: approximately 45 minutes. Chilling time: 2 hours.

†*COLD CURRIED MUSHROOM SOUP

SERVES 6

2 to 3 scallions, sliced, reserving
   the green tops
3 tablespoons butter or margarine
2½ tablespoons flour
½ teaspoon curry powder
2½ cups hot water

2½ cups hot milk
1 pound mushrooms, chopped
   fine
2 teaspoons salt
2 egg yolks
½ cup heavy cream

In a saucepan sauté the sliced scallions in the butter or margarine over low heat for 7 to 8 minutes, or until they are soft. Add the flour and curry powder and cook over moderate heat, stirring until well blended. Remove the pan from the heat and add the water and milk, stirring constantly. Add the mushrooms and salt. Return to the heat and simmer, partially covered, for 30 minutes. In a bowl beat the egg yolks with the heavy cream and beat in 2 cups of the soup in a steady stream. Return the mixture to the pan and cook over moderately low heat, stirring, for 5 minutes, or until the soup thickens and begins to coat the spoon. Allow to cool, stirring several times, and chill for 2 hours. Serve the soup in chilled bowls and sprinkle each serving with the reserved snippings of green scallion tops.

Preparation and cooking time: approximately 1 hour 15 minutes. Chilling time: 2 hours.

†*COLD CURRIED VEGETABLE SOUP

SERVES 6

2 tablespoons butter
1 tablespoon curry powder
6 cups clear chicken stock (see page 276)
1 teaspoon brown sugar
2 cups green beans, cooked (string or runner)

1 cup peas, cooked
½ cup scallions, minced
1 tomato, peeled, seeded and chopped

In the top of a double boiler, over hot water, combine the butter and curry powder and cook for 10 minutes. Add the chicken stock and brown sugar and heat until the sugar is dissolved. Remove the pan from the heat, and stir in the green beans, peas, scallions and tomato. Cool the soup and chill it.

Preparation and cooking time: approximately 45 minutes. Chilling time: 3 hours.

FIRST COURSES

---

†EGG MOUSSE

SERVES 8

10 eggs
One 15-fluid ounce Crosse &
Blackwell clear consommé
madrilène
2 teaspoons Worcestershire
sauce
2 teaspoons mushroom
ketchup‡

Salt and pepper
2 teaspoons capers (optional)
½ cup heavy cream
½ cup fresh mayonnaise or Hell-
man's mayonnaise
1 cucumber, sliced thin, or one 3½-
ounce jar of black Danish lump-
fish roe

Hard-boil the eggs, then mash them roughly in a bowl with a fork to a crumbly but not creamy consistency. Add half the consommé, season with Worcestershire sauce, mushroom ketchup, salt and

‡ Mushroom ketchup can be bought at most specialty food shops or ordered from Maison Glass, 52 East 58 Street, New York, New York 10022.

†*CURRIED PEA AND AVOCADO SOUP

SERVES 6

3 tablespoons butter or margarine
¼ cup onion, chopped fine
1 teaspoon curry powder
2 cups shelled fresh green peas
1 teaspoon chervil
Salt and pepper to taste
2 cups chicken stock or broth

2 avocados to make 6 teaspoons
   avocado pulp and 6 slices avocado brushed with lemon
   juice
1 cup light cream
Salt and white pepper to taste

In a saucepan melt the butter or margarine and sauté the onion with the curry powder until the onion is tender but not colored. Add the peas, chervil, salt and pepper to taste and chicken stock or broth. Simmer the peas, covered, for 15 to 25 minutes, or until they are tender. Put the peas and liquid in the container of a blender or food processor with the avocado pulp and purée, scraping down the sides with a rubber spatula. Transfer the mixture to a saucepan. Stir in the light cream and heat the soup, stirring occasionally. Season with additional salt and white pepper to taste and top each serving with a slice of avocado.

Preparation and cooking time: approximately 45 minutes. Chilling time: 2 to 3 hours.

pepper, and capers, if desired. Beat the cream and mayonnaise together and fold into the egg mixture. Pour into an 8-inch soufflé dish and chill for at least 5 hours. When thoroughly chilled, arrange sliced cucumber on the top, cover with the remaining consommé and continue to chill until the additional consommé has jelled. Or, if you like lumpfish, *wait until just before serving,* and spread the lumpfish over the top of the egg mousse so that it makes a nice thick covering and save the remaining consommé for another use. *Important:* If you put the lumpfish on too long before serving, it stains the mousse gray.

Preparation time: 30 minutes. Chilling time: 5 to 7 hours.

††EGGS IN TOMATOES FLORENTINE

SERVES 6

6 ripe but firm tomatoes	6 tablespoons bread crumbs
Salt and pepper	Oregano, to taste
6 tablespoons butter or margarine	Creamed spinach (see page
6 eggs	56)

Preheat oven to 400° F.

Slice off the top of each tomato, then cut around the inner shells to release the pulp. Remove the pulp and reserve for use in another dish, lightly salt the inside of the shells and invert the shells on a rack. Allow the shells to drain for about 30 minutes. Put 1 teaspoon of butter or margarine into each tomato, arrange the tomatoes in a lightly buttered ovenproof dish, and bake them in the preheated oven for 10 minutes. Remove from the oven, break 1 egg into each tomato, pour 1 teaspoon of melted butter over each egg, and lightly salt and pepper the egg whites. Bake the tomatoes, covered loosely with foil, for 10 minutes longer, or until the egg whites are just set. Remove from oven and turn up heat to broil. Mix the bread crumbs and oregano together and top each egg with 1 teaspoon of the mixture and a few dots of softened butter. Cook the tomatoes under a preheated broiler for 1 minute, or until the crumbs are lightly colored and the egg whites are completely set. Serve the tomatoes on a bed of creamed spinach.

Preparation and cooking time: approximately 1 hour.

†CREAMED SPINACH

---

2 pounds fresh spinach, well washed and
   trimmed
2 cloves garlic, chopped fine
¼ cup butter

1 cup heavy cream
Nutmeg to taste
Salt and pepper to taste

In a large saucepan filled with boiling salted water, cook the spinach for 5 to 6 minutes, or until it is tender. Drain the spinach and refresh it under running cold water until it is cool. Squeeze all the water from the spinach and chop fine. In a large enamel frying pan, sauté the garlic in the butter until it is golden, then add the spinach and cook over moderately high heat, stirring, until the moisture has evaporated. Add ⅓ cup cream and simmer the mixture, until it is hot and the cream is well reduced. Add the rest of the cream, one half at a time, allowing the first addition to reduce before adding more. Season the spinach with nutmeg, salt and pepper.

Preparation and cooking time: approximately 1 hour.

††HERBED EGGS MORNAY

SERVES 6

6 hard-boiled eggs
6 mushrooms, sautéed and chopped fine
1½ teaspoons butter, softened
½ teaspoon salt
Dash of cayenne

¼ cup parsley and chives
   combined, chopped
   fine
2 cups Mornay sauce (see
   below)
6 individual scallop
   shells or ramekins

Preheat oven to 350° F.

Halve the eggs lengthwise. Remove the yolks, rub them through a sieve and mix them with the mushrooms, butter, salt and a dash of cayenne. Using a pastry bag fitted with a decorative tube, force the mixture into the egg whites, heaping it as high as possible. Add chopped parsley and chives to the Mornay sauce and spread a layer of the sauce in each scallop shell. Arrange the stuffed eggs on the sauce and set them in the preheated oven for approximately 15 minutes.

Preparation and cooking time: 45 minutes plus 1 hour to make Mornay sauce.

††MORNAY SAUCE

MAKES APPROXIMATELY 3 CUPS

1 tablespoon onion, chopped fine
¼ cup butter
2 tablespoons flour
3 cups milk, scalded
¼ teaspoon salt
3 white peppercorns

Sprig of parsley
Pinch of nutmeg
3 lightly beaten egg yolks
1 tablespoon light cream, heated
2 tablespoons grated Parmesan
   or Swiss cheese

In a saucepan sauté the onion in 2 tablespoons of the butter until it is soft. Add the flour, mix well, and cook the roux slowly, stirring constantly, until it just starts to turn golden. Gradually add the milk and cook the mixture, stirring vigorously with a wire whisk, until it is thick and smooth. Add salt, peppercorns, parsley and nutmeg. Cook the sauce slowly, stirring frequently, for about 30 minutes, or until it is reduced by one-third. Strain the sauce through a fine sieve. Mix the egg yolks with the hot cream and combine them with the sauce. Cook the sauce, stirring constantly, until it just reaches the boiling point. Add the remaining butter and the grated cheese.

†MADAME JACQUES DE BEAUMARCHAIS'S OEUFS CHIMAY

SERVES 6

9 eggs, hard-boiled
2 shallots, chopped
¾ cup button mushrooms, chopped
  fine
1 tablespoon butter or margarine
2 heaping tablespoons
  chopped parsley

2½ tablespoons heavy cream
1¼ cups béchamel or basic
  white sauce (see page 278)
1 tablespoon grated Gruyère

Halve the eggs lengthwise and put the yolks through a very fine sieve. Sauté the shallots and mushrooms in butter, add to the sieved egg yolks and blend with the parsley and cream. Put the mixture into the hollows of the egg whites and cover with a layer of béchamel sauce. Arrange the eggs in an ovenproof dish, sprinkle with grated cheese and brown under a hot broiler for 2 to 3 minutes or until golden.

Preparation and cooking time: approximately 45 minutes.

†OEUFS EN COCOTTE WITH TRUFFLES

SERVES 6

Melted butter, to brush ramekins
6 to 12 eggs, depending on size
6 tablespoons heavy cream

Sprinkling of truffles, chopped
fine, or canned truffle
peelings
6 slices of foie gras or pâté
12 slices hot buttered toast

Preheat oven to 350° F.

Brush 6 individual ramekins with melted butter, then break 1 or 2 eggs into each one and add 1 tablespoon of heavy cream. Sprinkle the eggs with the truffles. Place the ramekins in a shallow pan of boiling water, cover them with foil and cook the eggs in a preheated oven for 10 to 12 minutes, or until the whites are set. Top each ramekin with a slice of foie gras or pâté and serve hot with 2 pieces of hot buttered toast.

Preparation and cooking time: approximately 20 minutes.

†THE EARL OF GOWRIE'S OEUFS EN COCOTTE WITH DUCK JELLY

SERVES 4

The next time you cook a duck, pour off and reserve the juices. Chilled, these will produce duck lard excellent for frying onions or potatoes. Underneath there will be a couple of tablespoons of jelly that will make ordinary oeufs en cocotte à la crème something special.

Melted butter, to brush ramekins
4 teaspoons duck jelly
4 leaves fresh tarragon
8 tablespoons heavy cream

4 to 8 eggs
4 teaspoons butter
Salt and pepper to taste

Preheat oven to 375° F.

Brush 4 individual ramekins with melted butter. Place 1 teaspoon of duck jelly and 1 tarragon leaf at the bottom of each ramekin (dried tarragon will not do. Substitute fresh parsley and chives if necessary). Add 1 tablespoon of heavy cream and set the ramekins in a flameproof baking dish half filled with simmering water, over moderate heat. When the cream is hot break 1 or 2 eggs into each ramekin. Pour 1 tablespoon of cream over each egg and top with a teaspoon of butter. Place on the middle shelf of the hot oven and bake for 7 to 10 minutes. The eggs are done when they are just set but still tremble. They will set a little more when the ramekins are removed, so don't overcook. Season with salt and pepper.

Preparation and cooking time: approximately 20 minutes.

†OEUFS EN COCOTTE WITH SOUR CREAM

SERVES 6

6 tablespoons butter, melted   *6 teaspoons sour cream*
8 teaspoons toasted bread crumbs   *3 teaspoons chives, snipped fine*
6 eggs

Preheat oven to 350° F.

Butter 6 individual ramekins and into each put 1 tablespoon melted butter and 1 teaspoon toasted bread crumbs. Break 1 egg into each ramekin and sprinkle with the remaining bread crumbs. Arrange the ramekins in a baking dish half filled with boiling water, and bake in the oven for 10 minutes. Pour 1 teaspoon of sour cream mixed with ½ teaspoon of chives over each egg and serve immediately.

Preparation and cooking time: approximately 15 minutes.

†PEAS WITH EGGS AND TOMATO SAUCE

SERVES 4

1 medium onion, chopped
1 medium carrot, chopped
2 tablespoons butter or vegetable oil
¾ cup chicken stock or broth
½ cup tomato sauce (see below)
4 tablespoons mushrooms, chopped
1 tablespoon parsley, chopped

¼ teaspoon Worcestershire
sauce
Salt to taste
1 pound fresh or frozen peas
4 eggs
White pepper to taste

In a frying pan sauté the onion and carrot in the butter or vegetable oil until they are soft. Add the chicken stock, tomato sauce, mushrooms, parsley, Worcestershire sauce and salt to taste and simmer the mixture, covered, for 5 minutes. Add the peas and cook, covered, for 20 minutes. With the back of a spoon make 4 indentations in the mixture and crack an egg into each one. Sprinkle the white of each egg with salt and white pepper to taste and continue to cook, covered, for 2 to 3 minutes or until the eggs are set.

Preparation and cooking time: approximately 1 hour 30 minutes.

TOMATO SAUCE

4 tablespoons olive oil
1 medium onion, chopped fine
2 shallots, chopped fine
1 garlic clove, chopped fine
6 tomatoes, coarse-chopped
1 bay leaf

¼ teaspoon thyme
1 clove
Salt and pepper to taste
1 tablespoon sugar
Ground cuminseed to taste

In a heavy saucepan heat the olive oil and add the onion, shallots and garlic. Cover the pan and cook the vegetables over very low heat for about 15 minutes, or until they are soft but not browned. Add the tomatoes, bay leaf, thyme, clove and salt and pepper to taste, and simmer the sauce over low heat for about 20 minutes. Put the sauce through a fine sieve and add the sugar and cuminseed. Heat the sauce slowly.

†CHEDDAR CORN SOUFFLÉ

SERVES 6

1½ tablespoons butter or margarine
2 tablespoons flour
2 cups hot milk
1 cup grated Cheddar cheese
1 teaspoon dry mustard

½ teaspoon salt
1 cup canned or frozen corn
   kernels
3 egg yolks, lightly beaten
3 egg whites, beaten until stiff

Preheat oven to 375° F.

In a saucepan melt the butter, remove the pan from the heat and stir in the flour. Gradually add hot milk and cook the sauce over low heat, stirring constantly, for 5 minutes or until it is smooth and thick. Add the cheese, dry mustard and salt, and cook the mixture, stirring, until the cheese has almost melted. Remove the pan from the heat and stir the corn kernels into the cheese mixture. Add the egg yolks and fold in the egg whites. Pour the mixture into a 1½-quart soufflé dish, buttered and floured, and set the dish in a pan of hot water. Bake the soufflé in the preheated moderate oven for 45 minutes or until the top is firm and brown.

Preparation and cooking time: approximately 1 hour 30 minutes.

††CHEESE PUFFS WITH HERBED TOMATO SAUCE

APPROXIMATELY 20 PUFFS

½ cup water
½ cup milk
6 tablespoons butter, cut into pieces
½ teaspoon salt
¼ teaspoon white pepper
1 cup flour

3 eggs
¾ cup grated Emmentaler
  cheese
Vegetable fat and vegetable
  oil for frying

In a heavy saucepan combine the water and milk, butter, salt and white pepper, and bring the liquid to the boil over high heat. Reduce the heat and add the flour. Beat the mixture with a flat wooden spoon until it leaves the sides of the pan and forms a ball. Transfer the dough to the bowl of an electric mixer. With the mixer at high speed beat in the eggs, one at a time, beating well after each addition. Then beat in the cheese. In a deep fryer heat to 360° F. enough vegetable oil and vegetable fat in equal amounts to measure 3 inches. Dip 2 tablespoons into the fat and with them shape balls of dough. Lower the balls into the fat and fry them, in batches, turning them several times, until they are lightly browned. Drain the puffs on paper towels and serve them immediately with an herbed tomato sauce (see below).

Preparation and cooking time: approximately 45 minutes.

†*QUICK HERBED TOMATO SAUCE

3 garlic cloves, chopped fine
¼ cup olive oil
One 32-ounce can Italian plum
  tomatoes
1½ teaspoon salt

Few grinds fresh black pepper
2 to 3 fresh basil leaves or 1½ teaspoons dried basil
1 teaspoon grated orange zest
1 tablespoon tomato paste

In a heavy saucepan sauté the garlic cloves in the olive oil over medium heat for 1 minute. Add the tomatoes and cook them over rather high heat for 10 minutes. Add the salt, pepper, fresh or dried basil, orange zest and tomato paste. Allow the sauce to cook for another minute or two. Leftover sauce freezes well.

Preparation and cooking time: approximately 15 minutes.

†CURRIED CREAM CHEESE AND HAM RAMEKIN

SERVES 8

One 15-ounce can Crosse & Blackwell clear consommé madrilène
One 6-ounce package Philadelphia cream cheese
Juice of 1 lemon

2 cloves garlic, crushed
1 teaspoon curry powder
1 teaspoon Worcestershire sauce
3 slices cooked ham
Handful of snipped chives

In a blender or food processor put half of the consommé, the cream cheese, lemon juice, garlic, curry powder and Worcestershire sauce, and mix until well blended. Slice the ham into julienne strips and line the bottom of 8 individual ramekins with them. Pour in the cream cheese mixture, leaving a ¼-inch space at the top of each ramekin. Put in the refrigerator until the mixture sets, or approximately 1 hour. Then sprinkle the chives on top of each ramekin and cover with the rest of the consommé. Put back into the refrigerator for another hour, or until the additional consommé has set.

Preparation time: 10 minutes. Chilling time: 2 hours.

†POTTED CHEESE

SERVES 12

1 pound Cheddar cheese
3 tablespoons scallions, chopped
3 tablespoons parsley, chopped
1 teaspoon Dijon mustard
Salt to taste

2 tablespoons softened butter
2 tablespoons sherry
Dash of Tabasco and dash of Worcestershire sauce

Grate the cheese into a bowl. Season it with the scallions, parsley, mustard and salt. Beat in the butter, sherry, Tabasco and Worcestershire sauce. Stir the mixture until it becomes creamy, then pack it into a jar or crock and refrigerate it until ready to use. Serve the potted cheese at room temperature with crusty bread.

Preparation time: approximately 10 minutes.

†*CHICKEN LIVER AND CAPER PÂTÉ

SERVES 6 TO 8

1 pound chicken livers
3 shallots, chopped fine
½ cup sweet butter
1½ tablespoons sherry
1½ tablespoons Cognac
2 teaspoons salt

¼ teaspoon nutmeg
¼ teaspoon pepper
Pinch each of thyme, basil and marjoram
Half of a 3-ounce bottle of capers
3 to 4 tablespoons clarified butter (see page 275)

Sauté the chicken livers and shallots in the butter for 3 to 4 minutes, or until the livers are browned on the outside but pink inside. Transfer to a bowl. Stir the sherry and Cognac into the butter remaining in the pan and pour over the livers. Season with salt, nutmeg, pepper and herbs. Combine well and purée the mixture, about a third at a time, in a blender or food processor. Add the capers but do not blend, so that they give a slightly rough texture to the pâté. Spoon into an earthenware terrine, cover the surface with clarified butter and chill for 12 hours. Serve with hot buttered toast.

Preparation and cooking time: 30 minutes. Chilling time: 12 hours.

†*KIPPER PÂTÉ

SERVES 4 TO 6

1 pound frozen kipper fillets	*3 tablespoons light cream*
1 clove garlic, crushed	*Salt and pepper to taste*
6 tablespoons olive oil	*Lemon slices for decoration*

Poach the kippers in water for 10 minutes, or until they are just cooked. Drain and remove the skins, then put the cooked flesh into a saucepan and beat with a wooden spoon to break it up. Beat in the garlic and heat gently, stirring to prevent sticking. Add the olive oil gradually, beating well between each addition. Beat in the cream. Remove from the heat and season. Turn the mixture into individual ramekins or a small soufflé dish. Decorate with lemon slices, cover and refrigerate for up to 2 or 3 days.

Preparation and cooking time: 30 minutes. Chilling time: 4 hours.

†*PÂTÉ WITH OLIVES, PINE NUTS AND PROSCIUTTO

SERVES 6

1 pound pork, ½ pound veal and ¼
   pound pork fat, ground together
⅓ cup black olives, pitted and
   chopped
¼ cup lightly toasted pine nuts,
   chopped
¼ cup prosciutto, diced
¼ cup fresh white bread crumbs
2 tablespoons dry vermouth

1½ teaspoons basil,
   preferably fresh
½ teaspoon dried thyme
¼ teaspoon pepper
1 very small garlic clove
½ teaspoon salt
1 egg, lightly beaten
½ pound bacon, sliced thin

Preheat oven to 350° F.

In a large bowl combine the ground meat with the olives, pine nuts, prosciutto, bread crumbs moistened in the vermouth, basil, thyme and pepper. In a mortar crush the garlic together with the salt. Add it to the meat mixture and blend thoroughly. Add the egg and mix thoroughly again. Line the bottom of a 10-inch loaf pan with half the bacon. Turn the meat mixture into the pan and press it down firmly. Cover the top of the mixture with the remaining bacon. Bake the pâté in the preheated moderate oven for 1½ hours. Weight the pâté, allow it to cool and chill for 12 hours. Unmold the loaf onto a serving dish and remove the bacon. Serve at room temperature.

Preparation and cooking time: 2 hours. Chilling time: 12 hours.

††DILLED CRÊPES WITH SMOKED SALMON

SERVES 6 TO 8

1 pint sour cream
8 slices smoked salmon
8 sprigs fresh dill

Preheat oven to 350° F.

Make entree crêpes (see below). To serve immediately, spread each crêpe as it is made with a thin layer of sour cream and top the cream with a slice of smoked salmon. Fold the crêpes in quarters and serve them on a heated dish, topped with sprigs of dill. If you make the crêpes in advance, stack them on an ovenproof dish as they are done and cover them with a round of foil. Reheat for approximately 10 minutes in the preheated moderate oven before serving. Then proceed as above. *Do not heat after smoked salmon has been added.*

*ENTREE CRÊPES

¾ cup flour	½ teaspoon salt
¾ cup milk	2 tablespoons butter, melted and cooled
3 eggs	3 tablespoons snipped dill
¼ cup water	1 cup clarified butter (see page 275)

In a blender combine all the ingredients except the butter and dill, and blend for 30 seconds, scraping down the batter from the sides of the container. Add the melted and cooled butter and blend for a few seconds more. Transfer the batter to a bowl and allow it to stand, covered, for at least 1 hour. Add the snipped dill. Heat a 6-to-7-inch crêpe pan and brush it lightly with clarified butter. Pour in about 3 tablespoons of batter, quickly tilting and rotating the pan so that the batter covers the bottom in a thin layer, and return any excess batter to the bowl. Cook the crêpe over moderately high heat until the underside is browned, turn it with a spatula and brown the other side. Transfer the crêpe to a plate and make crêpes from the remaining batter in the same manner. These crêpes may be frozen, with a sheet of either foil or waxed paper between each crêpe, and reheated.

Preparation and cooking time: 1 hour 30 minutes.

††CRAB SOUFFLÉ

SERVES 6

2 tablespoons grated onion
3 tablespoons butter
3 tablespoons flour
⅔ cup milk, scalded
3 egg yolks, lightly beaten
1 tablespoon chopped parsley
2 teaspoons lemon juice
¾ teaspoon salt

½ teaspoon paprika
Pepper to taste
1¼ cups cooked lump crab meat,
    fresh or canned
4 egg whites
Pinch of salt
Hollandaise sauce (see page 296)

Preheat oven to 375° F.

In a saucepan cook the onion in the butter over moderate heat, stirring, for 1 minute. Add the flour and cook the roux, stirring, for 2 minutes. Remove the pan from the heat and stir in the scalded milk. Cook the sauce, stirring, for 2 minutes. Transfer to a bowl and stir in the egg yolks, parsley, lemon juice, salt, paprika and pepper to taste. Stir in the crab meat. In another bowl beat the egg whites with a pinch of salt until stiff. Fold a quarter of the whites into the crab mixture, then gently but thoroughly fold in the rest. Butter a 1-quart soufflé dish and tie a band of waxed paper, doubled and buttered, around it to form a standing collar extending 2 inches above the rim. Turn the crab mixture into the dish and bake the soufflé for 35 to 40 minutes, or until it is puffed and golden brown. Serve with hollandaise sauce.

Preparation and cooking time: approximately 1 hour 15 minutes.

††MARINATED MUSSELS

SERVES 6

*3 pounds mussels, well scrubbed
(see note page 34)*
½ cup onion, sliced thin
1 lemon, sliced thin
¼ cup dry white wine
¼ cup lemon juice

¼ cup olive oil
*½ teaspoon whole mixed
pickling spice*
1 garlic clove, crushed
Salt and pepper to taste
Sprinkling of minced parsley

Preheat oven to 400° F.

Arrange the mussels in a shallow baking pan and place them in a preheated hot oven for 5 minutes, or until they open. Allow the opened mussels to cool, shell them, reserving their liquid, and discarding any that have not opened, and remove the black rims. Transfer the mussels to a deep dish just large enough to hold them in 2 layers and strain and reserve the mussel liquid. Spread the sliced onion and sliced lemon over the mussels. In a small saucepan bring the reserved liquid, dry white wine, lemon juice, olive oil, mixed pickling spice and crushed garlic to the boil and simmer the mixture for 10 minutes. Add salt and pepper to taste, and allow the marinade to cool. Strain the cooled marinade over the mussel mixture and sprinkle the dish with minced parsley. Toss the mussels with the marinade and chill, covered, for 48 hours.

Preparing mussels and cooking time: approximately 1 hour. Chilling time: 48 hours.

†DEVILED SARDINES

SERVES 4

1 egg yolk
1 teaspoon Dijon mustard
1 teaspoon dry mustard
Juice of 1 lemon
Few drops Tabasco sauce
Few drops Worcestershire sauce

3 cans skinless and boneless
  sardines
1 cup fresh white bread crumbs
4 slices white bread, trimmed of
  crusts
2 to 3 tablespoons butter
Lemon wedges

Preheat the broiler.

Mix together the egg yolk, Dijon mustard and dry mustard, lemon juice, Tabasco and Worcestershire sauces. Drain the sardines, coat them with the sauce and roll each fish in the bread crumbs. Place the sardines under preheated broiler for 2 minutes on each side, or until they are crusty, or sauté them in a little heated oil until they are lightly browned. Sauté the slices of white bread in butter until they are crisp. Serve the sardines on fried bread with lemon wedges.

Preparation and cooking time: approximately 30 minutes.

†SCALLOPS AND MUSHROOMS IN
LEMON DRESSING

SERVES 8

1 pound small scallops
2 tablespoons minced onion
1 bay leaf
¼ teaspoon salt
Pepper to taste

1 pound firm white mushroom caps,
  sliced thin
3 tablespoons lemon juice
½ cup olive oil
Salt and pepper to taste
Chopped parsley

In a saucepan combine the scallops, onion, bay leaf, salt and pepper to taste and add enough water to cover. Bring the water to the boiling point over moderately low heat, turn off the heat and allow the scallops to stand, covered, for 5 minutes. Transfer the scallops and onion, with a slotted spoon, to a bowl. Put the sliced mushrooms in another bowl. Put the lemon juice in a small bowl and add the olive oil in a stream, beating. Add salt and pepper to taste, and toss the scallops in one half of the dressing, then the mushrooms in the remaining dressing. Combine the mushrooms and scallops in a serving dish and sprinkle them with chopped parsley. Chill the dish for 4 hours.

Preparation and cooking time: approximately 30 minutes. Chilling time: 4 hours.

†MRS. ANTHONY LUND'S TARAMASALATA

SERVES 6

"This can be made by hand if no electric mixer is available, but it is a lot of work. I've often used the non-bottled cod's roe which comes whole in a sort of orange skin. This should make it better but, in fact, does not unless the roe is very moist and easily detachable from its skin. Again, the jar is labor-saving."

> *6 slices white bread, crusts removed*   *8 tablespoons olive oil*
> *1 jar smoked cod's roe*   *Juice of 1 lemon*
> *¼ onion, grated*   *Heavy cream to taste*
> *1 clove garlic*

Soak the bread in water. Squeeze dry and beat it with the cod's roe in a mixer (not a liquidizer) until it is as free of lumps as possible. Add the onion and garlic, then start adding olive oil and lemon juice, alternately, in small amounts, rather like making mayonnaise, beating all the time until the mixture is smooth. Finish off with a little heavy cream. The more cream you add, the blander the taramasalata will become, so it is totally a question of taste. Chill in the refrigerator, as it must be served very cold on hot toast.

Preparation time: approximately 30 minutes. Chilling time: 1 to 2 hours.

††GINGERED TUNA PUFFS

SERVES 6 TO 8

One 7-ounce can of tuna fish
3 tablespoons mayonnaise
2 ounces cream cheese
1 tablespoon grated fresh ginger
root

Salt and pepper to taste
Small cream puffs of choux pastry
(see below)

Make small bite-sized cream puffs of pâté à choux. Split the puffs and fill them with a mixture of all the above ingredients.

*PÂTE À CHOUX (CHOUX PASTRY)

MAKES 18 TO 20 PUFFS

1 cup water
½ cup butter
1 teaspoon sugar

½ teaspoon salt
1 cup plus 2 tablespoons flour
4 large eggs

Preheat oven to 375° F.

In a small saucepan bring the water, butter, sugar and salt to the boil. Add the flour all at once and beat well with a spoon. Remove the pan from the heat for a moment and beat the mixture briskly. Beat the batter over very low heat until it forms a ball and leaves the sides of the pan. Remove the pan from the heat and beat in the eggs, one at a time, beating well after each addition, until the dough is smooth and glossy. Cool the paste slightly. Shape it into small puffs on a lightly buttered baking sheet with a pastry tube or a teaspoon. Bake the puffs in the preheated oven for 15 to 20 minutes or until they are light brown and dry.

Preparation and cooking time: approximately 1 hour 30 minutes.

††EGGPLANT SOUFFLÉ

SERVES 6

3 medium-sized eggplants
Salt and pepper to taste
Handful of bread crumbs
6 tablespoons butter
Pinch of nutmeg

3 tablespoons flour
1 cup hot milk
6 egg yolks
6 egg whites, beaten stiff

Preheat oven to 350° F.

Peel and halve the eggplants, sprinkle them with salt and allow to stand for 30 minutes. With 1 tablespoon butter, grease a 1-quart soufflé dish and sprinkle the bottom and sides with a light coating of bread crumbs. Wipe the salt from the eggplants, cut into cubes and steam for 10 to 12 minutes, or until they are soft. Sauté the steamed eggplant in 2 tablespoons of butter, over low heat, stirring frequently, until all the excess moisture has evaporated. Purée the eggplant, put it in a bowl, season with salt and pepper and add the nutmeg. In a saucepan blend the flour with the remaining butter to make a roux and stir for a few minutes. Do not allow the flour to brown. Gradually add the hot milk and cook the sauce over low heat, stirring constantly, until it thickens. Combine the sauce with the eggplant and add the egg yolks one at a time, beating hard after each addition. Fold in the egg whites and turn the mixture into the prepared soufflé dish. Set the dish in a baking pan partially filled with hot water and bake in moderate preheated oven for 30 to 40 minutes, or until the soufflé is puffed and golden brown. Serve immediately.

Preparation and cooking time: approximately 2 hours.

†EGGPLANT WITH GINGER AND SESAME SEEDS

SERVES 6

One 2-pound eggplant, peeled and cut into ½-inch cubes
½ cup sesame seeds
4 scallions, sliced thin
1 tablespoon fresh ginger root, peeled and grated

½ teaspoon salt
3 tablespoons sesame oil
2 teaspoons lime juice

Preheat oven to 350° F.

Drop the eggplant cubes into a large saucepan filled with boiling salted water, cook them for 3 to 4 minutes or until they are barely tender, and drain well. Spread the sesame seeds on a baking sheet and toast them in the oven until they are lightly browned. In a blender grind the seeds until they are almost a paste. Combine the ground sesame seeds with the scallions, grated ginger root and salt. In a frying pan sauté the eggplant cubes in sesame oil over moderately high heat, tossing them frequently, for 5 minutes. Add the sesame-seed mixture and sauté the eggplant for 2 to 3 minutes more, or until the mixture is heated through. Stir in the lime juice. This dish may be served hot or cold and may also be used as a vegetable with roast lamb.

Preparation and cooking time: approximately 1 hour.

†MRS. RORY McEWEN'S AVOCADO AND CAVIAR MOUSSE
(*which she originally got from Jonathan Routh*)

SERVES 4

> 2 ripe avocados
> 1 small onion, chopped fine
> 1 large jar Danish lumpfish roe (or fresh caviar)
> 2 lemons, quartered

Mash the avocados and onions together in a bowl and put in the refrigerator to chill for 1 hour. Just before serving gently stir in almost all the lumpfish roe or caviar and put into a soufflé dish. Note: If the lumpfish roe or caviar is put in too long before it is served, the mousse becomes gray in color. Spread the remaining lumpfish roe or caviar on top of the mousse and serve with lemon quarters, hot toast and butter. The mixture should be made not long before serving, but if making it several hours in advance, bury an avocado stone in the middle of the avocado-and-onion mixture to keep it from turning brown.

Preparation time: 15 minutes. Chilling time: 1 hour.

†MR. BRIGGS'S AVOCADO RAMEKIN
(*A recipe given to me by Peter Coats*)

SERVES 8

3 ripe avocados
One 15-fluid-ounce can Crosse &
   Blackwell clear consommé
½ lemon

2 tablespoons heavy cream
½ cup chopped walnuts
8 slices crisp lean bacon,
   crumbled

Put the avocado flesh in a liquidizer or food processor with three-quarters of the can of consommé, a good squeeze of lemon (to keep avocado from turning brown) and the cream. Half fill 8 individual ramekins with about half the avocado mixture and allow it to set in the refrigerator. When set, add the chopped walnuts and allow to set again. Add the remaining avocado mixture to almost fill the ramekins and set again, then pour on a very thin layer of consommé. Set, then sprinkle very crisp bacon bits on top and keep in the refrigerator until ready to serve.

Preparation time: 15 minutes. Chilling time on and off: approximately 2 hours.

†AVOCADOS WITH HOT SAUCE

SERVES 6

¾ *cup salad oil*
¼ *cup tarragon vinegar*
2 *teaspoons sugar*
½ *teaspoon salt*
A dash of Tabasco sauce
2 *hard-boiled eggs, sieved*

1 *tablespoon chopped chives*
1 *tablespoon chopped parsley*
1 *teaspoon dry mustard*
½ *teaspoon Worcestershire sauce*
3 *avocados, halved and stone removed*

In a saucepan combine the salad oil, vinegar, sugar, salt and Tabasco sauce. Bring the mixture to the boil, remove it from the heat and stir in the eggs, chives, parsley, dry mustard and Worcestershire sauce. Spoon the hot sauce into the cavities of the unpeeled avocado halves.

Preparation and cooking time: approximately 30 minutes.

†BARONESS DACRE'S CURRIED MELON AND SHRIMP

SERVES 8

4 cantaloupes
6 to 7 teaspoons curry powder
½ cup heavy cream

½ cup mayonnaise
Two 6-ounce cans of shrimp or 12
ounces frozen shrimp

Halve the melons, scoop out the flesh into small balls and reserve the shells. Mix the curry powder with the heavy cream, mayonnaise and shrimp. Add the melon and put the entire mixture back into the melon shells. Cool in refrigerator before serving.

Preparation time: 20 minutes. Chilling time: 1 to 2 hours.

†BAKED STUFFED MUSHROOMS

SERVES 6 TO 8

16 large mushroom caps
3 tablespoons butter
3 slices prosciutto, minced
3 eggs, beaten
2 cups milk

1 teaspoon salt
Pinch of pepper
2 tablespoons grated Cheddar cheese
(optional)

Preheat oven to 350° F.

Scrub or peel the mushroom caps and sauté them in butter. Stuff the sautéed mushrooms with the prosciutto and place them in a shallow baking pan. Combine the eggs, milk, salt and pepper and pour over the mushrooms. Sprinkle with cheese if you wish. Put the pan in a dish of hot water and bake for 1 hour or until the custard is set and a knife stuck into the center comes out clean. Cut into squares. Serve with hot toast.

Preparation and cooking time: approximately 1 hour 30 minutes.

†MUSHROOM CAVIAR

SERVES 6 TO 8

2 small onions, chopped fine
3 tablespoons olive oil
¾ pound mushrooms, trimmed and
  chopped fine

1½ tablespoons lemon juice
1½ tablespoons sour cream
2 teaspoons chopped chives
Salt and pepper to taste

Sauté the onions in oil until they are soft but not brown. Stir in the mushrooms and cook them, stirring frequently, until they are tender. Remove the mixture from the heat and stir in the lemon juice, sour cream, chives, and salt and pepper to taste. Chill the mixture in the refrigerator for 1 hour. Serve it with slices of Scandinavian crispbread.

Preparation and cooking time: approximately 30 minutes. Chilling time: approximately 1 hour.

†MUSHROOM SOUFFLÉ

SERVES 6

¾ pound mushrooms, washed, drained
  and chopped very fine
1 cup milk
2 tablespoons butter
2 tablespoons flour
Salt and pepper to taste
Ground mace to taste

5 egg yolks, lightly beaten
5 egg whites, beaten stiff
  but not dry
1 tablespoon Madeira
Sprinkling of fine bread
  crumbs

Preheat oven to 350° F.

Put the mushrooms into a saucepan with the milk and bring to the boil. Lower the heat and simmer the mushrooms for 15 minutes. In a heavy saucepan melt the butter, add the flour and cook the roux over low heat for a few minutes. Stir in the mushrooms and milk and cook the sauce, stirring constantly, for about 5 minutes. Season with salt, pepper and a little mace to taste, remembering that the flavor will be diluted by the egg whites in the soufflé. Mix the beaten egg yolks into the sauce, and bring the mixture just to the boiling point. Allow it to cool a little, stirring constantly at first to prevent the egg yolks from curdling. Fold in the stiff egg whites and the Madeira. Pour the mixture into a 3-pint soufflé dish, buttered and sprinkled with fine bread crumbs. Bake the soufflé in the moderate preheated oven for about 30 minutes, or until it is puffed and lightly brown on top.

Preparation and cooking time: approximately 1 hour 30 minutes.

†POLISH BAKED MUSHROOMS

SERVES 4
A good vegetarian luncheon dish

½ *pound mushrooms*
2 *teaspoons lemon juice*
1 *tablespoon onion, minced fine*
3 *tablespoons butter*
¼ *teaspoon salt*
Pinch of fresh-ground black pepper
1 *tablespoon flour*

2 *tablespoons fresh-grated*
   Parmesan cheese
1 *cup heavy cream*
2 *egg yolks, lightly beaten*
2 *tablespoons fine white*
   bread crumbs

Preheat oven to 425° F.

Butter 4 individual ramekins. Wash the mushrooms and cut off their stems. Slice thin and sprinkle with the lemon juice to prevent discoloration. In a saucepan with a tightly fitting lid simmer the mushrooms and onion in 1 tablespoon of butter until soft. Season with salt and pepper. Stir in the flour and grated Parmesan cheese and cook about 3 minutes. Spoon the mushroom mixture into the prepared ramekins. Mix the cream and egg yolks together and pour over the mushrooms. Sprinkle with the bread crumbs and dot with the remaining butter. Place the ramekins in a shallow baking dish half filled with hot water and bake in the preheated oven about 10 minutes, or until golden brown. Serve immediately.

Preparation and cooking time: approximately 30 minutes.

††MRS. ARTHUR SCHLESINGER'S SPINACH QUICHE

SERVES 4 TO 6

2 pounds washed fresh spinach	*Dash of pepper*
2 tablespoons chopped shallots	*Dash of nutmeg*
4 tablespoons butter	*1 9-inch partially baked pastry*
3 eggs, lightly beaten	*shell (see page 82)*
½ pint heavy cream	*½ cup Gruyère cheese, grated*
½ teaspoon salt	

Preheat oven to 375° F.

Blanch the spinach in boiling water for 1 minute. Remove, dry well and chop fine. Sauté the shallots in 1 tablespoon of butter until soft. In a bowl combine the shallots, spinach, eggs, cream, salt, pepper and nutmeg and mix until blended. Transfer to a partially baked pastry shell, sprinkle with Gruyère and dot with the remaining butter. Bake for 25 to 30 minutes, or until puffed and slightly brown on top.

Preparation time: 30 minutes. Cooking time: approximately 30 minutes.

SHORT PASTRY

1½ cups flour	*⅓ cup butter*
¼ teaspoon salt	*2 tablespoons vegetable shortening*
¼ teaspoon sugar	*3 tablespoons cold water*

Preheat oven to 400° F.

Put the flour, salt and sugar in a bowl. Rub in the butter and vegetable shortening gently with your fingertips until the mixture resembles oatmeal. Stir in the water, a little at a time, until the dough holds together. Chill for at least 1 to 2 hours. Roll out the dough and put in a 9-inch, loose-bottomed pie plate that is 1½ inches deep, or a scalloped tart pan. Do not stretch the pastry. Flute the edges of the pastry shell, prick the bottom with a fork, line with aluminum foil and fill with dried beans to prevent shrinkage. Bake for 8 minutes, or until pastry is set. Remove beans and foil, prick with a fork again and bake 2 to 3 minutes longer.

Preparation and cooking time: approximately 1 hour. Chilling time: 1 to 2 hours.

FISH

Fish should be broiled 10 minutes per inch of depth, measured at the thickest point. For shrimp with a thickness of approximately ½ inch, a broiling time of 5 minutes is perfect. A ⅓-to-⅔-pound fish is adequate for each person.

†CRAB CAKES

SERVES 6

1 cup crumbled day-old bread
¼ cup mayonnaise
2 teaspoons Dijon mustard
Dash each of cayenne and black
  pepper

Salt to taste
1 pound crab meat
Vegetable oil, to coat pan

In a bowl combine the crumbled bread, mayonnaise, mustard, cayenne, black pepper and salt. Work the crab meat in gently, being careful not to allow it to flake, and shape the mixture into cakes. Heat a frying pan coated with vegetable oil and add the crab cakes. Sauté them for 3 to 5 minutes, turning once, or until they are hot and golden brown on both sides. Serve crab cakes hot.

Preparation and cooking time: approximately 30 minutes.

††CRAB MOUSSELINE IN SCALLOP SHELLS

SERVES 6

3 egg yolks
1 tablespoon lemon juice or dry
  vermouth
½ cup butter, melted and hot
¾ pound mushrooms, sliced
3 tablespoons butter
1 tablespoon lemon juice

¼ teaspoon garlic salt
1½ pounds cooked crab meat
1 pound canned artichoke hearts,
  drained
2 tablespoons Cognac
½ cup heavy cream
Six 6-inch scallop shells, buttered

Rinse out the container of a blender with hot water to heat it and drop in the egg yolks and the lemon juice or vermouth. Blend the mixture for a few seconds. With the motor running, slowly add the ½ cup melted butter in a fine stream and blend the sauce until it is smooth. Turn the hollandaise into a bowl. In a large frying pan sauté the mushrooms in the 3 tablespoons butter with the lemon juice and garlic salt for 2 to 3 minutes. Add the crab meat and heat it, stirring lightly, until it is well coated with the butter drippings. Add the artichoke hearts. Sprinkle the mixture with the Cognac and cook until the juices are reduced by half. Divide the mixture among the buttered scallop shells. Whip the heavy cream until it is stiff and fold it into the hollandaise to make mousseline sauce. Spread it over the crab mixture and put the shells under the broiler for 2 to 3 minutes to brown the tops.

Preparation and cooking time: approximately 45 minutes.

††MUSSELS IN WHITE WINE

SERVES 2

4 pounds mussels, well scrubbed
  and beards removed (see note
  page 34)
1½ cups water
½ cup white wine
1 small onion, chopped fine

2 stalks celery, chopped fine
4 whole peppercorns
¼ teaspoon salt
1 egg yolk
½ cup heavy cream
½ cup chopped parsley

Put cleaned mussels into a large saucepan with the water, white wine, onion, celery, peppercorns and salt, and steam, covered, shaking the pan frequently, for 7 minutes, or until the mussels open. Transfer them with a slotted spoon to a deep serving dish and cover. Reduce the broth by half over high heat. Carefully pour the broth and vegetables into a small saucepan, leaving any sand in the bottom of the first saucepan. In a bowl lightly beat the egg yolk with the heavy cream and stir in ½ cup of the mussel broth. Stir the egg mixture into the remaining broth and heat the sauce but do not allow it to boil. Pour the sauce over the mussels and sprinkle them with parsley.

Scrubbing and bearding mussels: approximately 1 hour. Preparation and cooking time: approximately 1 hour.

†HERBED SHRIMP IN GARLIC BUTTER

SERVES 6

36 large shrimp, shelled and
  deveined, leaving tails intact
1 tablespoon salt
1 teaspoon oregano
1 teaspoon thyme

½ pound butter or margarine,
  softened
4 cloves garlic, crushed
1 tablespoon minced parsley
¼ pound mushrooms, sliced

Preheat oven to 375° F.

Put shrimp in a bowl and toss them with the salt, oregano and thyme. Chill, covered, for at least 20 minutes. In another bowl cream together half the softened butter or margarine, the crushed garlic cloves and minced parsley. In a frying pan sauté the sliced mushrooms in the other half of the butter or margarine for 3 to 4 minutes, or until they are browned. Divide the shrimp among 6 large individual ramekins and top them with the mushrooms. Dot with the garlic butter and bake in the preheated oven for 12 minutes, or until they are pink. Serve with wild rice (see page 216).

Preparation and cooking time: approximately 1 hour 30 minutes.

†SHRIMP FONDUE

SERVES 4

> 2 pounds raw shrimp, peeled
> Cooking oil

Rinse the shrimp in cold water and pat dry in paper towels. Arrange them on a dish. Half fill a fondue pan with bland cooking oil and heat it to boiling point. Adjust the heat to keep the oil bubbling hot during the cooking process. At the table each person spears a shrimp on a long fork and dips it into the oil, twirling the fork until the shrimp is cooked. The shrimp is then dipped into a sauce and eaten immediately.

The following sauces are particularly suitable, as is the piquant mayonnaise on page 96.

GARLIC SAUCE

> 2 cups fresh mayonnaise and 1 teaspoon dill
> ¼ cup lemon juice Salt to taste
> 1 clove garlic, crushed

Mix all the ingredients together, chill and serve very cold.

CURRY SAUCE

1 teaspoon butter *1 teaspoon curry powder*
2 tablespoons flour *1 cup chicken consommé*

In a saucepan melt the butter. Stir in the flour and curry powder and cook the mixture over low heat for a minute or two. Add the consommé and continue to cook the sauce over low heat, stirring constantly, for about 15 minutes. Strain through a sieve and serve hot or cold.

†SPICED SHRIMP EN BROCHETTE

SERVES 6

2 pounds raw shrimp, shelled *1 tablespoon chopped mint*
and deveined *leaves*
1 cup olive oil *1 tablespoon chili powder*
3 cloves garlic, crushed *Salt and pepper to taste*
2 tablespoons tarragon vinegar *2 cups uncooked rice (or 6 cups*
1 tablespoon turmeric *cooked)*

Put the shrimp in a bowl and cover them with a mixture of the oil, garlic, vinegar, turmeric, mint leaves and chili powder. Add salt and pepper sparingly, and marinate the shrimp in the refrigerator for several hours or overnight. Drain the shrimp, reserving the marinade, and thread them on skewers. Place the spiced shrimp under the broiler for 4 to 5 minutes, turning the skewers and basting once or twice with the marinade. Serve them hot with a bowl of marinade and rice.

Preparation and cooking time: approximately 20 minutes. Marinating time: 8 to 12 hours.

†STIR-FRIED SHRIMP AND PEAS

SERVES 4

2 cups (after shelling) fresh green
   peas, or 1½ cups frozen peas
2 to 3 slices fresh ginger root,
   chopped fine
1½ tablespoons egg white
1½ teaspoons cornstarch
½ teaspoon salt

1 pound uncooked shrimp,
   peeled and deveined
3 tablespoons peanut oil
2 tablespoons chicken stock or
   broth
1½ tablespoons sherry
1 teaspoon soy sauce

In a saucepan cook the green peas in enough salted water to cover for 10 minutes. Drain and reserve the peas. In a shallow dish mix the ginger root with the egg white, cornstarch, and salt. Coat the shrimp with the egg-white mixture. In a frying pan heat the peanut oil until it is very hot. Add the shrimp and stir-fry them for 2 to 3 minutes, or until they are barely cooked. Add the peas, chicken stock or broth, sherry and soy sauce and cook the mixture for 2 to 3 minutes, or until the peas are hot but still crisp.

Preparation and cooking time: approximately 1 hour.

†SCALLOPS AND BACON EN BROCHETTE

SERVES 6

1½ pounds small scallops, cut into
   pieces
½ cup white wine
½ cup soy sauce
½ cup olive oil
2 cloves garlic, chopped fine

Peel of 1 lemon, grated
Chopped parsley
½ pound lean bacon, sliced
   and cut into ¼-inch squares
Melted butter

Preheat the broiler.

Wash and dry the scallops and cover them with a mixture of the wine, soy sauce and olive oil. Allow them to marinate for about 20 minutes and drain them. Make a mixture of the garlic, lemon peel and parsley. Roll each piece of scallop in this mixture and thread the scallops on skewers, alternating them with pieces of bacon. Broil the scallops for about 15 minutes, turning them frequently, until they are just cooked but not dry. Brush with melted butter and serve.

Preparation and cooking time: approximately 1 hour.

††LADY ELIZABETH VON HOFMANNSTHAL'S POACHED SEA BASS

SERVES 6 TO 8

COURT BOUILLON

4 sprigs parsley
7½ cups water
2 bay leaves
2½ cups dry white wine
Tarragon to taste
Thyme to taste
4 tablespoons white wine vinegar
5 to 6 teaspoons salt
3 large onions, sliced thick
10 whole black peppercorns

2 carrots, cut into 1-inch chunks
1 pound fish trimmings, in a
    muslin bag
4 celery stalks, cut into chunks

One 3-pound sea bass
Beurre blanc (see page 90)
Mayonnaise fines herbes (see
    page 90)

Bring all the ingredients for the court bouillon to the boil in a saucepan over high heat. Partly cover, reduce heat and simmer for 30 minutes. Set aside to cool. Strain the cooled bouillon into a fish kettle. Wash the bass inside and out in cold running water. Without drying it, wrap the bass in a piece of wet muslin, which must be quite a lot larger than the fish, and tie the knots very close to the fish, leaving the ends free to lower the bass into the kettle. Tie the ends of the muslin around the handles of the kettle so that the fish is covered by an inch of liquid. Cover and bring to a very low simmer for about 15 minutes. Remove the fish in the muslin, skin one side gently, remove to a serving dish and skin the other side. Serve hot with beurre blanc, or cold with mayonnaise fines herbes (see below).

Preparation and cooking time: approximately 1 hour 30 minutes.

†BEURRE BLANC

SERVES 6 TO 8

> *2 tablespoons shallots, chopped fine*
> *9 tablespoons white wine vinegar*
> *Salt and fresh-ground pepper, to taste*
> *1 pound butter*

Combine the shallots, vinegar and salt and pepper in a saucepan and reduce until only a quarter of the liquid remains. Then beat in the butter, 1 tablespoon at a time, whisking constantly, until all is absorbed and the mixture is white and slightly foamy.

MAYONNAISE FINES HERBES

1 to 2 egg yolks
2 tablespoons lemon juice
½ teaspoon salt
½ teaspoon pepper
¼ teaspoon dry mustard

1 to 2 tablespoons mixture of parsley,
chervil, tarragon and chives,
chopped fine
¾ cup salad oil

In a blender mix the egg yolks, lemon juice, salt, pepper, mustard and herbs for 1 minute, then add the oil in a steady stream through the hole in the lid while the motor is running, and blend for 20 seconds.

✝✝CREAMED HALIBUT WITH CAVIAR
(OR LUMPFISH ROE)

SERVES 6·

1 cup minced onion	*Salt and pepper to taste*
1 cup minced celery	*Flour, for dredging*
1 cup minced carrots	*1 teaspoon cornstarch*
½ cup butter	*1 tablespoon water*
½ cup chopped parsley	*½ cup heavy cream*
3 bay leaves, crushed	*2 tablespoons lemon juice*
2 cloves	*5 tablespoons Danish black lumpfish*
½ teaspoon salt	*roe or caviar*
¼ teaspoon white pepper	*Salt to taste*
1 cup dry white wine	*Sieved hard-boiled eggs*
Six ¾-inch-thick halibut steaks	*Minced chives*

In a heavy frying pan sauté the onion, celery and carrots in ¼ cup of
the butter for 5 minutes. Add the chopped parsley, bay leaves, cloves,
salt and white pepper and cook, covered, over low heat for 15 minutes. Add ½ cup of the dry white wine and simmer for 5 minutes
longer. Purée the mixture through the fine disk of a food mill into
a bowl or in a food processor. Sprinkle the halibut steaks with salt
and pepper and dredge them in flour. In another heavy frying pan
sauté the fish in the remaining ¼ cup of butter for 3 minutes on each
side, or until they are golden. Transfer the fish to a dish and keep
them warm. Pour off the butter from the pan and add the remaining
½ cup of wine. Bring this to the boil and boil it for 1 minute, or
until it is reduced to ¼ cup. In a cup dissolve the cornstarch in the
water, stir in the heavy cream and add the mixture, with the puréed
vegetables, to the frying pan with the wine. Bring the mixture to a
simmer over moderate heat, stirring. Reduce the heat to low, stir in
the lemon juice, 3 tablespoons of lumpfish roe or caviar and salt to
taste. Pour the sauce over the fish steaks, top each one with 1 teaspoon
of the remaining lumpfish roe or caviar and sprinkle with sieved
hard-boiled eggs and minced chives.

Preparation and cooking time: approximately 1 hour 45 minutes.

†FRESH HERRING BAKED IN BEER

SERVES 6

10 to 12 fresh herring, heads and tails removed
Pinch of ground allspice for each fish
Pinch of ground cloves for each fish
Salt and pepper to taste

1 medium onion, sliced thin
¾ cup beer
¾ cup white wine vinegar

Preheat oven to 450° F.

Clean the herring and drain them carefully. Sprinkle each herring with the allspice, ground cloves, salt and pepper. Arrange the fish in a shallow baking dish and wedge bits of the sliced onion between them. Pour a mixture of the beer and vinegar over the fish—the liquid should barely cover them. Cover the dish and bake in the preheated oven for 25 minutes.

Preparation and cooking time: approximately 1 hour.

†BROILED HERRING ROE

SERVES 6

12 whole herring roe
Butter
1 or 2 cloves garlic, cut in half or ½ onion, raw
12 slices lean bacon

Preheat the broiler.

Flatten the herring roe to make them easier to handle. Butter the broiler rack and rub it with the cut garlic or onion. Arrange the roe on the prepared rack and top each one with a slice of bacon. Broil for about 5 minutes, or until the roe is just tender.

Preparation and cooking time: approximately 30 minutes.

†BROILED MARINATED MACKEREL

SERVES 6

¼ cup olive oil
¼ cup onion rings, sliced thin
2 tablespoons lemon juice
1 teaspoon salt

¼ teaspoon thyme
¼ teaspoon pepper
6 small mackerel (12 ounces each)
2 to 3 tablespoons melted butter

Preheat broiler.

In a shallow baking dish combine the olive oil, onion rings, lemon juice, salt, thyme and pepper. Add the mackerel and allow them to marinate in the refrigerator, turning them once, for 1 hour. Drain the mackerel, and broil, basting them twice with the melted butter, for 5 minutes on each side.

Preparation and cooking time: approximately 15 minutes. Marinating time: 1 hour.

††MACKEREL WITH FENNEL

SERVES 6

3 bunches fennel, bases trimmed,
  stalks and leaves removed
  and reserved
Two 1½-to-2-pound mackerel
Salt and pepper to taste
3 cloves garlic, sliced

7 tablespoons butter
2 tablespoons olive oil
3 tablespoons of the reserved
  fennel leaves, snipped
3 tablespoons chopped parsley
Peeled lemon slices

Peel the fennel stalks and cut the bulbs and stalks into slices ½ inch thick and 1½ inches long. Cut diagonal slashes in both sides of each mackerel and sprinkle them with salt and pepper. In a flameproof dish just long enough to hold the fish, sauté the sliced garlic cloves in 4 tablespoons of the butter and the olive oil over high heat until the garlic is golden. Remove the pan from the heat, add the reserved fennel leaves and allow the mixture to cool for 10 minutes. Add the mackerel to the garlic and fennel mixture and marinate them, turning occasionally, for 30 minutes. In a saucepan blanch the fennel slices in boiling salted water for 2 minutes and drain them. In another saucepan combine the fennel slices with the remaining 3 tablespoons butter and salt and pepper to taste and cook them, covered, over low heat for 15 minutes, or until they are tender. Scrape the marinade from the fish, sprinkle with salt and pepper and fill the cavities with the remaining fennel leaves. Broil the mackerel 4 inches from the broiler, basting them once, for 10 minutes. Transfer the fish to a heated dish and arrange the fennel slices around them. Sprinkle with chopped parsley and arrange peeled lemon slices around the dish.

Preparation and cooking time: 1 hour. Marinating time: 30 minutes.

†BAKED SALMON

SERVES 6

¼ cup scallions, minced	One 2-pound salmon steak
¼ cup celery, minced	Dry mustard to taste
¼ cup parsley, minced	Salt and pepper to taste
1 bay leaf	½ cup dry vermouth
	Lemon-mustard sauce (see page 95)

Preheat oven to 350° F.

Butter a small gratin dish, sprinkle it with the scallions, celery and parsley, and top with the bay leaf. Sprinkle the salmon steak with mustard, salt and pepper. Arrange the salmon in the dish and add the dry vermouth. Cover with buttered foil and poach the fish in the preheated oven for 35 minutes, or until it flakes easily when tested with a fork. Serve it with lemon-mustard sauce.

Preparation and cooking time: approximately 45 minutes.

††LEMON-MUSTARD SAUCE

MAKES APPROXIMATELY I CUP

½ recipe béchamel sauce (see page 278)   Dry mustard to taste
1 egg yolk, lightly beaten   Salt and pepper to taste
Juice of 1 lemon

In a saucepan reduce the béchamel sauce over moderately high heat, stirring constantly, to ¾ cup. Remove the pan from the heat. In a dish combine the egg yolk with 1 tablespoon of the hot béchamel, and whisk it back into the remaining sauce. Stir in the lemon juice, dry mustard, salt and pepper.

†COLD SALMON WITH PIQUANT MAYONNAISE

SERVES 8

One 3½ pound salmon
Salt
Boiling water
Piquant mayonnaise (see page 96)

Rub the salmon with salt. Set the fish on an oiled rack and lower it into a fish kettle containing 1½ inches boiling water. Cover the kettle tightly and steam the salmon for about 45 minutes, or until the flesh flakes at the touch of a fork. If necessary, add more boiling water during the cooking to maintain the original level. Allow the salmon to cool for 30 to 45 minutes and chill it thoroughly. Serve cut into large wedges, with piquant mayonnaise on the side.

Preparation and cooking time: 1 hour 45 minutes. Chilling time: 2 hours.

†PIQUANT MAYONNAISE

MAKES APPROXIMATELY 3½ CUPS

2 eggs

2 cloves garlic, slivered

1½ teaspoons Worcestershire sauce

½ teaspoon dry mustard

Cayenne, paprika and black
   pepper to taste

Juice of 1½ lemons

3 cups salad oil

Break the eggs into a bowl and beat in the garlic, Worcestershire
sauce, dry mustard, cayenne, paprika and black pepper. Using a wire
whisk or electric mixer, beat in the lemon juice alternately with the
salad oil. Beat continually, adding the oil drop by drop at first and
then in a steady stream, until the mayonnaise has thickened sufficiently. This can also be made in a blender.

†*FIONA CHARLTON-DEWAR'S KEDGEREE

SERVES 6 TO 8

1 pound long-grain rice, cooked

6 hard-boiled eggs, chopped

¾ pound cooked salmon, fresh or
   canned, flaked

1 to 2 tablespoons curry powder

1 teaspoon ground ginger

1 tablespoon mango chutney

1 tablespoon tomato paste

2 dashes Tabasco sauce

Salt and pepper to taste

1¼ cups lightly whipped
   heavy cream

½ cup raisins

½ cup chopped walnuts

2 teaspoons commercial mixed
   herbs

With a fork, mix together the cooked rice, chopped eggs and flaked
salmon. Combine the curry powder, ginger, chutney, tomato paste,
Tabasco sauce, salt and pepper with the whipped cream and pour
this into the rice mixture. Add the raisins, walnuts and herbs, and

mix in gently with a fork. Serve hot or cold. To reheat, place in a 275° oven for about 30 minutes.

Preparation and cooking time: approximately 30 minutes.

†SALMON AND CUCUMBER EN BROCHETTE

SERVES 6

2 to 2½ pounds salmon steak, cut into 1-inch cubes

2 medium cucumbers, sliced ½ inch thick

Oil

Salt and pepper to taste

Lemon butter (see below)

Preheat broiler.

Alternate cubes of salmon with slices of cucumber on skewers. Brush them lightly with oil and season with salt and pepper. Place the skewers under the broiler for approximately 10 minutes, turning them 2 or 3 times during the cooking so that the heat penetrates the fish evenly. Serve with lemon butter or hollandaise sauce (see page 296).

Preparation and cooking time: approximately 45 minutes.

*LEMON BUTTER

½ pound sweet butter, cut into small pieces
4 heaping tablespoons parsley, chopped fine
Lemon juice to taste

Beat the butter until it becomes creamy, then add the parsley and lemon juice. Roll in greaseproof paper or foil and store in the refrigerator. Cut off in slices as required. Lemon butter freezes beautifully and can be used with any broiled fish.

††SALMON AND SOLE PAUPIETTES

SERVES 6

½ pound raw fresh salmon, skinned and boned

2 eggs

½ cup parsley, chopped fine

Salt and pepper to taste

6 uniform fillets of raw sole (or any white fish)

1½ cups dry white wine

4 tablespoons butter or margarine

1½ tablespoons flour

12 small button mushroom caps

6 canned artichoke hearts, heated

Few sprigs fresh tarragon, or 1 teaspoon dried tarragon

Put the salmon through a food chopper, add the eggs and parsley. Put the mixture through the chopper twice more and pound it until it is smooth. Add salt and pepper to taste. Spread this mousse preparation evenly on the fillets of sole, roll the fillets and secure them with wooden toothpicks. Lay them side by side in a saucepan and add the white wine. Simmer the fish gently, basting frequently, until it flakes at the touch of a fork. Transfer the fillets to a heatproof serving dish and reserve the wine. In a small saucepan melt 2 tablespoons of the butter. Stir in the flour and cook the roux for a minute or two. Do not allow it to brown. Stir in the reserved wine and cook, stirring, until the sauce is smooth and thick. Sauté the mushroom caps and artichoke hearts lightly in the remaining butter with a little fresh tarragon. Pour the sauce over the paupiettes, surround them with the artichoke hearts and arrange mushroom caps on the fish. Add the tarragon butter to sauce. Serve very hot.

Preparation and cooking time: approximately 1 hour.

††SALMON STEAKS IN CAPER SAUCE

SERVES 6

¾ cup carrots, sliced	Six 1-inch-thick salmon steaks
½ cup celery, sliced	Salt and pepper to taste
¼ cup shallots, sliced	1 cup dry white wine
4 or 5 sprigs parsley	½ cup fish stock or canned clam broth
¾ teaspoon fennel seed	3 egg yolks, beaten
½ teaspoon thyme	Capers to taste
2 tablespoons butter	Minced parsley

Preheat oven to 350° F.

In a large frying pan sauté the carrots, celery, shallots, parsley, fennel seed and thyme in the butter for 2 minutes. Cover the frying pan and cook the mixture over low heat for 10 minutes. Spread the vegetables in a large flameproof dish. Season the salmon steaks with salt and pepper and arrange them on the vegetables. Add the white wine and fish stock or clam broth, and bring the liquid to a simmer over low heat. Cover the dish tightly with aluminum foil and bake the salmon in the preheated oven for 15 minutes, or until it flakes easily when tested with a fork. Transfer the salmon steaks to a heated dish and keep them warm. Strain and reserve the braising stock. Slowly pour the egg yolks into the braising stock, beating constantly with a whisk. Pour the sauce into a heavy saucepan and cook it over low heat, stirring constantly, until it has thickened and is smooth. Do not allow it to boil. Fold in the capers. Pour the sauce over the salmon steaks and sprinkle with minced parsley.

Preparation and cooking time: approximately 45 minutes.

†SMELTS PROVENÇALE

SERVES 4, OR 8 AS A FIRST COURSE

½ cup onion, chopped fine | Salt and cayenne to taste
3 cloves garlic, minced | Dash of sugar
3 tablespoons olive oil | 24 cleaned smelts
2 cups tomato paste | Salt and pepper
½ cup lemon juice | Chopped parsley
¼ cup chopped parsley | Lemon wedges
½ teaspoon oregano

Preheat oven to 400° F.

Sauté the onion and garlic in 2 tablespoons of the olive oil until soft. Stir in the tomato paste, lemon juice, parsley, oregano, salt, cayenne and sugar. Bring the mixture to the boil and remove from heat. Dip the cleaned smelts in the remaining olive oil and arrange in 1 layer in an oiled baking dish and sprinkle with salt and pepper. Pour the tomato mixture over the smelts and bake in the preheated oven for 12 to 15 minutes. Allow the smelts to cool in the sauce and then chill. Garnish with parsley and lemon wedges.

Preparation and cooking time: approximately 50 minutes. Chilling time: 1 to 2 hours.

†FILLETS OF SOLE WITH CURRY SAUCE

SERVES 2

4 large ripe tomatoes, peeled, | Salt and pepper to taste
   seeded and coarse-chopped | 4 fillets of sole
1 large onion, chopped | Flour
5 tablespoons butter or margarine | ¼ cup heavy cream
1½ teaspoons curry powder | Parsley, chopped fine
Pinch of sugar

In a saucepan combine the tomatoes with the onion and 2 tablespoons of the butter or margarine, and cook the mixture over low heat for 40 to 45 minutes, or until it is very thick. Stir in the curry powder, sugar, salt and pepper to taste. Remove the mixture from the heat and set it aside. Dust the fillets with flour and sauté them in the remaining butter or margarine over moderate heat until they are golden brown on both sides. Season the fillets with salt and pepper to taste and arrange them on a heated dish. Stir the heavy cream into the tomato-and-curry mixture, bring the sauce to the boil, and pour it over the fish. Sprinkle the dish with parsley.

Preparation and cooking time: approximately 1 hour 20 minutes.

†BAKED TROUT WITH GARLIC BUTTER

SERVES 4

Four 10-ounce trout	*1 tablespoon minced parsley*
Salt and pepper to taste	*1 teaspoon minced shallots*
¼ pound butter, softened	*¼ cup dry white wine*
1 clove garlic, crushed	*Snipped dill*

Preheat oven to 400° F.

Sprinkle the trout with salt and pepper. In a bowl combine the butter, garlic, minced parsley, minced shallots and salt and pepper to taste, and spread a quarter of the mixture into the cavity of each trout. Put the fish in a shallow baking dish just large enough to hold them, pour in the white wine, and bake the fish, covered with a buttered sheet of waxed paper and a sheet of aluminum foil, in the preheated oven for 20 minutes, or until they flake easily when tested with a fork. Spoon the pan juices over the fish and sprinkle snipped dill on top.

Preparation and cooking time: approximately 1 hour.

†BAKED TROUT WITH HAZELNUTS

SERVES 2

Two 8-ounce trout, cleaned
White pepper to taste
Salt to taste
Flour
1 egg, lightly beaten
½ cup lightly toasted ground
* hazelnuts*

4 tablespoons clarified butter (see
* page 275)*
¼ cup hazelnuts, slivered thin
1 teaspoon lemon juice
Lemon slices
Chopped parsley

Preheat oven to 450° F.

Wipe the trout with a damp cloth, and sprinkle with white pepper and salt to taste. Dust them with flour and dip them into the beaten egg. Coat them with the ground hazelnuts. In a shallow baking dish just large enough to hold the fish, heat 2 tablespoons of the clarified butter in the preheated oven for 3 minutes. Add the fish and bake them for 15 to 20 minutes or until they flake easily. In a small frying pan lightly sauté the slivered hazelnuts in the remaining clarified butter until they are lightly browned. Add the lemon juice and salt to taste. Pour the sauce over the trout and top with lemon slices and chopped parsley.

Preparation and cooking time: approximately 40 minutes.

†BAKED TROUT WITH TARRAGON

SERVES 4

One 5-to-6-pound trout
1½ tablespoons butter
Salt and pepper to taste
Flour

½ cup dry white wine
1 tablespoon fresh tarragon leaves or
* dried tarragon*

Preheat oven to 400° F.

Measure the trout at the thickest part. Rub it well with butter, sprinkle with salt and pepper to taste and dust lightly with flour. Put the fish in a buttered baking dish, add the wine and tarragon leaves and bake in the preheated oven for 10 minutes per measured inch of thickness. Baste 2 or 3 times with the pan juices during the cooking and add more wine and melted butter if necessary.

Preparation and cooking time: approximately 20 to 30 minutes depending on size.

††CATALAN FROGS' LEGS

SERVES 4

12 pairs frogs' legs	*1 egg, lightly beaten*
Milk	*½ cup beer*
½ cup flour	*1 egg white, beaten until stiff*
¼ teaspoon salt	*Flour, for dredging*
2 cloves garlic, crushed	*Hot deep-frying oil*
1 tablespoon butter, melted	*Piquant sauce (see page 104)*
1 tablespoon chopped parsley	

Soak the frogs' legs in milk to cover for 1 hour. Sift the flour and salt together into a small bowl and add the crushed garlic cloves, melted butter, chopped parsley and egg. Combine the mixture well, gradually stir in the beer and allow the batter to stand for 1 hour. Fold the beaten egg white into batter. Drain the frogs' legs, dredge them in flour and coat them with the batter. Fry them, a few at a time, in hot deep oil (375° F.) for 2 minutes, or until they are golden, and drain them on paper towels. Serve the frogs' legs with piquant sauce.

Preparation time: 2 hours 30 minutes. Cooking time: approximately 30 minutes.

PIQUANT SAUCE FOR THE FROGS' LEGS

MAKES 3½ CUPS

2 slices white bread, diced, with
  crusts removed
1 cup plus 1 tablespoon olive oil
1 tomato, peeled, seeded and
  chopped
½ cup dry red wine

¼ cup red-wine vinegar
12 blanched almonds, toasted
2 large cloves garlic
1 teaspoon salt
½ teaspoon cayenne
½ teaspoon allspice

In a saucepan, sauté the bread cubes in 1 tablespoon of the olive oil until they are golden. Transfer the bread to a blender and add all the rest of the ingredients. Blend the sauce until it is smooth. Return to the saucepan and serve hot.

Cooking time: approximately 10 minutes.

GAME AND POULTRY

The following are a few important rules in game cookery.

1. An old game bird has no place in cookery except when used for stuffing, forcemeat, preparing stock, pâté or casseroles.

2. The signs of youth in a pheasant are gray feet and a flexible breastbone. Also, as is true in a partridge, the very end of the large feather of the wing should be pointed; if round, the bird is old.

3. When roasting, it is advisable to "bard," that is, to cover the breast of the bird with slices of bacon, larding pork fat or ham fat to protect it against the intensity of the heat as well as to enhance its flavor and tenderness. The larding fat should be removed when the bird is half done so that the breast will be delicately browned.

4. A few drops of rum, brandy, Madeira, sherry or even Calvados will always enhance a game sauce. Never try to use whisky, which does not go with game.

5. Game should be cooked and served at once. All dark meats are served rare—white meats well done.

Timetable for Cooking Game

Venison		According to size 25 minutes per pound plus an additional 25 minutes
Large game	Roasted	20 to 40 minutes
	Broiled	15 to 20 minutes
Small game	Roasted	20 to 30 minutes
	Broiled	15 to 25 minutes
Large birds	Roasted	40 to 75 minutes
	Broiled	15 to 25 minutes
Small birds	Roasted	10 to 15 minutes
	Broiled	10 to 15 minutes

Grouse should be eaten in a fresh state, unless otherwise indicated. If the bird is old, hang it for up to one week. It is best to roast a large grouse, but small ones may be prepared in a variety of ways. It takes about 25 to 30 minutes to roast.

Both pheasant and partridge should be "mortified," *i.e.,* hung, for up to a week—the right time for cooking when the bird begins to decompose. Then its aroma is developed and combines with an oil that requires a slight degree of fermentation to develop. Pheasant and partridge should be roasted or grilled for about 25 to 40 minutes.

Quail are always prepared in their fresh state. They should be plump with white and firm fat. They are delicious roasted, especially on a spit, which is, unfortunately, rare these days. Quail will roast or grill in 15 minutes. Veal stock is particularly good to use when preparing any quail dish.

Wild duck, without exception, should be cooked and served rare. Ducks are seldom blanketed with slices of fat, as they are fatty in themselves. However, it is always a good idea to stuff them with an onion and an orange to absorb any fishy taste they may have. Discard the stuffing before serving. Fat from the roasted wild duck should be poured off as soon as it collects. It should *not* be used for basting unless otherwise indicated. Instead, a basting liquid made with water, game stock or meat stock, to which a little butter has been added, should be used. Ducks should be cooked in a very hot oven (400 to 500° F.) unless otherwise indicated.

†††GROUSE À LA MUSCOVITE

FOR 1 PERSON

The best, traditional way of cooking grouse is to roast it. But there are many different ways of preparation and this Russian recipe is particularly interesting.

4 chestnuts, peeled (see page 137)
½ cup bread soaked in Smitane sauce (see page 108)
1 plump grouse, cleaned and singed, liver reserved
2 tablespoons ground pistachio nuts
Pinch of dried tarragon
Salt and pepper to taste

Fat salt pork, for barding
Polish or Russian vodka
1 tablespoon chives, chopped fine
Sauce of 2 tablespoons bread crumbs, ¼ cup brandy or vodka to taste and ½ cup hot butter
2 artichoke bottoms, sautéed
Triangles of fried bread

Preheat oven to 400° F.

In a bowl combine the peeled chestnuts, the bread (soaked in Smitane sauce and slightly squeezed), the grouse liver mashed with a fork and the pistachio nuts, the whole seasoned to taste with the dried tarragon, salt and pepper. Stuff the grouse with this mixture and sew up the cavity. Cover the bird with a thin layer of fat salt pork rubbed or sprinkled with vodka, then with chopped chives. Roast for about 35 to 45 minutes, keeping the bird rather underdone. Baste occasionally with the sauce made from the bread crumbs, brandy or vodka and hot butter. Serve the bird as it is, without removing the pork fat, with artichoke bottoms sautéed in butter and interspersed with triangles of fried bread. Serve with red-currant jelly in a separate dish and additional Smitane sauce if you wish.

SMITANE SAUCE
MAKES APPROXIMATELY 1 CUP

2 small onions, minced fine	1 cup sour cream, scalded
1 generous tablespoon butter	Salt and pepper to taste
½ cup dry white wine	Lemon juice to taste

Sauté the minced onion in the butter, stirring constantly over low heat until soft but not browned. Add the white wine, stir and continue to cool until the liquid has reduced completely. Add the sour cream, stirring constantly, until well blended; allow to simmer gently for a good 5 minutes. Strain through a fine sieve. Then and only then, season with salt and pepper. Just before serving add a little lemon juice if a sharp sourness is desired.

Preparation and cooking time: approximately 1 hour 30 minutes.

††CASSEROLED PARTRIDGE WITH PORT WINE SAUCE

SERVES 6

6 young partridge	36 tangerine sections
Gin	½ cup butter
Salt and pepper	Port wine sauce (see page 109)

Clean and wipe the partridge with a damp cloth. Rub it inside and out with gin, then with salt and pepper. Put 6 tangerine sections inside each bird and truss as you would a young roasting chicken. Cook in plenty of butter in a covered casserole over moderate heat, turning occasionally to brown all sides, for 25 to 30 minutes. Serve on a hot round dish in a circle with ridged potato chips in the center and port wine sauce served separately.

PORT WINE SAUCE

MAKES APPROXIMATELY 2 CUPS

1 cup port wine, good red nonvintage
1 teaspoon shallots, minced very fine
Small sprig of thyme
Juice of 2 oranges
Few drops lemon juice

¼ teaspoon grated orange rind
Salt and cayenne to taste
1 cup good beef stock or brown stock (see page 279)
1 scant tablespoon flour

Combine the port wine, minced shallots, thyme, orange juice, lemon juice, grated orange rind, salt and cayenne in a saucepan and reduce the liquid to half over high heat. Strain through a fine cloth or sieve, return to the heat and add the beef stock, to which has been added the flour stirred in a little water. Bring to the boil, skim and allow the sauce to simmer a good 5 minutes before straining into a sauceboat. This sauce is suitable for any game, particularly wild duck.

Preparation time: approximately 30 minutes. Cooking time: approximately 1 hour.

††PARTRIDGE À LA CREOLE

SERVES 6

FOR THE SAUCE:

¼ cup butter
1 cup sliced onion
1 cup sliced green pepper (with seeds and white ribs removed)
6 sprigs parsley
One 13-ounce can tomatoes
1 cup button mushrooms
1 cup small green pitted olives, each split in two

1 cup meat stock mixed with ½ cup sweet white wine
Salt and pepper to taste
2 whole cloves
Pinch of thyme leaves

6 partridge
6 slices fried bread

Preheat oven to 400° F.

Melt the butter in a large frying pan, add the onion and cook for a full 10 minutes, stirring frequently. Do not allow the onion to brown. Add the green pepper, mix well, and cook for a good 5 minutes, stirring very often, then add all the remaining ingredients. Combine gently but thoroughly and allow the sauce to simmer very slowly over low heat, stirring occasionally for about 30 minutes or until vegetables have reduced to a thick sauce. Truss the partridge as for roasting and arrange in a casserole, as in a nest, in the Creole sauce. Cover tightly and roast in the preheated oven for 30 minutes. Lift out the birds. Arrange the Creole dressing nestlike on a large platter and into each nest place a bird. Surround the edge of the platter with small triangles of fried bread. Serve with currant, grape or guava jelly. When serving each person place a piece of bread on each plate, cover with the Creole sauce and place a partridge on top.

Preparation and cooking time: approximately 1 hour 20 minutes.

✝ROAST PARTRIDGE ON TOAST

SERVES 6

3 to 6 partridge, according to size
Salt and pepper to taste
Butter
Strips of barding pork, 1 for each
    partridge
1 to 2 teaspoons butter for each
    bird
2 tablespoons water for each
    bird
6 slices toast
Sherry

Preheat oven to 450° F.

Clean the partridge, reserving their livers, and with a soft string truss the legs of each bird close to the body. Sprinkle the partridge with salt and pepper to taste and rub well with butter. Wrap a thin sheet of barding pork around each bird and tie with a string. Place the birds on their sides in a roasting pan and roast them in the preheated oven for 10 to 15 minutes. Turn them on their other side and roast them for 10 to 15 minutes more. Baste frequently with the pan juices. Turn the birds on their backs and roast them for 10 to 15 minutes longer, or until they are well done. Not a tinge of pink should show in the juices that run out of the cavity when the birds are lifted from the pan. Remove the barding pork from the birds and reserve it.

To make the sauce, skim the fat from the pan juices and add the butter and water. Reduce the mixture to the desired consistency over direct heat, stirring in all the brown bits that cling to the pan. Strain the sauce and pour into a heated sauceboat. Serve a whole or half bird, according to size, on toast spread with the reserved livers, cooked, mashed and seasoned with a little sherry. Top the partridge with the reserved brown pork fat, cut into pieces, and serve the sauce separately.

Preparation and cooking time: approximately 1 hour 45 minutes.

††THE HONORABLE MRS. JAMES OGILVY'S DEVILED PHEASANT

SERVES 4 TO 6

You can also use this recipe to prepare deviled chicken or leftover turkey.

2 pheasant	*2 bay leaves*
1 large carrot, chopped	*1¼ cups heavy cream*
1 large onion, chopped	*One 8½-ounce jar mango*
1 clove garlic	*chutney*
1 sprig each of thyme and parsley	*4 tablespoons Worcestershire sauce*

Preheat oven to 300° F.

Clean the pheasant and place them in a casserole with the carrot, onion, garlic, parsley and herbs. Cover the birds with water and cover casserole. Bring to the boil and simmer gently until tender—from 30 to 45 minutes. Strip the meat from the bones and put it back in the juices so that the meat does not become dry. Meanwhile, whip the heavy cream stiff and leave it in the refrigerator for approximately 1 hour until it becomes quite hard, then beat in the chutney and Worcestershire sauce and keep cool in the refrigerator until ready to use. Place the meat, *thoroughly drained of* cooking juice, in the dish in which it is to be served. Cover with the cream mixture and put in the preheated oven for 10 minutes to heat through. *Hint:* The birds can be cooked in the morning and the rest of the preparation done about 1½ hours before dinner, but remember to keep the stock in which the birds were first cooked for reheating.

Preparation and cooking time: approximately 1 hour 15 minutes.

††GEORGIAN-STYLE PHEASANT

SERVES 4 TO 5

2 cups walnut halves	⅓ cup butter
2½ pounds white seedless grapes	1½ teaspoons salt
Two 3-pound pheasant	¼ teaspoon pepper
Juice of 6 blood oranges	⅓ cup butter
¾ cup sweet muscatel wine	4 tablespoons flour
¾ cup strong cold tea	Walnuts

Preheat oven to 375° F.

Soak the walnut halves in enough boiling water to cover for 3 to 4 minutes. Remove and discard the skins. In a blender purée the grapes and force them through a sieve. Put the pheasant in an ovenproof casserole just big enough to hold them. Add the nuts, grape purée, orange juice, wine and tea, butter, salt and pepper. Bake, covered, in the preheated oven for 50 minutes, or until tender. Reserve the cooking liquid. Carve the pheasant, arrange on a platter and surround with walnuts. Keep warm while you make the sauce. Strain the reserved cooking liquid into a saucepan and reduce to 1½ cups. Make beurre manié by blending ⅓ cup of butter with 4 tablespoons of flour. Add to the sauce a little at a time, stirring after each addition until the sauce is thickened. Coat the pheasant with some of the sauce and serve the rest separately. Serve with straw potatoes.

Preparation and cooking time: approximately 2 hours.

†BROILED PHEASANT WITH DEVILED BUTTER SAUCE

SERVES 6

Six 1½-pound pheasant, split, with *1 cup fine bread crumbs*
backbones and breastbones *Watercress*
removed *Deviled butter sauce (see*
Salt and pepper to taste *page 115)*
2 to 3 tablespoons melted butter

Preheat broiler.

Flatten the pheasant slightly between 2 sheets of waxed paper with the flat side of a cleaver. Season them with salt and pepper and brush them well with melted butter. Put the pheasant, breast side up, on the rack of a broiling pan, and broil them, 5 inches from the heat, for 8 to 9 minutes. Turn the birds breast side down. Brush them with additional melted butter, sprinkle each one with 2 tablespoons fine bread crumbs and dribble a little more butter over the crumbs. Broil the pheasant for 2 to 3 minutes more, or until the crumbs are browned. Turn the birds breast side up, sprinkle each one with 2 tablespoons bread crumbs and a little melted butter and broil them for 2 minutes more. Arrange a bed of watercress on a warm serving dish and top with the roasted pheasant. Serve with deviled butter sauce.

Preparation and cooking time: approximately 45 minutes.

DEVILED BUTTER SAUCE

MAKES APPROXIMATELY I CUP

½ *pound sweet butter*
⅓ *cup white-wine vinegar*
1 tablespoon fresh tarragon or
  1¼ teaspoons dried tarragon
¼ *teaspoon salt*
Few grinds fresh black pepper
2 tablespoons cold water

3 egg yolks, lightly beaten
2 tablespoons sour gherkins,
  chopped fine
1 to 2 tablespoons Dijon mustard
1 tablespoon chopped parsley
Salt and pepper to taste

In a saucepan melt the butter and allow it to cool. In a heavy saucepan cook the vinegar, tarragon, salt and pepper over moderately high heat until the mixture is reduced to a moist glaze. Remove the pan from the heat, add cold water and stir around the pan. Add the egg yolks, stirring with a wire whisk. Set the pan over low heat and beat, lifting the pan from the heat now and then to prevent the sauce from getting too hot, until it has thickened. Add the cooled butter, 2 tablespoons at a time, beating well after each addition. Add the gherkins, mustard, parsley, salt and pepper to taste.

Preparation and cooking time: approximately 30 minutes.

┼┼┼JELLIED PHEASANT PIE

SERVES 6

2 pheasant
½ *pound lean pork, ground with*
  1 medium onion

Salt and pepper to taste
½ *pound lean bacon*
Pheasant stock (see page 280)

Preheat oven to 300° F.

Cut the breasts from the pheasant, remove all the skin and membranes and cut the meat into small, thick slices. Reserve the giblets and trimmings for pheasant stock. Put the slices of meat between 2 pieces of waxed paper and pound them until they are well flattened. Spread the slices ⅛ inch thick with the ground pork and onion and season with salt and pepper. Line a heatproof shallow dish with thin slices of lean bacon and cover them with the pheasant meat. Cover with more slices of bacon and pour in enough pheasant stock to fill the dish halfway. Cover the dish with a lid, or several thicknesses of foil, and set it in a larger baking pan half filled with water. Cook the pie in the preheated oven for 2 hours, adding water to the baking pan as necessary to maintain the water level. Reduce about 3 cups of pheasant stock by half and add it to the pie to fill the dish to the rim. Cool the pie. Cover the top with waxed paper and put a light weight on top of it. Chill the pie until it is firm. Remove the paper and carefully skim any fat from the top of the pie. Serve cold, cut into slices.

Preparation and cooking time: approximately 2 hours 45 minutes. Chilling time: 2 hours.

†PHEASANT IN BOURSIN

SERVES 4 TO 6

1 pheasant
2 tablespoons butter or oil
1 large package garlic Boursin cheese
¾ cup sour cream or plain yogurt

1 clove garlic
2 teaspoons arrowroot
¾ cup red wine
Chicken stock, to cover
Salt and pepper to taste

Preheat oven to 350° F.

In a casserole brown the pheasant in the butter or oil. In a bowl mix the Boursin with the sour cream. Crush the garlic clove into this mixture and blend in the arrowroot and red wine. Pour the mixture over the browned pheasant. Add enough chicken stock to cover, and simmer in the preheated oven for 45 minutes to 1 hour, or until tender. Add a lot of pepper and salt to taste.

Preparation and cooking time: approximately 1 hour 30 minutes.

††ROAST PHEASANT WITH CHESTNUT STUFFING

SERVES 6

*1 pound fresh lean pork, cut
into pieces*
*1 pound fresh fat pork, cut
into pieces*
1 pound boiled chestnuts, chopped
1 cup fresh bread crumbs
¼ cup Madeira
*3 to 4 truffles, chopped, or one
6-ounce truffle peelings*
1 teaspoon salt

*¼ teaspoon commercial
poultry seasoning*
*3 small pheasant, cleaned and
dressed*
Salt to taste
Softened butter
6 tablespoons Madeira
6 rounds of bread
Watercress

Preheat oven to 350° F.

Put the pieces of lean pork and fat pork twice through the finest blade of a food chopper. Combine the ground pork with the chopped chestnuts and add the bread crumbs, ¼ cup Madeira, truffles, salt and poultry seasoning. Wipe the pheasant inside and out with a damp cloth. Stuff the cavities with the chestnut mixture and skewer the openings. Truss the birds and sprinkle them with salt. Rub the birds with softened butter and arrange them on a rack in a roasting pan. Roast them in the preheated oven for 15 minutes. Add 6 tablespoons Madeira and roast the birds for 30 minutes more, basting them every 10 minutes with the pan juices. Fifteen minutes before serving put the rounds of bread in the pan to brown and absorb the juices. Arrange the pheasant on a bed of watercress in a hot dish and surround with the rounds of bread and ridged potato chips.

Preparation time: approximately 1 hour. Cooking time: 1 hour.

✝✝✝NORMANDY QUAIL

SERVES 6

6 large cooking apples	*6 tablespoons Calvados*
6 quail	*Basic pie pastry (see below)*
½ cup butter	*1 egg yolk, beaten*
12 cardamom seeds	*Clarified butter (see page 275)*

Preheat oven to 370 to 400° F.

Cut the tops off the apples, core and carefully scoop out most of the flesh from both pieces, without piercing the skin. Sauté the quail quickly in 2 tablespoons of the butter until golden brown. Place 1 tablespoon in each apple shell and top with a quail. Add 2 cardamom seeds to each apple and 1 tablespoon Calvados. Cover each apple with its top. Wrap each quail-stuffed apple in pie pastry and paint the pastry with the egg yolk. Arrange the pastries on a sheet of foil and bake for 30 to 35 minutes, or until lightly browned. Serve with hot clarified butter.

Preparation and cooking time: approximately 1 hour 30 minutes (without making pie pastry).

*BASIC PIE PASTRY

3 cups flour	*½ cup cold butter, cut into pieces*
2 teaspoons sugar	*¼ cup vegetable fat*
½ teaspoon salt	*5 to 6 tablespoons iced water*

In a bowl sift together the flour, sugar and salt. Add the cold butter bits and vegetable fat and blend the mixture until it resembles meal. Add just enough iced water to form a dough, toss the mixture until the water is incorporated and form the dough into a ball. Wrap it in waxed paper and chill for at least 1 hour.

††QUAIL FLAMBÉ

SERVES 4

4 quail	2 ounces pâté de foie gras
4 slices lean bacon	4 slices fried bread
8 oysters, with their juice	½ cup Cognac

Preheat oven to 400° F.

Tie a slice of bacon around the breast of each quail. Put the birds in a shallow roasting pan and roast in the preheated oven for about 15 to 20 minutes, or until they are tender. Heat the oysters in their own juice until the edges begin to curl. Drain, chop them into coarse pieces and mix with the pâté de foie gras. Spread the mixture on the fried bread. At serving time place a quail on each piece of toast, warm the brandy, spoon it over the birds and ignite.

Preparation and cooking time: approximately 45 minutes.

††ROAST WILD DUCK

SERVES 6

3 Mallard ducks	2 tablespoons flour
1 shallot, chopped	1 tablespoon mushroom ketchup‡
A blade of mace, or 1 teaspoon dried mace	1 tablespoon bottled HP sauce or Escoffier Sauce Diable
2 whole cloves	Grated zest of 1 orange and 1
Pinch of cayenne	lemon
2 tablespoons butter	Juice of ½ lemon

Preheat oven to 475° F.

Clean the birds, reserving the giblets, and truss the legs close to the body. Preheat a roasting pan in the oven, place the duck in the

‡ Mushroom ketchup can be bought at most specialty food shops or ordered from Maison Glass, 52 East 58 Street, New York, New York 10022.

hot pan and roast them, breast side up, for about 8 to 12 minutes per pound. Remove the duck from the oven and allow them to stand for about 10 minutes. Remove the breasts, discarding the remainder, and keep the breasts warm without further cooking. Make a strong stock by combining the giblets, shallot, mace, cloves, cayenne and adding water to cover. Cook the stock until it is well flavored and somewhat reduced and strain it. In a saucepan melt the butter, stir in the flour, and cook the roux over low heat for 30 seconds. Add the strained stock to the roux, stirring constantly. Add all the rest of the ingredients and simmer the sauce for 10 minutes. Cut the breast meat of the duck into thin slices and arrange on a heated serving dish. Strain the sauce into a heated sauceboat and serve it very hot with the duck.

Preparation time: approximately 30 minutes. Cooking time: roasting time depending on weight plus 45 minutes.

††JUGGED HARE

SERVES 6 TO 8

One 5- to 6-pound hare
2 teaspoons salt
½ teaspoon fresh-ground pepper
6 tablespoons flour
¼ cup butter
2 tablespoons olive oil
4 cups chicken stock
2 tablespoons lemon juice
1 onion stuck with 2 cloves

Bouquet garni (6 sprigs parsley,
*   1 bay leaf, ½ teaspoon thyme,*
*   10 black peppercorns)*
1 cup red wine
Salt and pepper to taste
Beurre manié (2 tablespoons
*   butter, 2 tablespoons flour)*
2 tablespoons chopped parsley

Preheat oven to 325° F.

Cut the hare into 12 serving pieces and dry well. Season the meat with the salt and pepper and dredge in flour. In a heavy flameproof casserole brown the hare on all sides in the butter and oil. Add the chicken stock, lemon juice, onion, bouquet garni and half the red wine. Season with salt and pepper to taste and bring to the boil. Bake the casserole, covered, in the preheated oven for 2½ hours. Add the rest of the red wine and bake for 30 minutes more, or until the hare is tender. Transfer the meat to a hot serving dish and keep warm. Strain the sauce through a sieve into a saucepan, skimming off as much fat as possible. Reduce the sauce over high heat to 3½ cups and thicken with beurre manié. (For this, knead together the butter and flour and stir into the sauce.) Season to taste and pour over the hare. Sprinkle with 2 tablespoons chopped parsley, and serve with boiled potatoes and red-currant jelly.

Preparation and cooking time: approximately 4 hours 15 minutes.

††SADDLE OF VENISON

SERVES 8

One 5-to-6-pound saddle of venison, larded with ¼ pound fresh pork fat cut into ¼-inch-wide strips
3½ cups buttermilk
½ cup butter
2 tablespoons oil
1 teaspoon salt

1 teaspoon crushed juniper berries
½ teaspoon fresh-ground pepper
½ cup white wine
Pepper sauce (see page 286)
Salt and pepper to taste

Soak the venison in the buttermilk for 24 hours. Preheat oven to 450° F. Drain the meat and dry it thoroughly. In a roasting pan or baking dish just large enough to hold the venison, sear it on all sides in ¼ cup of the butter and the oil. Rub the venison with salt, crushed juniper berries and ground pepper. Roast the meat in the preheated oven for 20 minutes per pound. Reduce heat to moderate (350° F.) and roast for 25 to 30 minutes longer, or until the top is brown and crisp and the inside slightly pink. Transfer the venison to a serving dish. Skim off as much fat as possible from the roasting pan and set on high heat. Add the white wine and stir in the brown bits clinging to the pan. Reduce the wine by half, add the pepper sauce and cook, stirring, until it is well blended. Strain the sauce, add salt and fresh-ground pepper if necessary. Swirl in the remaining ¼ cup butter cut into bits.

Preparation time: 24 hours. Cooking time: approximately 1 hour 30 minutes.

†*BAKED CINNAMON CHICKEN

SERVES 8 TO 10

3 frying chickens, each 3 to 3½ pounds, cut into quarters	*¼ cup lemon juice*
	4 teaspoons cinnamon
1 cup dry sherry	*2¼ teaspoons garlic salt*
¾ cup clear honey	*1¾ teaspoons curry powder*

Preheat oven to 375° F.

Arrange the pieces of chicken in a single layer in a large shallow roasting pan, or in 2 smaller pans. In a bowl mix together the sherry, honey, lemon juice, cinnamon, garlic salt and curry powder. Pour the marinade over the chicken and chill for 12 hours, basting several times. Bake the chicken in its marinade in the preheated oven, basting every 15 minutes, for 1¼ hours, or until it is tender. (If the pan juices evaporate, add a little water.) Remove the chicken to a heated dish and keep it hot. If the juices are not lightly syrupy, reduce them over direct heat, stirring constantly. Adjust the seasoning and pour the sauce over the chicken.

The cooked chicken may be frozen in a baking pan large enough to accommodate all the pieces in a single layer with the pan juices poured over it. After the chicken has frozen solid, remove the frozen block from the dish, wrap it in freezer-weight foil or in a freezer bag and store. To serve the frozen chicken, return it to the dish in which it was frozen. Cover the dish and heat in the preheated oven for 30 minutes. Remove the cover and continue to bake 20 minutes longer, or until it is hot. If necessary, reduce the pan juices as described above.

Marinating time: 12 hours. Cooking time: approximately 2 hours.

†CHICKEN HASHED IN CREAM

SERVES 4

3 tablespoons butter
1 medium onion, grated
3 tablespoons flour
1 cup chicken stock
1½ cups light cream
¾ teaspoon curry powder

1 pound cooked white-meat chicken,
  minced
One 10-ounce can water chestnuts,
  coarse-chopped
Salt to taste

Melt the butter in a saucepan. Add the onion and cook over low heat for 5 minutes. Stir in the flour. Slowly add the chicken stock, light cream and the curry powder (or more to taste). Whisk until thickened. Add the chicken meat, water chestnuts and a little salt to taste. Cook, stirring occasionally, for about 5 minutes or until heated through.

Preparation and cooking time: approximately 30 minutes.

†CHICKEN IN YOGURT MARINADE

SERVES 6 TO 8

1 teaspoon saffron threads, crushed
2 tablespoons boiling water
½ cup lemon juice
2 tablespoons fresh ginger root,
  peeled and chopped
2 tablespoons garlic, chopped
1 tablespoon salt
2 tablespoons coriander seed

1 teaspoon cumin seed
¼ teaspoon chili powder
1 cup plain yogurt
¼ cup peanut oil
Two 2½-to-3-pound roasting
  chickens, each cut into 6
  pieces
½ cup melted butter

In a small dish soak the crushed saffron threads in the boiling water. Put the lemon juice, ginger root, garlic, salt, coriander seed, cumin seed and chili powder in a blender and blend until the mixture is smooth. Transfer to a bowl and combine with the yogurt, peanut oil and saffron mixture. Slash each piece of chicken in several places and rub the marinade well into each piece. Allow the chicken to marinate, covered, at room temperature overnight. Broil the chicken, basting it 4 times with melted butter, for 15 minutes on each side, or until it is done.

Marinating and preparation time: approximately 12 hours 30 minutes. Cooking time: approximately 30 to 45 minutes.

††*CHICKEN ROUXINOL

SERVES 4

2 *cloves garlic*
1½ *cups white wine*
1½ *cups crushed (not ground) almonds*
½ *cup lard*
1 *medium onion, chopped*
1 *teaspoon cayenne*

1½ *dried chili peppers or 1 teaspoon chili powder*
2 *ounces Spanish chorizo sausage or any spicy sausage*
One 3-*pound chicken, quartered*
Salt and pepper to taste
2 *bay leaves*

This dish improves with reheating and can be made the night before serving. Crush the cloves of garlic and mix them with the white wine and crushed almonds. Allow the mixture to stand for about 1 hour so that the almonds and garlic soak up the wine. In a casserole melt the lard, add the onion and brown slightly. Add the cayenne, chili peppers or powder and the chorizo (important: make a slit lengthwise in the sausage to keep it tender while cooking). Cover the casserole and allow it to simmer on low heat for 3 to 4 minutes, or until the chorizo is tender. Add the chicken to the mixture in the casserole and continue to cook on low heat for 25 minutes. (If the chicken is not young and tender, cook it longer *but not quicker*, otherwise it will fall apart.) Add the wine mixture to the casserole and season with salt and pepper. Remove the lid and continue cooking until the sauce thickens (about half an hour). Add the bay leaves and allow to cool. Reheat the following day. This dish is particularly suitable for buffets.

Preparation time: 1 hour 30 minutes. Cooking time: approximately 1 hour 30 minutes.

†CHICKEN WITH CHICKPEAS

SERVES 4

2 onions, chopped fine
3 tablespoons olive oil
¼ teaspoon ground turmeric
One 2½-pound chicken, quartered
1½ cups chicken stock

2 tablespoons lemon juice
3 cloves garlic, minced
Salt and pepper to taste
One 10-ounce can chickpeas, drained

In a casserole sauté the onions in the olive oil until soft but not brown. Add the turmeric. Brown the chicken pieces in the onion mixture. Add the chicken stock, lemon juice, garlic, and salt and pepper to taste. Cover and simmer for 30 minutes. Add the chickpeas and continue to simmer, partially covered, for 30 minutes, or until the chicken is tender.

Preparation and cooking time: approximately 2 hours.

†CHICKEN WITH LEMON

SERVES 4

1 lemon studded at ½-inch intervals with whole cloves
Olive oil
3 onions, coarse-chopped
One 3-pound chicken, cut into serving pieces

½ cup chicken stock or chicken broth
Salt and pepper to taste
¼ cup raisins
¼ cup toasted pine nuts

Put the clove-studded lemon in a wide-mouthed jar and cover it with olive oil. Cover the jar and allow the lemon to stand for at least 7 days. Remove the lemon, reserving the oil. Remove and discard the cloves and slice the lemon thin. In a large, deep, heavy frying pan or casserole, sauté the chopped onions in 3 tablespoons of the reserved oil until soft. Transfer the onions with a slotted spoon to a dish. In the same frying pan or casserole, brown the chicken over moderately high heat, adding more of the reserved oil if necessary. Add the chicken stock or chicken broth, the onions, lemon slices, and salt and pepper to taste. Bring the liquid to the boil and simmer the chicken, covered, for 25 to 30 minutes, or until it is just tender. Add the raisins and toasted pine nuts and cook for 2 minutes more.

Marinating time: 7 days. Cooking time: approximately 1 hour.

†LEMON CHICKEN WITH TARRAGON SAUCE

SERVES 4

One 3½-pound roasting chicken	*1 tablespoon flour*
1 lemon, quartered	*1 cup chicken stock*
1 bunch fresh tarragon	*Juice of 1 lemon*
Salt and pepper to taste	*1 tablespoon tarragon vinegar*
2 tablespoons butter or margarine	*¼ cup heavy cream*

Preheat oven to 350° F.

Stuff the chicken with the lemon quarters and half the bunch of tarragon, reserving the other half. Truss the chicken and season it with salt and pepper to taste. Roast the bird in the preheated oven for 1½ hours, or until it is tender. In a saucepan melt the butter or margarine and stir in the flour as smoothly as possible. Add the chicken stock, reserved tarragon, lemon juice and tarragon vinegar. Bring the sauce to the boil and simmer for 5 to 8 minutes. Pour in the heavy cream and season the sauce with salt and pepper to taste. Cut the chicken in half, discard the stuffing and strain the sauce over it.

Preparation and cooking time: approximately 2 hours.

††CIRCASSIAN CHICKEN AND KASHA

SERVES 6 TO 8

8 chicken breasts, skinned and
   cut in half
Water
Dry white wine
1 whole onion
1 bay leaf
Several peppercorns

Salt to taste
2½ cups walnuts
Pinch of cayenne
2 onions, chopped
2 tablespoons butter
Kasha (see below)

Put the chicken breasts in a deep saucepan with a mixture of water and dry white wine to cover, the whole onion, bay leaf, peppercorns and salt to taste. Poach the chicken breasts, covered, over low heat for 15 to 20 minutes, or until they are tender. Let them stand in the broth until needed. In the container of a blender, blend the walnuts with a pinch of cayenne until the nuts are mealy. Sauté the 2 chopped onions in the butter until they are tender and golden. Stir in the walnut mixture and add enough of the strained chicken broth to make a thick sauce. Simmer the sauce for several minutes. Drain the chicken breasts, arrange them on a bed of kasha, and cover with the sauce.

Preparation and cooking time: approximately 1 hour.

†KASHA

1½ cups kasha
1 egg
3 cups chicken broth or stock

Salt to taste
¼ cup butter

In a heavy frying pan heat the kasha for 1 minute. Stir in the egg and cook the mixture, stirring constantly over low heat, until it is dry and the grains are well coated with egg. Add the chicken broth or stock and salt to taste. Cook the kasha over low heat, covered, for about 30 minutes, or until the grains are tender and all the broth is absorbed. Add the butter and toss the mixture with a fork to separate the grains.

Preparation and cooking time: 45 minutes to 1 hour.

†GINGER CHICKEN

SERVES 3 TO 4

5 tablespoons fresh ginger root, peeled and chopped fine	*2 tablespoons sherry*
¼ cup soy sauce	*Salt and pepper to taste*
9 tablespoons peanut oil	*One 2½-pound roasting chicken, cut into 8 pieces*
2 tablespoons scallions, chopped fine	*2 teaspoons sugar*
	1 teaspoon cornstarch

In a bowl combine the ginger root, soy sauce, 6 tablespoons of the peanut oil, the chopped scallions, sherry and a dash of salt and pepper. Coat the pieces of chicken well with the ginger mixture and allow them to marinate at room temperature, turning the pieces occasionally, for at least 1 hour. Drain the chicken and reserve the marinade. In a frying pan sauté the chicken in the rest of the peanut oil for 15 to 20 minutes, or until it is tender. Transfer the chicken to a plate and keep it warm. Combine the reserved marinade with the sugar and cornstarch and stir it into the frying pan. Cook the mixture, stirring, until it has thickened. Return the chicken to the frying pan and heat it in the sauce for 2 to 3 minutes, or until it is hot.

Preparation and marinating time: 1 hour 30 minutes. Cooking time: approximately 45 minutes.

†ANTHONY WEST'S GOOD CHICKEN RECIPE

SERVES 6 TO 8

One 4½-to-6-pound roasting chicken
Salt and pepper to taste
Chicken liver and heart, chopped
1 medium onion, chopped
⅔ cup fresh bread crumbs
¼ cup olive oil
½ pound butter

5 slices fatty bacon
1 tablespoon olive oil
Juice of 1 lemon
1 tablespoon Calvados or
Cognac and hard cider
mixed

Preheat oven to 375 to 400° F.

This chicken is to be cooked on a rack in a heavy enamel casserole. Rub the bird inside and out with salt and pepper. Combine the chopped liver and heart and the onion and sauté the mixture in the olive oil until the onion is soft but not browned. Add bread crumbs, stuff the bird with this mixture and put it on the rack. Cut the butter into ⅛-inch-thick slices and arrange them on the breastbone and between the legs and breast of the bird. Cover the whole bird with the bacon slices, 2 running lengthwise and 3 across. Pour the olive oil over the bird, followed by the lemon juice and the Calvados. Cover the casserole and place in the preheated oven. The chicken will be ready in about 1 hour, during which time you need to give it no further thought. When the casserole is opened the bird will be rosy and the bacon pink and the cook's first thought is that it has not been properly cooked. This is not so. The bird will prove to be especially tender and delicious. This is a very good way to cook a chicken that is to be eaten cold. Cider or apple juice can be substituted for the lemon juice.

Preparation and cooking time: approximately 2 hours.

††MOORISH CHICKEN AND RICE

SERVES 4 TO 6

One 3½-to-4-pound chicken
4 onions, sliced
Salt and pepper to taste
½ cup seedless raisins

9 tablespoons butter
½ cup blanched almonds, coarse-
  chopped
1½ cups rice

Preheat oven to 350° F.

Simmer the chicken with 1 onion in water almost to cover for 30 to 45 minutes or until the chicken is tender. Season the chicken with salt and pepper to taste and reserve it. Discard the onion, measure the cooking liquid and reserve 3 cups. Sauté the raisins in 3 tablespoons of the butter over low heat for several minutes. Strain the butter into a casserole, reserving the raisins. Sauté the chopped almonds in 3 more tablespoons of butter over low heat until they are golden. Strain the butter into the same casserole, reserving the almonds. Sauté 2 or 3 onions in 3 additional tablespoons of butter until they are tender and golden. Strain the butter into the same casserole, reserving the onions. To the butter in the casserole add the reserved chicken liquid, season the mixture with salt and pepper to taste and bring to the boil. Stir in the rice and cook it for 15 minutes, until it is almost cooked. Transfer the casserole to the oven and bake the rice for approximately 10 minutes, or until it is lightly browned and fluffy. Carve the chicken and arrange it on a heated serving dish. Cover it with the reserved onions. Combine the rice with the reserved raisins and almonds and serve it over the chicken and onions.

Preparation and cooking time: approximately 2 hours.

†VIENNESE FRIED CHICKEN WITH SWEET AND SOUR SAUCE

SERVES 2 TO 3

¼ cup flour
½ teaspoon curry powder
¼ teaspoon salt
Pinch of nutmeg
1 egg yolk
3 tablespoons milk
1 egg white, beaten until stiff

One 2-pound chicken, cut into serving pieces
1 clove garlic
Salt to taste
Frying oil
Sweet and sour sauce (see below)

In a bowl combine the flour, curry powder, salt and nutmeg. Stir in the egg yolk mixed with the milk until the batter is smooth. Fold in the egg white. Rub the skin of the chicken pieces lightly with a cut garlic clove and salt. Dip the chicken pieces into the batter and fry them in moderately hot deep fat (350° F.) for about 10 minutes or until they are cooked through and golden. Drain them on paper towels. Serve the chicken with sweet and sour sauce.

Preparation and cooking time: approximately 45 minutes to 1 hour.

SWEET AND SOUR SAUCE

MAKES APPROXIMATELY 1 CUP

½ cup tomato ketchup
½ cup brown stock (see page 279) or beef broth

2 tablespoons vinegar
1 strip of bacon rind
2 to 3 drops Tabasco sauce

In a small saucepan combine all the ingredients except the Tabasco sauce. Reduce the mixture over high heat to ¾ cup, remove the bacon rind and add the Tabasco sauce.

†CHICKEN LIVERS IN DEVIL SAUCE

SERVES 6

1½ pounds chicken livers
¼ cup butter
3 tablespoons shallots, chopped fine
1 cup white wine
½ cup heavy cream

2 tablespoons Worcestershire
   sauce
2 tablespoons bottled
   Escoffier Sauce Diable
Anchovy paste to taste
Dash of Tabasco sauce

Preheat oven to 450° F.

In a frying pan sauté the chicken livers in the butter over high heat until they are browned. With a slotted spoon transfer the livers to a shallow ovenproof dish and keep them warm. Add the shallots to the pan juices and cook them, stirring, until they are golden. Add the white wine, reduce it by half over high heat, and pour the wine and shallots over the livers. Whip the heavy cream until it is almost stiff and beat in the Worcestershire sauce, Sauce Diable, anchovy paste, and Tabasco sauce. Continue to beat the cream until it is smooth and spoon it over the livers. Bake the dish in the oven or glaze it under the broiler for 3 to 5 minutes or until the cream is pale gold. Serve immediately.

Preparation and cooking time: approximately 30 minutes.

†CHICKEN LIVERS IN MADEIRA SAUCE

SERVES 4 TO 6

1 pound chicken livers
Milk to cover
Salt and pepper to taste

Flour, for dredging
2 tablespoons butter

FOR THE SAUCE:

2 tablespoons butter   3 tablespoons Madeira
½ cup flour   ½ teaspoon minced parsley
1 cup chicken stock

Clean the chicken livers and soak them for ½ hour in the milk. Drain and dry. Sprinkle with salt and pepper; dredge with flour and sauté in the butter for 2 to 3 minutes. They should be brown on the outside but still pink inside. To prepare Madeira sauce, brown the butter in the flour. Gradually add the chicken stock (or water with a bouillon cube), the Madeira, minced parsley, salt and pepper, stirring continually. Reheat the livers in the sauce and serve.

Preparation and cooking time: approximately 45 minutes.

†BROILED GINGERED SQUAB

SERVES 2

1 tablespoon fresh ginger root,   2 squabs, split and slightly
   peeled and minced   flattened
2 teaspoons coriander seed   Butter
1 teaspoon coarse salt   Salt
½ teaspoon ground cloves   ¾ cup dry white wine
3 tablespoons butter, softened

In a mortar pound the ginger root, coriander seed, coarse salt and ground cloves until the spices are pulverized and mixed. Blend the spices into the softened butter. Carefully loosen the skin from the breast meat of the squabs and, with a small knife, cut 3 or 4 deep incisions in each breast half. Force a little of the spiced butter into each incision, replace the skin and press it down. Repeat the process on the thighs and legs, making 2 or 3 incisions in each thigh and 2 in each leg. Allow the squabs to stand for 1 hour, then rub them with butter and salt and arrange them on a rack in a flameproof dish.

Broil skin side up for 12 minutes about 3 inches from the heat. Turn them on their other side, and broil, basting 3 times at 3-minute intervals with a mixture of any remaining spiced butter melted with the white wine, or 9 minutes more, or until they are tender and crisp.

Preparation and marinating time: 1 hour 30 minutes. Cooking time: approximately 30 minutes.

†STUFFED SQUAB

SERVES 6

2 tablespoons shallots, chopped	Salt and pepper to taste
¼ cup butter or margarine	1 cup white wine
1¼ pounds mushrooms, trimmed and chopped fine	6 small squabs
	Lemon juice
2 tablespoons chopped fresh tarragon or 1 tablespoon dried tarragon	White wine

Preheat oven to 425° F.

Sauté the shallots in the butter or margarine for several minutes, or until they are tender. Stir in the mushrooms and cook over low heat, stirring frequently, until they are tender. Season the mixture with the chopped fresh tarragon or dried tarragon and salt and pepper to taste. Add ½ cup of the white wine and continue to cook until the mixture forms a heavy paste. Remove the stuffing from the heat and reserve it. Wipe the skin and body cavities of the squabs with a damp cloth. Spoon the mushroom stuffing into each body cavity and truss the squabs with soft cord. Rub the skins with lemon juice, arrange the squabs in a shallow roasting pan, and roast them in the oven, basting frequently with the remaining white wine and the pan juices, for 35 to 45 minutes, or until they are tender. Remove the cord from the squabs, arrange them on a heated platter and serve with Brussels sprouts and chestnuts (see page 182).

Preparation and cooking time: approximately 1 hour 20 minutes.

††BROILED DUCK WITH MOLASSES MARINADE

SERVES 4

⅓ cup molasses
⅓ cup lemon juice
⅓ cup soy sauce
¼ cup sherry
2 tablespoons Dijon mustard
1 tablespoon ginger syrup or
   melted ginger marmalade

1½ teaspoons ground ginger
1 egg yolk
One 4-to-5-pound duck
4 teaspoons vegetable oil (approximately)

Preheat the broiler.

Make the marinade by whisking together all the ingredients except the duck and the oil in a small bowl. Rinse and dry the duck, quarter it, trim the fat and put the pieces into a large deep dish. Pour the marinade over the duck pieces and allow them to stand at room temperature for 3 to 4 hours. Drain the duck and reserve the marinade. Pat the duck pieces dry and put them, skin side down, on the rack of a preheated broiler about 4 inches from the heat. Pour about 1 teaspoon oil over each piece of duck and broil the pieces for 15 minutes. Baste them with the reserved marinade and broil them, basting once, for 15 minutes more. Turn the pieces skin side up and broil them, basting once, for 20 minutes.

Preparation and marinating time: 4 hours. Cooking time: 1 hour.

†ROAST DUCK WITH HONEY BUTTER

SERVES 4

This recipe can also be used to prepare chicken, goose or turkey.

1 cup clear honey
¼ pound sweet butter,
   cut into pieces

Juice of ½ lemon
One 3½-to-4-pound roasting duck
Salt and pepper to taste

Preheat oven to 450° F.

Heat the honey in a saucepan. Remove the pan from the heat and add the butter, stirring, until it has melted. Add the lemon juice. Truss the duck and sprinkle the cavity and skin with salt and pepper. Put it in a shallow dish and pour a little honey butter into the cavity and over the duck, rubbing it in well. Allow the duck to stand at room temperature for 3 to 4 hours. Transfer it to a small flameproof roasting pan and lay it on one side, coating it with some more of the honey butter. Roast it in the oven for 10 minutes. Turn it onto the other side, coat it with some more of the honey butter, reserving the remainder, and roast it for 10 minutes more. Reduce the heat to 350° F. and continue to roast the duck, turning it and basting it with the reserved honey butter every 15 minutes, for about 1¼ hours or until the juices from the thigh run clear. Transfer the duck to a serving dish and keep it warm. Pour off most of the fat from the roasting pan, reserving it for other uses, and reduce the juices over high heat until they are thick and form a glaze. Then pour in the remainder of the honey butter. Stir constantly over moderate heat for about 1 minute, but no longer or the sauce will burn and turn into a kind of caramel. Pour the sauce over the duck or serve separately.

Marinating time: 3 to 4 hours. Cooking time: approximately 1½ hours.

††ROAST DUCKLING WITH PEACHES

SERVES 6

One 5-pound duckling
Salt and pepper to taste
Lemon juice
A few celery leaves
1 onion, sliced
1½ cups dry white wine
1 tablespoon honey
2 teaspoons cornstarch

1 cup chicken stock
1 cup peach brandy or Cognac
3 tablespoons sugar
2½ tablespoons vinegar
6 ripe peaches, peeled, stoned and halved, or substitute canned if fresh peaches are not available

Preheat oven to 325° F.

Wash the duckling inside and out with cold water, dry it carefully and sprinkle with salt and pepper. Rub the cavity with lemon juice and put in it a few celery leaves and the onion. Prick the skin. Place the duckling breast side up, on a rack in a roasting pan, and cook it in the preheated oven for 1 hour. Drain the fat from the pan, add the white wine and continue to roast the bird, basting frequently, for 40 minutes, or until it is tender and the legs move easily. (Allow 20 minutes cooking time per pound.) If you like a very crisp skin, brush the duck with 1 tablespoon of honey 15 minutes before taking it from the oven *and do not baste it again*. Remove it from the pan and keep warm. Skim all the fat from the pan. Dissolve the cornstarch in the chicken stock and add this to the pan with the peach brandy or Cognac. Bring the mixture to the boil, stirring constantly. Strain the sauce through a fine sieve. Caramelize the sugar with the vinegar and add to the sauce. Put the peaches in a saucepan, pour the sauce over them and poach for 5 minutes. Correct the seasoning. Put the duck on a serving dish, surround it with poached peaches and pour the sauce over the duck.

Preparation and cooking time: approximately 2 hours.

††ROAST STUFFED TURKEY

SERVES 12 TO 14
One 8-to-10-pound turkey

FOR THE STUFFING:

2 pounds chestnuts	1 pound cooking apples,
1¼ cups milk	peeled, cored and sliced thin
1 cup water	1 turkey liver, chopped
3 teaspoons salt	½ pound softened butter
One 6-ounce piece of bacon, diced	

Preheat oven to 350° F.

To make the stuffing: remove the shells from the chestnuts by cutting a cross on the flat side of each nut and heating them in the oven. When the shells begin to curl back from the cuts, allow the chestnuts to cool a little and peel. Put the peeled chestnuts in a saucepan with enough cold water to cover and boil for about 3 to 4 minutes. Drain them and carefully remove the brown inner skin. Heat the milk with ½ cup of the water and the salt, and when it is hot but not boiling, add the chestnuts, one by one, as they are peeled. Bring the liquid to the boil, lower the heat and let the chestnuts cook at a low simmer for about 15 minutes. Drain them carefully, keeping them as whole and unbroken as possible. Put the diced bacon in a saucepan with the remaining ½ cup of water, bring it to the boil and simmer for 5 to 6 minutes. Drain, and put the bacon in a heavy frying pan, add the sliced apples, cover and cook them over low heat for about 5 to 10 minutes or until the apples are softened. Add the chopped turkey liver and the whole chestnuts, and mix well.

Cool the stuffing completely, fill the cavity of the turkey, sew up the opening and truss the bird. Spread softened butter on the turkey and roast it in a 300° F. oven for 3 hours, or until it is well browned and the juices from the thighs are pale when pierced. Baste the turkey frequently with the pan juices, adding a small amount of stock if necessary. Place the turkey on a hot dish and skim most of the fat from the juices in the roasting pan. Add several tablespoons of cold water to the juices, stirring well. Serve.

Preparation time: 45 minutes for shelling chestnuts. Cooking time: approximately 4 hours 30 minutes.

††TRUFFLED TURKEY WITH TWO STUFFINGS

SERVES 16 TO 18

1 large truffle
Salt and pepper to taste
Cognac
One 12-to-15-pound turkey
Sausage stuffing (see page 140)

Shallot stuffing (see page 140)
Butter
½ cup melted butter combined with ½ cup white wine (optional)

FOR GIBLET SAUCE:

*The neck and giblets of the turkey,
cooked, chopped and reserved
together with their cooking
broth*
2 tablespoons flour

*Reserved truffle trimmings
Salt and pepper to taste
2 tablespoons Madeira or
Cognac*

Preheat oven to 300° F.

Cut 10 thin slices from the truffle, reserving all the trimmings, and sprinkle with salt and pepper and a little Cognac. Loosen the skin from the breast and thighs of the turkey by slipping your fingers carefully under the skin. Insert 4 truffle slices into each side of the breast and 1 into each thigh. Stuff the neck cavity of the bird with sausage stuffing, fold the neck skin under the body, and fasten it with a skewer. Stuff the body cavity loosely with shallot stuffing, cover the inside of the vent with a folded piece of foil and secure it with skewers. Truss the turkey, rub the skin with a generous coating of butter and sprinkle it with salt and pepper. Place the turkey, breast side up, on a rack in a shallow roasting pan and cover it loosely with foil. Roast the bird in the preheated oven for 1 hour. Remove the foil, turn it on one side and roast for 45 minutes longer, basting occasionally. (If there are not enough pan juices for basting, use the optional butter and the white wine mixture. Turn the turkey on the other side and roast it for 45 minutes longer or until it is done. While the turkey is roasting, place the neck and giblets in a saucepan with 1 cup of water and simmer gently for 20 minutes, chop and reserve them with their cooking broth. Transfer the turkey to a large warm dish and let it stand at room temperature for about 15 minutes. To make the giblet sauce, skim off all but 2 tablespoons of fat from the liquid in the roasting pan. Stir in the flour, as smoothly as possible, and the reserved broth, giblets and truffle trimmings, salt and pepper to taste. Cook the sauce over low heat, stirring constantly, for about 5 minutes. Then stir in the Madeira or Cognac. Remove the trussing cords from the turkey and serve.

Preparation and cooking time: approximately 3 hours 30 minutes.

*SAUSAGE STUFFING

2½ pounds fresh lean minced pork
¾ cup parsley, chopped fine
1 tablespoon Cognac
1 clove garlic, crushed
1 teaspoon thyme

1 teaspoon salt
1 teaspoon pepper
½ teaspoon fresh-ground nutmeg

Work all the ingredients together well. The stuffing will be solid enough to slice when the turkey is carved.

*SHALLOT STUFFING

¾ cup butter
10 cups bread crumbs, made from
    French or Italian bread
2 cups shallots, chopped fine
½ cup parsley, chopped

1 tablespoon tarragon
2 tablespoons salt
1 tablespoon fresh-ground
    black pepper

Melt the butter in a saucepan. Remove from the heat, stir in the bread crumbs, shallots, parsley, tarragon, salt and pepper, and combine well.

MRS. JEANNETTE DE ROTHSCHILD'S SPECIAL STUFFING

2 cups fresh white bread crumbs
1 medium onion, chopped fine
1 tablespoon fresh sage, crumbled, or
    2 tablespoons dried

Rind and juice of 1 orange
One 15-ounce can natural
    chestnut purée

Preheat oven to 350° F.

Combine the bread crumbs, onion and sage in a bowl. Chop the orange rind fine and add to the mixture. Add the orange juice and the chestnut purée. Mix together until smooth. Use to stuff 8 squabs or 1 large chicken and bake the rest in a small soufflé dish for about 15 minutes in preheated oven to use in place of a vegetable.

*WILD RICE AND SAUSAGE STUFFING

MAKES APPROXIMATELY 3½ CUPS
Good with pheasant, duck or squab.

1 cup wild rice (see page 216)	*1½ ounces sausage meat,*
¼ cup onion, minced	*crumbled*
¼ pound butter or margarine	*2 tablespoons minced parsley*
1 cup mushrooms, chopped	*½ teaspoon crumbled sage*
	Salt and pepper to taste

Steam the wild rice for approximately 25 minutes. In a frying pan sauté the onion in the butter or margarine until it is soft. Stir in the chopped mushrooms and sauté them until they are golden. Add the sausage meat and sauté the mixture for 2 to 3 minutes more, or until the sausage meat is cooked. Combine the rice with the onion, mushroom and sausage mixture, the minced parsley, sage and salt and pepper to taste.

Preparation and cooking time: approximately 1 hour 15 minutes.

MEAT

---

†BARBECUED STEAK

SERVES 6

Can be done either on an outdoor barbecue or in the broiler.

2½ to 3 pounds chuck steak, cut into
six 1-inch-thick steaks
½ cup dry red wine
1 teaspoon meat tenderizer

⅛ teaspoon garlic powder
¾ cup salad oil
3 teaspoons soy sauce
1 teaspoon cardamom

Arrange the steaks in an ovenproof dish. Combine the wine, meat tenderizer, cardamom, garlic powder, oil and soy sauce. Pour over the steaks and marinate for 1 hour at room temperature, turning the meat several times. Drain and reserve the marinade. Barbecue the steaks, turning once, for about 20 minutes or until they are cooked as you like them. Brush frequently with the reserved marinade while cooking.

Preparation time: 15 minutes. Marinating time: 1 hour. Cooking time: 30 minutes.

†BEEF RAGOÛT WITH BREAD DUMPLINGS

SERVES 4 TO 6

1½ cups onions, chopped

3 tablespoons sweet butter

3 tablespoons oil

2 pounds boneless beef chuck, cut into 1-inch cubes

⅔ cup dry red wine

2 tablespoons tomato paste

Rind of ½ lemon, minced

1 clove garlic, minced

1 teaspoon marjoram

½ bay leaf

3 cups (or more) brown stock (see page 279) or beef broth

Salt and pepper to taste

Bread dumplings (see page 144)

In a saucepan sauté the onions in the butter and oil until they are lightly browned. Add the beef cubes and sauté the mixture until the meat is well browned. Add the red wine and tomato paste and cook for 5 minutes. Add the lemon rind mixed with the minced garlic, marjoram, bay leaf and beef broth or brown stock, and simmer the ragoût, covered, adding more beef broth as necessary in order to keep ragoût covered with liquid, for 2 hours, or until the meat is tender. Add salt and pepper to taste and serve the ragoût with bread dumplings (see page 144).

Preparation time: 30 minutes. Cooking time: approximately 2 hours 30 minutes.

††BREAD DUMPLINGS

SERVES 6

1 small onion, minced
3 tablespoons butter
2 tablespoons minced parsley
1½ pounds stale hard rolls, cut into ½-inch cubes

1 cup milk
1 egg, lightly beaten
¼ cup flour
Salt to taste

In a small frying pan sauté the minced onion in the butter until it is golden. Stir in the parsley and toss the onion mixture with the bread cubes. Add the milk, heated to the boiling point, the egg, flour and salt to taste, and stir well. Shape the mixture with wet hands into 2 cylinders, each 2 inches in diameter, and plunge them into a large saucepan of simmering salted water. Simmer the dumplings, partially covered, for 15 minutes; turn them with 2 wooden spoons, and simmer them for 15 minutes more. Transfer the dumplings with slotted spoons to a board and immediately cut them with a thread into ½-inch slices. Serve on a heated dish.

Preparation time: 30 minutes. Cooking time: approximately 1 hour.

††CARBONNADE À LA FLAMANDE

SERVES 6

2½ pounds beef rump or chuck cut into 10 to 14 slices
3 tablespoons lard
2 to 3 large onions, sliced thin
3 tablespoons brown sugar
2 tablespoons red-wine vinegar
1 clove garlic, chopped fine

Pinch of thyme
1 bay leaf
Beer, to cover
1 large slice of French bread, spread thick with Dijon mustard

Flatten the beef slices with a cleaver. Brown the meat in the lard and put in a heavy casserole. In the fat remaining in the pan, lightly brown the onions, sprinkle them with the brown sugar and shake the pan over medium heat until they are caramelized. Sprinkle the onions with the vinegar and add the contents of the frying pan to the casserole. Add the garlic, thyme, bay leaf and enough beer to cover the meat completely. Place the bread slice on top of the meat, bring the carbonnade just to the boil, cover the casserole and simmer it over the lowest possible heat for about 2 hours, or until the beer is reduced by half. If the beer is not reducing fast enough, remove the lid for the last 15 minutes for cooking. The bread will completely dissolve, binding the sauce. Serve the carbonnade with steamed potatoes in their skins, scallions and cold beer.

Preparation time: approximately 25 minutes. Cooking time: approximately 2 hours 30 minutes.

†††COLD FILLET OF BEEF WITH SOUR-CREAM FILLING

SERVES 6

THE BEEF

1 carrot, chopped	¼ cup butter or margarine
1 stalk of celery, chopped	2 pounds fillet of beef
1 onion, chopped	Salt and pepper to taste

THE FILLING

One ½-pound piece of fat bacon, cut into ¾-inch cubes	1½ tablespoons reserved pan juices
1 tablespoon oil	1 tablespoon grated onion
1 clove garlic, crushed	1 tablespoon chopped chives
1 cup sour cream	Salt and white pepper to taste
	Watercress

Preheat oven to 500° F.

In a roasting pan just large enough to hold the beef, sauté the carrot, celery and onion in 2 tablespoons of the butter or margarine for 10 minutes, or until the vegetables are soft. Add the fillet of beef, sprinkled with salt and pepper, and dot it with 2 tablespoons of butter or margarine. Roast the fillet in the preheated oven for 20 to 25 minutes, depending on the thickness of fillet, for rare meat. Allow it to cool in the pan for 1 hour. Transfer the fillet to a serving dish, strain and reserve the pan juices.

To make the sour-cream filling, sauté the cubes of bacon in the oil with the garlic, until the bacon is crisp. Remove the bacon bits with a slotted spoon, drain them on paper towels, and discard the fat. In a bowl combine the sour cream with 1½ tablespoons of the reserved pan juices and the grated onion and chopped chives. Add the bacon bits and salt and white pepper to taste, and combine the mixture well. With a sharp knife cut a wedge along the length of the fillet, about 1½ inches wide and 1 inch deep, and remove it. Fill the cavity with as much filling as it will hold and pour the remainder into a dish and serve separately. Cut the fillet wedge crosswise into ¾-inch slices, reassemble the wedge and place it on top of the filling. Serve on a bed of watercress. To serve the beef, cut through the sliced top wedge of the fillet, the filling and the bottom section, forming complete ¾-inch slices.

Preparation and cooking time: approximately 1 hour 45 minutes.

†THE EARL OF GOWRIE'S STEAK AU POIVRE

SERVES 6

6 *tablespoons black peppercorns*
3 *tablespoons juniper berries*
1½ *pounds well-aged boneless*
    sirloin steak
Dijon mustard

2 *tablespoons clarified butter*
    (*see page 275*)
2 *tablespoons vegetable oil*
Brandy, to deglaze the pan

In a coffee grinder or a mortar, blend the black peppercorns and juniper berries. Coat one side of the steak with mustard and press the spices onto it so that the mustard holds them. Repeat the process on the other side and around the edges. Leave standing for 1 hour or more. Heat the clarified butter and oil in a heavy frying pan until it is very hot. Sear the steak for about 6 minutes on each side so that the meat forms a good brown springy crust and seals in the spices, but the inside remains rare. If some of the spice crust comes away in the cooking, fry a little more of the mixture and press it into the meat. When cooked place the meat on a large cold dish, set it aside until cool, then refrigerate. Slice very thick before serving. While the meat is cooling deglaze the pan juices with brandy, then set it aside for reheating. This dish is delicious served with leeks and potatoes. Sauté the cleaned and sliced leeks in butter for about 15 minutes or until they are quite soft. Mix them with a thin purée of potatoes.

Preparation and cooking time: approximately 30 minutes. Cooling time: approximately 1 hour.

†FILETS MIGNONS WITH MUSTARD SAUCE

SERVES 6

6 filets mignons	1 tablespoon clarified butter (see page
½ teaspoon cinnamon	275)
Salt and pepper to taste	1 tablespoon butter
⅔ cup olive oil	Reserved steak marinade
½ cup white vinegar	1 tablespoon Cognac
3 egg yolks	1 tablespoon Dijon mustard, or to taste
1 sprig of thyme	Pepper to taste
2 bay leaves	

Sprinkle the filets mignons with the cinnamon and salt and pepper to taste, and put them in a dish or bowl just big enough to hold them.

In a bowl, beat together the oil, vinegar, egg yolks, thyme and bay leaves. Pour the mixture over the steaks, cover and allow to marinate in the refrigerator for 4 hours, turning the meat several times. Remove and discard the thyme and bay leaves. Drain the steaks, reserving the marinade, and pat them dry with paper towels. In a large, heavy frying pan, cook the steaks in the clarified butter over high heat for 4 minutes on each side for rare meat. Transfer them to a heated dish and keep warm. Wipe the frying pan. Add the 1 tablespoon butter and melt it. Remove the pan from the heat and add the reserved marinade, the Cognac, Dijon mustard and pepper to taste. Stir the mixture vigorously for 1 minute or until it is hot, and pour over the steaks.

Preparation and marinating time: 4 hours 10 minutes. Cooking time: approximately 10 minutes.

†FONDUE BOURGUIGNONNE

A good dish for a summer party out of doors, or any informal supper party. The sauces can be made in advance and kept in the refrigerator until you need them, then served in cold, shallow bowls. Escoffier's Cumberland sauce is excellent, as are the 3 spicy sauces that follow, which you can make yourself. All you need then is a first-class rump steak (allowing ½ pound per person), cut into bite-size pieces, and a chafing dish filled with a mixture of half butter, half oil, kept very hot on top of a table burner (or you could use an electric frying pan). Spear the squares of meat with a fork and dip them in the hot fat until they are cooked as you like them. Then dip them into one of the spicy sauces. Serve with baked potatoes or French fries, which can be dipped into the fat at the last minute to make them extra crisp.

GARLIC MAYONNAISE
SERVES 6
Blend 3 crushed cloves of garlic with 2 egg yolks. Slowly add, drop by drop, ½ cup oil, beating constantly with a wire whisk or rotary beater until the sauce thickens. Slowly add a mixture of ½ cup oil, 1

teaspoon lemon juice, 1 teaspoon salt, ½ teaspoon cold water and a pinch of both white pepper and cayenne. Continue beating until the mixture is smooth. Chill before serving.

CHILI MAYONNAISE
SERVES 6

To 1 cup mayonnaise (see page 295), add ½ cup chili sauce, 2 tablespoons tomato paste, 1 tablespoon each of tarragon vinegar, chives, chopped fine, parsley, chopped fine, 1 teaspoon each of onion juice and Worcestershire sauce, salt and pepper to taste.

RÉMOULADE SAUCE
SERVES 6

To 2 cups mayonnaise (see page 295), add ½ cup sour pickle, chopped fine, and 2 tablespoons capers, chopped fine (both well drained), 3 hard-boiled eggs, chopped fine, and 1 tablespoon each of Dijon mustard and mixed chopped parsley, tarragon and chervil.

†††SPICED BEEF

SERVES 6

¼ cup dark-brown sugar	1 tablespoon whole allspice
3 to 4 pounds lean brisket of beef	1 tablespoon whole peppercorns
¼ cup juniper berries	¾ cup water
¼ cup coarse salt	

Preheat oven to 275° F.

With the fingertips firmly press the sugar into the beef, coating it on all sides. Put the meat in a large casserole and allow it to stand in the refrigerator, covered, for 2 days. In a mortar crush together the juniper berries, salt, allspice and peppercorns, or wrap the berries and spices in a towel and crush them with a rolling pin. Press 1 tablespoon of the spice mixture into the surfaces of the meat, cover it, and return to the refrigerator. *Repeat the spicing every day for 9 days.* Rinse the beef under running cold water to remove the spices clinging to it, discard any accumulated liquid in the casserole and return the meat to the casserole with the water. Bake the beef, covered, in the center of the preheated oven for 3½ hours, or until it is tender. Allow to cool to room temperature. Wrap in foil, put a weight on it, and refrigerate for 12 hours. Serve cold, cut into very thin slices. The beef will keep in the refrigerator, wrapped in foil, for about 4 weeks.

Marinating time: 12 days. Cooking time: 3 hours 3 minutes. Chilling time: 12 hours.

††*CRANBERRY BEEF STEW

SERVES 6 TO 8

¼ cup salt pork, blanched and diced

¼ cup sweet butter or margarine

½ cup shallots, chopped

1 clove garlic, chopped

Flour, for dredging

3 pounds beef chuck, cut into 2-inch cubes

1 pound cranberries

2 cups dry red wine

1 cup brown stock (see page 279) or beef broth

1 cup canned tomatoes, seeded and chopped

1 tablespoon sugar

½ teaspoon thyme

2 sprigs parsley

1 bay leaf

Salt and pepper to taste

½ pound mushrooms, sliced

¼ cup Madeira

1 tablespoon flour

In a heavy casserole sauté the diced salt pork in 2 tablespoons of the butter or margarine until it is browned. Remove the dice with a slotted spoon and reserve. Add the shallots and garlic to the casserole, and sauté until they are softened. Flour the cubed beef chuck, add to the shallots and garlic and brown over high heat for 3 to 4 minutes. Add the cranberries, red wine, brown stock or beef broth, the tomatoes, sugar, thyme, parsley, bay leaf, and salt and pepper to taste. Simmer, covered, for about 2 hours or until the meat is tender. In a frying pan sauté the sliced mushrooms in 2 tablespoons of butter or margarine over high heat until they are golden brown. Remove the meat from the casserole with a slotted spoon, arrange it on a dish and keep it warm. Strain the cooking liquid through a sieve into a bowl, pressing out as much juice as possible. Add the Madeira to the casserole, scraping up any bits clinging to the pan, and add the strained liquid, the mushrooms and 1 tablespoon of flour. Stir well, heat the sauce and pour it over the meat. Serve the stew with rice or boiled potatoes.

Preparation and cooking time: approximately 2 hours 30 minutes.

†DEREK HART'S STEW

SERVES 8

6 large onions, peeled and cut into chunks

2 tablespoons beef drippings or 2 tablespoons vegetable oil

2½ pounds top round, cut into chunks

Flour

1 pound tomatoes, peeled

1 pound carrots, peeled and sliced

½ bottle red wine

3¾ cups (or more) beef stock

Bouquet garni (6 peppercorns, sprig of parsley, 2 bay leaves)

2 pounds potatoes, peeled

Salt and pepper to taste

Chopped parsley

Preheat oven to 250° F.

Put the drippings or oil in a casserole over direct heat. Add onions and the meat, dredged in flour, and cook for a few minutes or until the meat is browned, stirring with a wooden spoon. Add the tomatoes and carrots. Pour in the red wine and top with stock to cover. Bring to a simmer, add the bouquet garni, cover and place in the preheated oven for 3 hours. About 1 hour before the stew is done, add the potatoes and salt and pepper to taste. If the juices evaporate, you may need to add a little extra stock. Sprinkle with chopped parsley before serving.

Preparation and cooking time: approximately 4 hours

†*YUGOSLAVIAN BEEF STEW

SERVES 8

2 pounds boneless chuck, cut into
   1½-inch cubes
2 tablespoons olive or vegetable oil
2 tablespoons butter or margarine
2 tablespoons paprika
1 pound canned tomatoes
½ pound string beans, cut into
   1½-inch lengths
½ pound zucchini, cut into
   ½-inch rounds

½ pound eggplant, peeled and
   cut into ½-inch cubes
10 whole black peppercorns
10 whole cloves garlic, peeled
3 carrots, peeled and cut into
   ⅓-inch rounds
2 onions, chopped
2 cups green pepper, chopped
2 bay leaves
Salt and pepper to taste

Preheat oven to 350° F.

In a flameproof casserole brown the meat in the oil and butter. Remove the casserole from the heat and sprinkle the meat with paprika. Add, in layers, the tomatoes, string beans, zucchini, eggplant, peppercorns and garlic, the carrots, onions, green pepper and bay leaves. Season the mixture with 1 tablespoon of salt or more, to taste, and pepper to taste, and bring it to the boil on top of the stove. Cover the casserole and bake it in the preheated oven for 2 to 2½ hours, or until the meat is tender.

Preparation and cooking time: approximately 3 hours 10 minutes.

†††CURRIED LEG OF LAMB

SERVES 8

One 5-pound leg of lamb, boned,
  rolled and tied (reserve
  the bones)
4 cups water
1 small onion, peeled and halved
1 stalk of celery with leaves
1 bay leaf
2 teaspoons salt
Pepper to taste
¼ cup safflower or vegetable oil

1 teaspoon dry mustard
½ teaspoon basil
½ teaspoon rosemary
2 tablespoons butter or margarine
2 tablespoons flour
1 tablespoon curry powder
1 teaspoon lemon juice
¼ cup Calvados, warmed

Preheat oven to 400° F.

In a large saucepan combine the lamb bones with the water, onion, celery, bay leaf, 1 teaspoon of the salt and pepper to taste. Bring the water to the boil and skim the froth from the surface. Simmer the broth, covered, for 3 hours and strain it into a bowl and reserve. In a small bowl combine the safflower or vegetable oil, the remaining teaspoon of salt, the dry mustard, basil, rosemary and pepper to taste. Arrange the rolled leg of lamb on a rack in a roasting pan and pour the seasoned oil over it. Roast it in a preheated oven for 1 hour 40 minutes for slightly rare meat. Transfer the meat to a heated dish. Skim the fat from the pan juices, put the roasting pan on top of the stove over moderate heat and add the butter or margarine to the juices. Stir in the flour and curry powder and cook the roux over moderately low heat, stirring, for 2 minutes. If you like the sauce hot, add more curry powder to taste. Remove the pan from the heat and add 2 cups of the reserved lamb stock, heated. Cook the mixture, stirring, for 3 to 4 minutes, or until it is the consistency of heavy cream. Stir in the lemon juice and transfer the sauce to a sauceboat. In a small saucepan ignite the warmed Calvados and pour it, flaming, over the lamb.

Preparation and cooking time: 3 hours 30 minutes.

††*GINGERED LAMB STEW

SERVES 6

¼ cup flour
2 tablespoons fresh ginger root,
    peeled and minced
1½ teaspoons salt
2 pounds boneless shoulder of
    lamb, cut into 1-inch cubes
1 onion, sliced
1 small clove garlic, minced

3 tablespoons butter or
    margarine
1 teaspoon whole coriander
1 teaspoon whole cloves
1 teaspoon whole peppercorns
2½ cups chicken stock
½ cup dry white wine
1 cup plain yogurt

In a shallow dish combine the flour with the ginger root and salt and dredge the lamb in the mixture. In a large frying pan sauté the sliced onion and minced garlic in the butter or margarine until they are just soft but not colored. In a mortar combine the coriander, cloves and peppercorns and pound them until they are fine. Add the spices to the onions in the pan and sauté over moderately low heat for 5 minutes. Transfer the onion mixture with a slotted spoon to a dish. Add the lamb to the pan and brown it on all sides over moderate heat, adding more butter or margarine if necessary. Return the onion mixture to the pan and add the chicken stock combined with the white wine. Simmer the stew, covered, stirring occasionally to prevent it from sticking, for 1 hour 15 minutes or until the lamb is tender. Stir in the yogurt and cook the stew, uncovered, over moderate heat for 10 minutes.

If you are going to freeze the stew, do not add the yogurt until it has been defrosted and is being reheated to serve.

Preparation and cooking time: approximately 2 hours 15 minutes.

††HERBED RACK OF LAMB

SERVES 3 TO 4

¾ teaspoon salt
½ teaspoon crushed dried rosemary
¼ teaspoon thyme
One 5-pound rack of lamb, trimmed,
  leaving a thin layer of fat on top
½ cup chopped celery
¼ cup chopped onion
½ cup chopped parsley

¼ cup white wine
¼ cup chicken stock
½ cup fresh bread crumbs
¼ cup shallots, chopped
  fine
1 tablespoon melted butter
  or margarine

Preheat oven to 500° F.

In a small bowl combine the salt, rosemary and thyme. Wipe the lamb with paper towels, score it lightly and rub it well with the herb mixture. Put the rack, fat-side down, in a shallow, flameproof baking dish just large enough to hold it, and roast it in the preheated oven for 8 minutes. Turn the rack fat-side up and roast it for 10 minutes more. Remove the lamb from the pan and drain off all the fat. In a baking dish combine the celery, onion and ¼ cup of the parsley. Put the lamb on the vegetables and roast it in a hot oven (400° F.) for 5 minutes. Add the white wine and chicken stock and roast the lamb for 5 minutes more. Remove the meat from the pan. Put the juices through a sieve and keep warm. Combine the bread crumbs with the shallots and the remaining parsley. Coat the fat side of the lamb with the bread-crumb mixture and with a broad spatula, press it against the meat so that it adheres. Sprinkle the crumbs with melted butter or margarine. Return the lamb to the baking dish and put it under the broiler for 2 to 3 minutes, or until the crumbs are golden. Serve the lamb with the reserved juices.

Preparation and cooking time: approximately 1 hour.

†HONEY-MARINATED ROAST LAMB

SERVES 6 TO 8

1 cup orange juice
¼ cup soy sauce
3 tablespoons clear honey
  (rosemary, if available)
1 sprig of rosemary
½ teaspoon ground ginger
½ teaspoon salt

½ green pepper, seeded and cut into
  1-inch pieces
1 clove garlic, bruised
One 3-to-3½-pound boned shoulder
  or leg of lamb, rolled and tied
Salt and pepper to taste

In a shallow dish combine the orange juice, soy sauce, honey, rosemary, ground ginger and salt with the green pepper and garlic. Place the shoulder or leg of lamb in the marinade and allow it to stand in the refrigerator, turning it occasionally, for 12 hours. Preheat oven to 450° F. Drain off the marinade and reserve it. Dry the meat and sprinkle it lightly with salt and pepper. Put the lamb in a small roasting pan and roast it in the preheated oven for 15 minutes. Reduce the heat to moderate (350° F.) and continue to roast the lamb, brushing it frequently with the reserved marinade, for 1 hour.

Marinating time: 12 hours. Cooking time: 1 hour 15 minutes.

††STUFFED SHOULDER OF LAMB

SERVES 6

¼ cup pine nuts
5 tablespoons butter or margarine
¼ cup celery, chopped fine
1 clove garlic, minced
1 shallot, minced

1½ cups cooked rice
2 tablespoons chopped mint
Salt and pepper to taste
One 3½-pound boned
  shoulder of lamb

Preheat oven to 400° F.

In a frying pan brown the pine nuts in 1 tablespoon of the butter or margarine. With a slotted spoon transfer the nuts to a bowl. Add 2 more tablespoons of the butter to the frying pan. Add the celery, minced garlic and minced shallots and sauté until the vegetables are soft. Add them to the pine nuts with the cooked rice and chopped mint. Toss the mixture together and add salt and pepper to taste. Spread the boned shoulder of lamb, smooth side down, on a board. Spread the stuffing mixture into the depressions left by the deboning and along the length of the meat, leaving margins along either side that are wide enough to fold over the stuffing. Fold the 2 long sides of the lamb over one another to form a roll and tie with string all along the length. Skewer or truss the short ends and the long seam to hold the stuffing in place during the cooking. Pat the meat dry. Then rub with 2 tablespoons soft butter and sprinkle it with salt and pepper. Roast the meat in the preheated oven for 30 minutes. Reduce the heat to moderate (350° F.) and roast for 1 hour more.

Preparation and cooking time: approximately 2 hours 45 minutes.

††LAMB AND VEAL KEBABS

SERVES 6

3 cloves garlic, chopped	Salt and pepper to taste
2 large onions, sliced	3 pounds lamb and 2 pounds veal,
2 tablespoons oil	shoulder or leg cuts, cut into
3 to 4 cups cider vinegar	1½-inch cubes
½ cup apricot jam	Oil, to baste
1 tablespoon curry powder	

Sauté the chopped garlic cloves and sliced onions in the oil until the onions are tender. Stir in the cider vinegar, apricot jam, curry powder and salt and pepper to taste. Cook the mixture until it comes to the boil, then allow it to cool thoroughly. In a deep earthenware bowl arrange the meat in layers alternately with the marinade. Marinate in the refrigerator for 4 to 5 days, turning the cubes once a day. Thread the cubes on skewers and broil them, turning occasionally and basting with oil, for approximately 15 minutes, or until they are tender. They taste even better broiled over a low charcoal fire.

Preparation and marinating time: 4 to 5 days. Cooking time: approximately 15 minutes.

†††LAMB CHOPS EN PAPILLOTE

SERVES 6

6 lamb chops, 1¼ to 1½ inches thick	*Butter*
1 tablespoon olive oil	*12 thin slices mildly smoked*
Duxelles (see page 344)	*ham*
12 pieces parchment paper, each 10	*Oil*
by 13 inches	*Minced parsley, to garnish*

Preheat oven to 450° F.

Have the chops trimmed as for rack of lamb. In a frying pan brown the fat edges of the chops in the olive oil. Then lay chops flat and brown them on each side for 1 to 2 minutes. Transfer them to a dish and cool. Make the duxelles. Cut 6 heart-shaped pieces of cooking parchment paper, each 10 by 13 inches, and butter the top sides. Fold the hearts in half, open them and put a thin slice of ham along the fold. Divide the duxelles into 12 parts and top each slice of ham with 1 part. Lay a chop on top, arranging it so that the straight side of the bone is nearest to the fold. Reserve a second piece of paper topped with ham and duxelles on top of each chop, and fold the paper around the chops. Starting at the rounded tops, crimp the edges, tightly shut all around and twist the bottom tips. Oil a baking sheet lightly and put the cases on it. Brush the cases lightly with more oil and bake in the center of the preheated oven for 12 to 15 minutes, or until the papers are puffed and lightly browned. Transfer the papillotes to a heated dish, open and sprinkle with minced parsley.

Preparation and cooking time: approximately 45 minutes.

†MARINATED LAMB CHOPS

SERVES 6

MARINADE

¼ cup olive oil

½ clove garlic, minced

½ teaspoon oregano

½ teaspoon salt

¼ teaspoon fresh-ground pepper

8 shoulder lamb chops

2 tablespoons Dijon mustard

1 tablespoon anchovy paste

Juice of ½ lemon

1 teaspoon oregano

½ clove garlic, mashed

Italian parsley, chopped, to garnish

In the bottom of a large shallow pan, combine the olive oil, minced garlic, oregano and salt and pepper. Put the lamb chops in the marinade and allow to stand, turning them occasionally, for at least 4 hours. In a bowl mix the rest of the ingredients except the parsley. Remove the chops from the marinade and spread one side with the mustard mixture. Broil the chops under the broiler or over charcoal, coated side up, for 3 to 4 minutes. Turn them, spread the other side with the mustard mixture and broil them until they are done to taste. Sprinkle the chops with parsley (the flat variety if possible), and serve immediately with a mixed green salad.

Preparation and marinating time: 4 hours 15 minutes. Cooking time: approximately 10 minutes.

††LAMB IN PEACH SAUCE

SERVES 6

One 2-pound boned leg of lamb,
   cut into 1-inch cubes
1 teaspoon cinnamon
1 teaspoon paprika
1 teaspoon salt
1 teaspoon pepper
⅓ cup peanut oil
1½ cups water

2 onions, chopped fine
3 tablespoons lemon juice
5 large peaches, halved and cut
   into thin slices
2 tablespoons butter
2 tablespoons lime juice
⅓ cup sugar
¾ cup water

Sprinkle the lamb cubes with the cinnamon, paprika, salt and pepper. In a heavy saucepan sauté the cubes in ¼ cup of the oil until they are brown. Add the 1½ cups of water and cook over low heat for about 25 minutes. In another pan sauté the onions in the remaining oil until they are golden. Stir in 1 tablespoon of the lemon juice and set aside. Sauté the peaches in the butter until they are slightly colored but not mushy. Combine the reserved onions and the lamb in a large casserole and arrange the peaches over the meat. Combine the lime juice and remaining lemon juice with the sugar and sprinkle the mixture over the ragoût. Add the ¾ cup water, cover the casserole and simmer the lamb for 20 minutes. Serve with steamed rice.

Preparation and cooking time: approximately 1 hour 45 minutes.

††LAMB WITH CUMBERLAND SAUCE

SERVES 8

1 whole rack of lamb
1 cup fresh bread crumbs
¼ cup chopped parsley
1 to 2 cloves garlic, minced

Salt and pepper to taste
2 tablespoons butter, melted
Cumberland sauce (see page 285)

Preheat oven to 500° F.

Trim and chine the lamb and score the fat. Sprinkle lightly with salt and pepper and roast in the preheated oven for 10 to 15 minutes, or a little longer if you like lamb well done. Combine the bread crumbs with the chopped parsley and garlic and salt and pepper to taste. Coat the fat side of the lamb with the bread mixture and sprinkle with the melted butter. With a broad spatula press the crumbs against the meat so that they adhere. Return the lamb to the oven and continue to roast for 10 minutes more, or until the crumbs form a brown crust. Serve with Cumberland sauce.

Preparation and cooking time: approximately 1 hour.

†BAKED PORK CHOPS

SERVES 4

Juice of ½ lemon
Juice of ½ orange
1 teaspoon grated lemon rind
1 teaspoon grated orange rind
¼ cup fresh mint, chopped
1 tablespoon sugar

1 teaspoon mixed allspice,
* cinnamon, rosemary and ginger*
Pinch each of salt, pepper, paprika
* and nutmeg*
4 large lean pork chops

Preheat oven to 300° F.

In the top of a double boiler, combine all the ingredients except the pork. Heat the mixture over simmering water until the sugar is dissolved. Place the pork chops in an oiled casserole with a lid. Spread the seasoned mixture over them and bake, covered, in the preheated oven for 2 hours.

Preparation and cooking time: 2 hours 25 minutes.

†ORANGE-MARINATED PORK

SERVES 6 TO 8

Juice of 6 oranges	½ teaspoon oregano
Juice of 1 lime	Salt and pepper to taste
Juice of ½ lemon	One 4-pound loin of pork
1 onion, sliced	2 to 3 cloves garlic, cut into slivers
1 bay leaf	

In a large ceramic or glass dish, combine all the juices. Add the sliced onion, bay leaf, oregano, salt and pepper to taste. Make small slits in the loin of pork and insert the slivers of garlic. Put the pork in the orange-juice mixture, turn it to coat it, and chill, covered with plastic wrap, turning occasionally, for 12 to 24 hours. Preheat oven to 350° F. Drain the pork, reserving the marinade, and put it on a rack in a roasting pan. Roast the pork in the preheated oven, basting it every 15 minutes with the reserved marinade and skimming off the fat, for 2 hours 30 minutes.

Preparation and marinating time: 12 to 24 hours. Cooking time: 2 hours 30 minutes.

†PORK MEDALLIONS WITH MUSTARD-CREAM SAUCE

SERVES 12

12 medallions, ¾ inch thick, from a loin of pork	⅓ cup vinegar
	8 peppercorns, crushed
Salt and pepper to taste	2 cups heavy cream
Flour	2½ ounces Dijon mustard
¼ cup butter or margarine	½ teaspoon salt

Flatten the medallions between 2 sheets of waxed paper until they are ½ inch thick. Sprinkle them with salt and pepper and dust with flour. In a frying pan sauté the medallions in 2 tablespoons of the butter or margarine for 4 minutes on each side. Transfer to a warm dish and keep them warm. Add to the frying pan the vinegar and peppercorns and boil the mixture, stirring in the brown bits that cling to the bottom and the sides of the pan, until it is reduced by two-thirds. Add the heavy cream and continue to simmer for 5 minutes longer, or until the sauce has thickened. Remove the pan from the heat and swirl in the mustard and the remaining butter or margarine. Season the sauce with ½ teaspoon salt or more, to taste, and pour it over the pork.

Preparation and cooking time: approximately 30 minutes.

††STUFFED SHOULDER OF PORK

SERVES 6 TO 8

One 4-pound shoulder of pork, boned
¾ cup dark rum
2½ cups fresh bread crumbs
1 cup milk
1 tablespoon chopped parsley
1 tablespoon chopped chives
½ teaspoon thyme

½ teaspoon sage
2 cloves garlic, chopped
1 bay leaf, crumbled
½ small hot red pepper, seeded and chopped
Salt and pepper to taste
1 cup chicken stock

Preheat oven to 325° F.

Score the pork at ⅛-inch intervals, put it in a dish, and add ½ cup of the rum.

To make the stuffing, soak the bread crumbs in the milk for 10 minutes and squeeze them dry. In another bowl combine the crumbs with the chopped parsley and chopped chives, thyme, sage, garlic, bay leaf, hot red pepper, and salt and pepper to taste. Drain the rum from the pork, add it to the bread-crumb mixture and toss lightly. Fill the cavity of the pork shoulder with the stuffing and tie it with string. Put the pork on a rack in a roasting pan and roast it in the preheated oven for 2½ hours. Transfer to a platter and keep warm.

Pour off the fat from the pan, add the remaining ¼ cup of rum, and cook it over moderately high heat, scraping up the brown bits that cling to the bottom and sides of the pan. Add the chicken stock and cook over high heat until the sauce is reduced to 1 cup. Serve the sauce separately.

Preparation and cooking time: approximately 3 hours.

†MRS. RALPH F. COLIN'S BAKED VIRGINIA HAM

SERVES 24

One 16-pound half-cooked baked
  Virginia ham
2 tablespoons flour
2 tablespoons stout or dark ale
1 cup brown sugar

Cloves
1¼ cups stout or dark ale, for
  basting
Red-currant sauce (see page
  165)

Preheat oven to 400° F.

Make diamond-shaped cuts in the skin of the ham and mix a paste of the flour, stout and brown sugar. Spread the paste over the top of the ham and stud it with cloves. Heat a clean roasting pan. Put the ham in the pan and roast in the preheated oven for 10 minutes. Add some more stout, reduce the heat to 350° F. and continue to cook for about 1 hour, basting well with stout every 10 minutes. When ready to serve, slice in thin cuts lengthwise across the top. Serve with red-currant sauce (see page 165). This is also delicious cold.

Preparation and cooking time: approximately 2 hours.

RED-CURRANT SAUCE

One 1-pound jar red-currant jelly
2 tablespoons vinegar
Pinch of dry mustard

1 cup seedless raisins
Salt and pepper to taste

Melt the red-currant jelly in a saucepan, then add the vinegar. When these have cooked together for a few minutes, add the pinch of dry mustard, the seedless raisins and the salt and pepper. When raisins are soft, the sauce is done. Serve hot.

††HAM CROQUETTES

MAKES APPROXIMATELY 16 CROQUETTES

6 ounces baked country ham, put
  through the medium blade of
  a food mincer
½ recipe for béchamel sauce
  (see page 278)
2½ tablespoons flour
⅔ cup toasted fresh bread crumbs
1 egg, beaten

1 tablespoon Worcestershire
  sauce
1 tablespoon minced parsley
½ teaspoon dry mustard
Salt and white pepper to
  taste
2 cups fresh bread crumbs
Oil for frying

Put the ham in a bowl. Make ½ recipe for béchamel sauce, using 2½ tablespoons flour in order to make the sauce very thick, and allow it to cool to room temperature. Add the béchamel sauce to the ham along with the toasted bread crumbs, beaten egg, Worcestershire sauce, minced parsley, dry mustard, salt and pepper to taste. Combine the mixture well and form it into 1-inch balls. Roll the balls in fresh bread crumbs, put them on a plate and chill for 30 minutes. Fry the croquettes in 2 batches, in hot deep oil (360° F.) for 30 seconds, or until they are browned. Transfer them with a slotted spoon to paper towels to drain, and serve immediately.

Preparation time: 1 hour 30 minutes. Cooking time: approximately 8 minutes.

†BAKED SPARERIBS

SERVES 4

½ cup butter or margarine
⅓ cup soft brown sugar
¾ cup tomato ketchup
3 tablespoons lemon juice
1 tablespoon Dijon mustard

2 teaspoons HP sauce
2 teaspoons chili powder
2 teaspoons Worcestershire sauce
4 pounds pork spareribs
Salt to taste

Preheat oven to 350° F.

In a saucepan melt the butter or margarine and stir in the brown sugar. Remove from the heat and stir in the ketchup, lemon juice, mustard, HP sauce, chili powder and Worcestershire sauce. Sprinkle the spareribs lightly with salt, put them on a rack in a roasting pan and spread them with some of the sauce. Bake them in the preheated oven for 30 minutes. Continue baking the spareribs, spreading them with additional sauce every 15 minutes, for 1 hour or more, or until they are tender. Cut into serving pieces.

Preparation and cooking time: approximately 2 hours.

†HONEY-GLAZED SPARERIBS

SERVES 6

Two 3-pound racks of pork spareribs
Salt and pepper to taste
1 cup honey
3 tablespoons onion, chopped fine

3 tablespoons lemon juice
1 tablespoon curry powder
1½ teaspoons salt

Preheat oven to 350° F.

Sprinkle the racks of spareribs with salt and pepper, arrange them on a rack in a roasting pan and bake them in the preheated oven for 45 minutes. Drain off all the fat and put them on a rack in a baking pan. In a bowl combine the honey, the onion, lemon juice, curry powder and salt. Brush the spareribs with the honey mixture, and put them under the broiler for 10 minutes. Continue to broil, turning and brushing frequently with the honey mixture for about 25 minutes or until the ribs are well cooked, crisp and glazed. Cut the ribs into serving pieces.

Preparation and cooking time: approximately 1 hour 30 minutes.

†SPARERIBS IN BEER MARINADE

SERVES 4

1½ cups stout or dark ale
1 cup firmly packed
dark-brown sugar
1½ teaspoons chili powder
1 teaspoon ground cumin seed

1 teaspoon dry mustard
1 teaspoon oregano
4 pounds pork spareribs
Salt to taste

In a bowl combine the stout or dark ale with the sugar, chili powder, ground cumin seed, mustard and oregano and stir the mixture until the sugar has dissolved. Put the spareribs in 1 layer in a shallow pan, pour the marinade over them and allow the spareribs to marinate, chilled, turning them several times, for at least 12 hours. Preheat oven to 350° F. Transfer the spareribs to the rack of a roasting pan, sprinkle them with salt and coat them with some of the marinade. Bake in the preheated oven for 20 minutes. Baste with the marinade and continue to bake, basting with additional marinade every 15 minutes, for 1 hour more, or until the ribs are tender. Transfer the spareribs to a preheated broiler for 10 minutes, or until they are glazed. Cut into serving pieces.

Marinating time: approximately 12 hours. Cooking time: approximately 2 hours.

††*OSSO BUCO

SERVES 6

Six 2-inch-thick slices
   veal shin
Salt and pepper to taste
Flour, for dredging
⅓ cup olive oil
2 cloves garlic
1 large onion, chopped fine
1 large carrot, diced fine
1 large stalk celery, diced fine

½ cup dry white wine
4 tomatoes, coarse-chopped
Bouquet garni (parsley sprigs, 1
   small bay leaf, 6 peppercorns, all
   tied in cheesecloth)
1 teaspoon sugar
1 cup beef broth
Rind of 1 lemon, grated
1 tablespoon minced parsley

Preheat oven to 350° F.

Sprinkle the meat with salt and pepper. Dredge with flour and shake off the excess. Heat half the olive oil in a large, ovenproof, lidded casserole. Add 1 clove of the garlic and brown until golden. Remove, mince it and set aside. To the same oil add the veal shins and brown carefully on all sides without losing the marrow. Add the onion, carrot and celery and more oil if needed, and cook for about 4 minutes, stirring constantly so as not to burn the vegetables. Add the white wine and reduce the mixture for a minute or so. Add the tomatoes, bouquet garni and minced cooked garlic. Reduce briskly. Add the sugar only if the tomatoes are too acid. Pour in the broth, stir well and bring to the boil. Cover and place in the preheated oven for 1 hour. Uncover and correct the seasoning. Continue cooking uncovered for 10 to 15 minutes longer. Meanwhile, make gremolata by mincing the remaining clove of garlic and mixing it with the lemon rind and parsley. Transfer the osso buco to a heated platter and sprinkle the gremolata over the meat. Serve with rice.

Preparation and cooking time: approximately 2 hours.

††PAUPIETTES OF VEAL ON PEA PURÉE

SERVES 6

12 veal scallops, each
   about 3 by 5 inches
12 slices prosciutto (fresh or
   canned) or any other
   smoked ham
6 scallions, chopped fine
6 mushrooms, chopped fine
7 tablespoons butter or margarine
⅓ cup fresh bread crumbs

3 hard-boiled eggs, chopped
   fine
2 tablespoons chopped parsley
2 teaspoons arrowroot
¾ cup Marsala
1½ cups veal or chicken stock
Pea purée (see page 170)
Chopped parsley

Preheat oven to 350° F.

Pound the veal scallops between two sheets of waxed paper until they are very thin. Lay a thin slice of prosciutto on each slice of veal and trim it to size. Sauté the scallions and mushrooms in 2 tablespoons of the butter until they are soft, and combine them with the bread crumbs, eggs and parsley. Spread the veal and ham slices with the filling, roll them up, tucking in the ends neatly. Tie each paupiette in two places with string and brown them evenly on all sides in the remaining butter or margarine. Stir in the arrowroot. Heat the Marsala until it is reduced by half and pour it over the paupiettes in the pan. Add the veal or chicken stock. Cover the pan and simmer the paupiettes, turning them occasionally to prevent them from sticking, for 15 minutes, or until the meat is well done and the rolls are glazed. Spread a thick layer of pea purée in a shallow baking dish and level it with a spatula. With kitchen scissors or a small, sharp knife remove the strings from the paupiettes. Arrange the rolls on the pea purée. Spoon over the sauce in which the veal was cooked and heat the dish, if necessary, in the preheated oven. Sprinkle the paupiettes with parsley before serving.

Preparation and cooking time: approximately 1 hour 30 minutes.

PEA PURÉE

Two 10-ounce packages frozen
  peas, or 5 pounds green peas in
  the pod
½ cup boiling water
1 teaspoon sugar
1 teaspoon salt

Pinch of pepper
2 tablespoons sweet butter or
  margarine
4 tablespoons heavy cream
Salt and pepper, to taste

Shell the peas (if fresh), place them in a saucepan with the water and sugar, cover and boil for 8 to 10 minutes if fresh, for 5 minutes if frozen, or until tender. Drain, add the salt, pepper and butter, and toss lightly to mix. Purée the peas in a liquidizer at high speed, or put them through a food mill. Mix in the cream and add salt and pepper to taste.

Preparation and cooking time: approximately 20 minutes for frozen peas. Approximately 40 minutes for fresh peas.

†MRS. ANTHONY LEWIS'S VEAL GOULASH

SERVES 6 TO 8

¼ cup commercial beef
  suet
3 pounds shoulder of veal,
  cut into 1½-inch cubes
1 bay leaf
1 tablespoon caraway seeds
1 tablespoon dill seeds
1 tablespoon salt

½ tablespoon whole black
  peppercorns
2½ cups veal or beef stock
3 medium onions, sliced
3 tablespoons butter
2 tablespoons flour
⅓ cup cold water
4 tablespoons paprika, or more
1⅓ cups sour cream

In a deep saucepan render the beef suet. Add the veal cubes and brown. Add the bay leaf, caraway seeds, dill seeds and salt. Tie the peppercorns in a cheesecloth bag and add, together with the stock. Cover and cook slowly for 1 to 1½ hours, or until the meat is tender. Meanwhile, cook the onion rings in the butter until they are soft. Add them to the meat 20 minutes before the end of the cooking time. Blend the flour with the cold water and stir it into the cooking liquid. Stir until thickened. Discard the bag of peppercorns and remove the pot from the heat. Stir in paprika to taste and sour cream and heat thoroughly, but do not boil.

Preparation and cooking time: approximately 2 hours.

††ANTHONY WEST'S VEAL ROAST

SERVES 6 TO 8

One 4½-to-6-pound shoulder of veal, boned and rolled
Olive oil
Salt and pepper to taste
Garlic powder to taste
½ pound lean bacon, sliced

¾ cup Calvados, or brandy and hard cider mixed
2 tablespoons apple juice
1 cup heavy cream
Parsley or fresh dill weed, chopped, to taste

Preheat oven to 350° F.

Rub the veal with olive oil, salt and pepper and a discreet amount of garlic powder and cover with overlapping slices of the bacon. Place the veal in an enamel casserole on a rack, pour ¼ cup of the Calvados, or a combination of brandy and cider mixed, and the apple juice into the pan and roast for 1½ hours. Heat 2 to 3 tablespoons of the remaining Calvados in a small saucepan, light it and pour the flaming liquid over the roast. Lift the roast out of the casserole, remove its jacket of bacon and put it on a warmed dish. Remove the rack and beat the heavy cream into the liquor in the pan. Add chopped parsley or dill to taste. Carve as many slices of the veal as are likely to be needed, put them on the serving dish with the uncut veal at the end, pour on the sauce and serve.

Preparation and cooking time: approximately 2 hours.

†ANTHONY WEST'S KIDNEYS IN CREAM
AND CALVADOS

SERVES 6

6 veal kidneys, surplus fat removed   ¾ cup butter or margarine
Flour, for dredging   ½ cup Calvados
Salt and pepper to taste   Light cream to taste

The success of this dish depends on slicing the kidneys very thin and
cooking them in plenty of butter. Kidneys differ in size, so consult
your butcher. They must be very fresh. Slice the kidneys lengthwise,
removing the fatty cores. Combine the flour with salt and pepper to
taste and dredge the sliced kidneys in the seasoned flour. Melt the
butter in a pan large enough to hold all the kidneys at once and sauté
them for about 3 minutes. When done, transfer the kidneys to a warm
dish, lower the heat and add the Calvados to the pan. Stir well and
add enough light cream to make a light sauce. Pour over the reserved
kidneys and serve.

Preparation and cooking time: approximately 15 minutes.

††SAUTÉED VEAL KIDNEYS WITH CURRIED
RICE AND PEACHES

SERVES 6

6 veal kidneys, surplus fat removed   Curried rice and peaches (see
Salt and pepper to taste   page 173)
¾ cup butter or margarine   3 tablespoons parsley,
                                         chopped fine

Slit the kidneys lengthwise at the core side without cutting all the
way through; remove the core, and press them flat. Season with salt

and pepper to taste. In a large frying pan melt ½ cup of the butter and cook the kidneys, partly covered, over moderate heat for about 10 to 12 minutes on each side, or until they are golden brown and tender. Arrange them on the curried rice and peaches. Add ¼ cup butter and the chopped parsley to the pan juices. Heat until the butter foams and pour it over the kidneys.

Preparation and cooking time: approximately 15 minutes.

CURRIED RICE AND PEACHES

2 tablespoons butter
2 cups rice
3¾ cups chicken stock, boiling
2 tablespoons curry powder, or to taste

One 30-ounce can whole or halved white peaches (try to avoid the bright yellow ones)
Melted butter, for glazing

Preheat oven to 350° F.

In a flameproof casserole melt the butter, stir in the rice and toss until well coated. Add the chicken stock and curry powder and bring the liquid to the boil. Put the casserole, covered, in the preheated oven or over very low heat, and cook until the liquid is absorbed and the rice is tender. Turn the rice out onto a hot serving dish and toss it with a little more melted butter, using a long-tined fork. Lightly glaze the peach halves in the butter for 2 minutes. Arrange around the edge of the serving dish.

Preparation and cooking time: approximately 40 minutes.

†VEAL KIDNEYS IN PORT

SERVES 2

2 veal kidneys, surplus fat
   removed
½ cup butter
Salt and pepper to taste
1 teaspoon flour

¼ cup port
Parsley, chopped fine
2 slices of bread, cut into triangles and
   sautéed in butter

Slice the kidneys ⅛ inch thick and cut out as much of the white tubes as possible. Melt the butter in a frying pan and add the kidney slices and salt and pepper to taste. Cook, covered, for 2 to 3 minutes and remove the pan from the heat. Sprinkle the kidneys with the flour and port and stir briskly with a wooden spoon until the sauce is well blended. Serve on heated plates, sprinkled with chopped parsley and surrounded with the bread triangles.

Preparation and cooking time: approximately 25 minutes.

†MARINATED CALVES' LIVER

SERVES 4

¾ cup dry red wine
2 tablespoons red-wine vinegar
3 cloves garlic, crushed
1 teaspoon coarse salt
1 bay leaf, crumbled
Pepper to taste

1 pound calves' liver, sliced thin
3 slices lean bacon, diced
3 tablespoons olive oil or
   vegetable oil
2 tablespoons minced parsley

Combine the wine, vinegar, garlic, salt and bay leaf in a bowl, and add pepper to taste. Add the liver and allow it to marinate, stirring occasionally, for 1 hour. Transfer the liver with a slotted spoon to paper towels and pat it dry. Strain the marinade into a bowl and reserve it. In a frying pan sauté the bacon in the oil until it is crisp and transfer to paper towels to drain. Add the liver to the pan, cook it over high heat, turning once, for about 2 minutes on each side, or until it is browned on the outside but still pink within. Transfer it to a heated dish. Add the reserved marinade to the pan, stirring in the brown bits clinging to the bottom and the sides, and reduce over high heat to ½ cup. Pour the reduced sauce over the liver, sprinkle with bacon and minced parsley and serve.

Marinating time: 1 hour. Cooking time: 10 minutes.

VEGETABLES

---

††ARTICHOKES WITH HERBS

SERVES 6

6 artichokes
1 tablespoon vinegar or lemon juice
1 cup minced onion
3 tablespoons carrot, sliced thin
¼ cup olive oil or vegetable oil
3 tablespoons dry white wine

½ teaspoon thyme
1 bay leaf
Salt and pepper to taste
1 tablespoon anchovy
  essence‡
3 cloves garlic, minced

Cut off the stems of the artichokes and, with a sharp knife, trim the bottom leaves. Trim the remaining leaves with scissors. Plunge the artichokes into a bowl of water with either vinegar or lemon juice added to prevent browning. Drain the artichokes, place them in boiling water to cook for about 50 minutes or until tender. While the

‡ Anchovy essence can be bought at most specialty food shops or ordered from Maison Glass, 52 East 58 Street, New York, New York 10022.

artichokes cook, in a large, deep saucepan sauté the minced onion and sliced carrot in the oil until the onion is lightly colored. Add the dry white wine, thyme, bay leaf, salt and pepper to taste and the anchovy essence. Reduce the liquid over high heat by two-thirds, add the minced garlic cloves and continue to cook the sauce for 2 minutes longer. Add more salt and pepper if necessary. Transfer the artichokes with a slotted spoon to a serving dish. Serve the sauce separately and the artichokes at room temperature.

Preparation and cooking time: approximately 1 hour 30 minutes.

††EGGPLANT WITH HERBED TOMATO SAUCE

SERVES 6
Good with roast lamb or chicken.

3 large eggplant
Salt
3½ pounds tomatoes, peeled,
*   seeded and chopped*

4 tablespoons olive oil or vegetable
*   oil*
3 tablespoons parsley, minced
2 cloves garlic, minced
Salt and pepper to taste

Remove the stems and cut the eggplant in half lengthwise, then cut each half into ⅓-inch slices. Lightly score the slices on both sides, sprinkle them with salt and let them drain on paper towels for 30 minutes. In a frying pan cook the tomatoes in 2 tablespoons of the olive or vegetable oil over moderately high heat for 10 minutes, or until most of the liquid has evaporated. Reduce the heat to moderately low and simmer the tomatoes, stirring occasionally, for 45 minutes. Add the minced parsley, minced garlic, and salt and pepper to taste, and simmer the sauce for 10 minutes more. Remove from the heat and keep warm. Pat the eggplant slices dry with paper towels and, in a large covered frying pan, cook slices in the remaining oil, adding additional oil if necessary, until tender and turning to brown on both sides. Drain the eggplant on paper towels and arrange on a heated platter. Sprinkle them with salt and pepper and cover with the sauce.

Preparation and cooking time: approximately 1 hour 30 minutes.

†BEET GREENS VINAIGRETTE

SERVES 4

2 pounds beet greens	2 tablespoons olive oil or vegetable oil
1 large clove garlic, crushed and minced	1 tablespoon red-wine vinegar
	Salt and pepper to taste

Remove and wash the leaves from the beet greens. Shake off the excess water, put the leaves in a large saucepan, and cook them, covered, over moderate heat for 3 to 5 minutes, or until they are just tender. Drain the leaves and chop them fine. In a frying pan sauté the garlic in the oil for 1 minute. Stir in the beet leaves, vinegar, salt and pepper to taste, and cook for 3 to 4 minutes or until heated through.

Preparation and cooking time: approximately 15 minutes.

†BUTTERED BEETS WITH TARRAGON

SERVES 6

24 very small fresh beets	1 teaspoon fresh tarragon, chopped fine, or dried tarragon to taste
4 to 5 tablespoons butter or margarine	2 teaspoons lemon juice
½ teaspoon salt	Snipped chives

Cook the beets in boiling salted water for about 20 to 25 minutes, or until they are barely tender. Let them cool slightly and peel off the skins, roots and stems. (Never do this before cooking or the beet will "bleed" and become tough.) In a heavy saucepan heat the butter or margarine until the foam subsides. Add the beets, salt, tarragon and lemon juice. Shake the pan well and allow the beets to heat through. Serve on a heated platter with a sprinkling of snipped chives.

Preparation and cooking time: approximately 45 minutes.

†ORANGE-GLAZED BEETS

SERVES 8

32 very small fresh beets	1½ teaspoons orange juice
4 tablespoons butter	1 tablespoon grated orange rind
2 teaspoons sugar	

Trim all but 1 inch off the stems and put the beets in a large saucepan with water to cover. Bring to the boil and simmer for 15 to 20 minutes, or until tender. Plunge into cold water to stop the cooking process. Trim roots and stems, peel and cut into thin slices. In a large frying pan melt the butter over moderately high heat and add the beets, tossing to coat with butter. Sprinkle with sugar and cook for 2 to 3 minutes or until glazed. Transfer to a serving dish and toss gently in the orange juice and rind.

Preparation and cooking time: approximately 45 minutes.

†LIMA BEANS WITH SALAMI AND HAM

SERVES 4

1 onion, chopped fine	*1 pound shelled lima beans*
½ cup salami, chopped	*½ cup carrots, sliced*
½ cup smoked ham, sliced	*½ tablespoon tomato paste*
1 tablespoon olive oil	*Salt and pepper to taste*
2½ cups chicken stock	

Preheat oven to 300° F.

In a frying pan or casserole, gently cook the onion, salami and smoked ham (Parma is a suitable substitute) in the olive oil for about 5 minutes. Add the chicken stock, beans, carrots, tomato paste and salt and pepper to taste. Cover and cook in the preheated oven for about 1 hour, or until beans and carrots are tender.

Preparation and cooking time: approximately 1 hour 25 minutes.

†LIMA BEANS WITH GARLIC

SERVES 6

1½ pounds shelled lima beans	*1 teaspoon salt*
5 tablespoons olive oil or	*½ teaspoon fresh-ground pepper*
vegetable oil	*1½ teaspoons lemon juice*
2 cloves garlic, chopped fine	*1 tablespoon chopped parsley*

Cook the beans in boiling salted water for 3 to 5 minutes or until they are just tender. Drain them well in a colander. In a saucepan heat the oil and add the garlic, beans, salt and pepper. Toss the beans until they are well coated with oil and garlic. Just before serving add the lemon juice and chopped parsley. Serve in a heated dish.

Preparation and cooking time: approximately 20 minutes.

†LIMA BEANS WITH SOUR CREAM

SERVES 6

1½ pounds shelled lima beans   *¼ cup sour cream*
1½ tablespoons butter or margarine *Chopped parsley*
Salt and fresh-ground pepper
   to taste

Cook the beans in boiling salted water for 3 to 5 minutes or until they are just tender. Drain them well in a colander and let stand until they are cool enough to handle. Then, with a small paring knife, pierce the skins and slip them off. In a heavy saucepan reheat the beans in the butter or margarine and season with salt and fresh-ground pepper. Just before serving stir in the sour cream and heat the mixture for a moment, but do not let it come to the boil. Transfer the beans to a hot dish and sprinkle them with chopped parsley.

Preparation and cooking time: approximately 30 minutes.

††BROCCOLI WITH PINE NUTS AND CAPERS

SERVES 6 TO 8

3 pounds fresh broccoli   *½ cup water*
⅓ cup pine nuts   *3 tablespoons capers*
⅓ cup olive oil or vegetable oil *Salt and pepper to taste*
2 cloves garlic, minced

Remove and separate the flowerets from the broccoli stems. Peel the stems, halve them lengthwise if they are thick, and cut them cross-wise into ½-inch slices. There should be 8 cups of flowerets and stems. Plunge the broccoli into a large saucepan of boiling salted water and boil for 4 minutes. Drain the broccoli, refresh it under cold running water and spread it on paper towels to dry. In a large frying pan lightly brown the pine nuts in the oil. Add the garlic and sauté for 30 seconds, then transfer the mixture with a slotted spoon to a small dish. Add the broccoli to the pan and toss it gently over moderate heat for 2 minutes. Add the water and continue to cook the broccoli over high heat for 6 minutes, or until just tender. Add the sautéed pine nuts and garlic, the capers, salt and pepper to taste, and cook, uncovered, over high heat for 1 minute. Serve hot.

Preparation and cooking time: approximately 30 minutes.

††BRUSSELS SPROUTS WITH CHESTNUTS

SERVES 6
These are particularly good served with game.

*1 pound Brussels sprouts, outer leaves
    removed and stems trimmed
½ pound chestnuts, shelled
    (see page 137)*

*Salted water or beef stock
½ cup butter, melted
Salt and pepper to taste*

Wash the sprouts and make an incision in the bottom of each one. Blanch the chestnuts and simmer them, covered, in boiling salted water for about 30 minutes, or until they are just tender. Cook the sprouts in boiling salted water or beef stock to cover for about 15 minutes, or until they are tender. Drain the sprouts and sauté them in ¼ cup of the melted butter for a few minutes, or until they are well glazed. Sprinkle with salt and pepper to taste and turn them into a heated serving dish. Drain the chestnuts, toss with the remaining butter and arrange in a ring around the Brussels sprouts.

Preparation time: approximately 45 minutes (add 30 to 45 minutes for peeling chestnuts). Cooking time: approximately 1 hour.

†HUGARIAN BAKED SPROUTS

SERVES 6

These are particularly good served with game.

1 pound washed and cleaned
Brussels sprouts
½ medium-sized onion,
coarse-chopped
3 sprigs parsley, tied with
1 small bay leaf

1 whole clove garlic, peeled
2 eggs, well beaten
½ cup grated Emmentaler cheese
Salt, pepper and cayenne to taste

Preheat oven to 350° F.

Cook the sprouts with the onion, parsley and garlic in boiling salted water for just 10 minutes. Drain, and turn the sprouts into a buttered baking dish. Combine the eggs, cheese and seasonings and pour over the sprouts. Bake in the preheated oven for a good 10 minutes. Serve with gooseberry jelly and fresh toast.

Preparation and cooking time: approximately 45 minutes.

††CABBAGE AND BACON

SERVES 6

This is particularly good served with game.

1 medium head of cabbage
3 tablespoons butter or margarine
2 tablespoons water
2 ounces unsliced bacon or lean salt
pork, cut into small dice

1 bunch scallions trimmed
and cut into 1-inch lengths
Fresh-ground pepper to taste

Trim the outer leaves and the core from the cabbage and shred the leaves fine. In a heavy saucepan melt 2 tablespoons of the butter or margarine and add the cabbage and water. Cook, covered, over low heat for about 4 minutes. Sauté the diced bacon or salt pork in the remaining butter until it is browned and crisp. Drain on paper towels and reserve. Add the scallions to the fat in the pan and sauté until barely tender. Stir the cabbage into the frying pan, season with fresh-ground pepper and add the reserved bacon. Toss the cabbage over low heat until it is hot and serve.

Preparation and cooking time: approximately 45 minutes.

†††CABBAGE AND CHESTNUT PURÉE

SERVES 6

This is particularly good served with game.

2 pounds chestnuts	Salt and pepper to taste
Beef stock, to cover	2 teaspoons light cream (or an equal
2 tablespoons butter	amount of beef stock or butter)
½ tablespoon sugar	1 medium head of cabbage
	1 tablespoon butter or margarine

Preheat oven to 350° F.

With a sharp knife, cut a cross on the flat side of the chestnuts. Heat them in a moderate oven for 10 minutes, or until the shells curl back. Peel them while they are hot, and simmer in water to cover for 3 to 6 minutes. Drain the chestnuts and remove the inner skins at once. Simmer the peeled chestnuts in enough beef stock to cover, with 1 teaspoon butter and sugar, for about 30 minutes, or until they are very soft and fall apart. Crumble the hot chestnuts, add salt and pepper to taste and beat in 2 teaspoons cream (or beef stock or butter). Remove the core of the cabbage and cut into ¾-inch slices. Cook, covered, in a little boiling salted water for approximately 10 minutes or until tender. Drain the slices and cook them in the butter until most of the moisture has evaporated. Force the cabbage through a sieve or purée it in a blender, and combine it with the chestnut purée. Beat the mixture well until it is fluffy, adding a little more cream if necessary. Season with salt and pepper to taste and serve in a heated dish with 1 tablespoon of sweet butter.

Preparation and cooking time: approximately 2 hours 30 minutes.

††CHOPPED CABBAGE IN EGG AND LEMON SAUCE

SERVES 6
This is particularly good served with game.

1 large head of cabbage, cored	*3 egg yolks*
and chopped fine	*3 tablespoons lemon juice*
¼ cup water	*Chopped chives*
1 tablespoon butter	

Put the chopped cabbage in a large enamel or stainless-steel frying pan with the water and 1 teaspoon of butter and steam it, covered, for 5 minutes, or until it is just tender. Drain the cabbage and reserve 2 tablespoons of the cooking stock. Beat the egg yolks until they are light and gradually beat in the lemon juice and reserved stock. Combine the sauce with the cabbage in a saucepan and cook the mixture over very low heat, stirring constantly with a wooden spoon, for approximately 15 minutes or until it has thickened. Serve the cabbage in a warm dish, sprinkled generously with chopped chives and 2 teaspoons of butter.

Preparation and cooking time: approximately 30 minutes.

†RED CABBAGE WITH CHESTNUTS

SERVES 6

Serve with game or pork.

4 pounds red cabbage
5 tablespoons butter
2 pounds peeled chestnuts
   (see page 137) (or two 16-ounce
   cans whole French unsweetened
   chestnuts, drained)

1½ teaspoons salt
1 teaspoon fresh-ground
   pepper
Chicken stock

Wash the cabbage and shred fine. In a heavy pan melt the butter over medium heat. Add the cabbage, chestnuts, salt, pepper and enough chicken stock to cover. Simmer, covered, for 40 to 45 minutes.

Preparation and cooking time: approximately 1 hour (add 30 to 45 minutes if peeling chestnuts).

†MOROCCAN CARROTS

SERVES 4

2 pounds carrots, scraped
6 tablespoons butter
½ onion, sliced paper-thin
¼ cup white wine

½ teaspoon ground nutmeg
Handful soaked seedless raisins
2 tablespoons brown sugar

Cut the carrots into ¼-inch slices. Put them in a saucepan with the butter, onion, white wine and ground nutmeg and cook, covered, over very low heat for approximately 15 to 20 minutes or until tender but firm. Stir in the soaked raisins and brown sugar and shake pan gently until the dish is thoroughly warmed.

Preparation and cooking time: approximately 45 minutes.

†GINGERED CARROTS

SERVES 6

1 pound young carrots	*1 teaspoon ground ginger*
¼ cup butter	*Salt and pepper to taste*
1 tablespoon sugar	*1 teaspoon lemon juice*

Peel and trim the carrots and halve diagonally. Coat a frying pan with the butter, add the carrots and cover with a buttered round of greaseproof paper and the lid. Steam over low heat for 10 to 12 minutes, or until just tender. Remove the lid and paper and sprinkle the carrots with the sugar and ginger. Add salt and pepper to taste and cook for 1 to 2 minutes more, or until glazed. Toss with the lemon juice and serve.

Preparation and cooking time: approximately 30 minutes.

††HONEY-GLAZED CARROTS AND ONIONS

SERVES 6

12 medium-sized carrots, cut diagonally into ½-inch-thick pieces	*⅓ cup butter, melted*
	⅓ cup honey
	½ teaspoon tarragon
12 pearl onions, peeled	*Salt and white pepper to taste*
Chicken stock	

Preheat oven to 350° F.

In a large saucepan parboil the carrots and onions in chicken stock to cover for 10 minutes. With a slotted spoon remove the vegetables to a buttered shallow baking dish. Combine the melted butter with the honey and tarragon and pour over the vegetables. Sprinkle with salt and white pepper to taste and bake in preheated oven for 20 minutes, or until tender. Drain the juices into a pan and keep the vegetables warm. Cook the juices over high heat until reduced by half. Add the vegetables and shake the pan lightly until the vegetables are thoroughly coated with the glaze.

Preparation and cooking time: approximately 50 minutes.

†CAULIFLOWER WITH HERBS

SERVES 6

1 head cauliflower	*2 tablespoons chopped parsley*
Water or milk	*1 tablespoon chopped fresh thyme*
½ cup butter, melted	*or 1 teaspoon dried thyme*
1 tablespoon chopped chives	*1 tablespoon lemon juice*

Place the whole cauliflower, head up, uncovered, in about 1 inch of boiling water or milk (the milk will help to keep it white). Then reduce the heat to a simmer and cook, partially covered, for about 15 to 20 minutes or until the stalk is tender but still crisp. Drain well and transfer to a heated serving dish. Combine the melted butter with the herbs and lemon juice. Spoon over the cauliflower and serve at once.

Preparation and cooking time: approximately 30 minutes.

††ÉTUVÉE DE CÉLERI RAVE

SERVES 4

Serve as a first course or as a vegetable with roast lamb or veal.

1 head celeriac	*1 teaspoon Dijon mustard*
¼ cup butter	*Dash of tarragon vinegar*
Salt and pepper to taste	*2 sprigs parsley, chopped fine*

Peel the celeriac, rinse it and shred into fine strips. Cook in the butter in a frying pan for about 10 minutes, turning it over and over; towards the end of the cooking time, add the salt, pepper, mustard, vinegar and parsley. The celeriac should retain some of its crispness and bite.

Preparation and cooking time: approximately 30 to 40 minutes.

††CURRIED CORN AND ONIONS

SERVES 6

1 tablespoon butter or margarine	*Heavy cream*
¼ cup water	*5 teaspoons arrowroot*
3 large onions, peeled and cut into 1-inch slices	*1 tablespoon turmeric*
	½ teaspoon ground cumin seed
Ground mace to taste	*½ teaspoon salt*
Salt and pepper to taste	*½ teaspoon pepper*
2 cups fresh-cooked corn kernels, or canned or frozen	*¼ cup grated Parmesan cheese*

Preheat oven to 350° F.

Heat the butter or margarine and water in a large frying pan and cook the onions, covered, over very low heat until they are transparent and tender but not mushy. Drain the onions, reserving the cooking broth, and put them in a buttered baking dish. Sprinkle the slices with ground mace, salt and pepper to taste, and cover with the corn. Combine the reserved onion broth with enough cream to make 1½ cups liquid. Blend in the arrowroot, turmeric, cumin seed, salt and pepper and cook over low heat until thick and smooth. Spoon the sauce over the onions and corn, sprinkle with grated Parmesan and bake in the preheated oven for approximately 5 minutes or until the cheese bubbles and is lightly browned.

Preparation and cooking time: approximately 30 minutes.

††FENNEL, MUSHROOM AND TOMATO

SERVES 4

2 heads of fennel
1 clove garlic, crushed
⅓ cup olive oil or vegetable oil
6 tomatoes, peeled, seeded and sliced
1 teaspoon dried basil or, if possible, 1 tablespoon fresh basil

¾ pound mushrooms, sliced
¼ cup chicken stock or broth
1½ teaspoons salt
¼ teaspoon pepper
1 tablespoon fennel leaves, snipped
1 tablespoon parsley, chopped

Trim the bases and remove the stalks from the fennel; remove and reserve the leaves. Peel the stalks and cut the bulbs and stalks into julienne strips 1½ inches long and ¼ inch thick. In a large frying pan cook the fennel strips and garlic in the oil over moderate heat, stirring, for 5 minutes. Add the tomatoes and basil, and cook, covered, for 5 minutes longer. Increase the heat slightly, remove the cover and cook the vegetables for 5 to 6 minutes more, or until the liquid has almost evaporated. Stir in the mushrooms, chicken stock or broth, salt and pepper, and simmer for 10 to 15 minutes, or until the moisture is almost absorbed and the mushrooms are tender. Sprinkle with the reserved fennel leaves and parsley. Serve at room temperature.

Preparation and cooking time: approximately 1 hour.

†STRING BEANS AMANDINE

SERVES 6

2 pounds string beans · · · · · 1 cup butter
¾ cup almonds, sliced thin

Cook the beans in boiling salted water for 5 to 8 minutes or until tender but crisp. Drain and rinse under cold water. In a frying pan sauté the almonds in ¼ cup of the butter until delicately brown and crisp. Remove from the pan and set aside. In another frying pan toss the beans in the rest of the butter. Add almonds and shake the pan to distribute them. Correct seasoning and serve.

Preparation and cooking time: approximately 45 minutes.

††STRING BEANS IN SOUR-CREAM SAUCE

SERVES 8

9½ cups water · · · · · · · Salt and pepper to taste
2 tablespoons salt · · · · · Sour-cream sauce (see page
2½ pounds string beans · · · · 192)
4 teaspoons butter or margarine · Snipped chives or parsley

In a large saucepan bring the water to the boil. Add the salt and drop in the beans. Return the water to the boil over high heat and cook the beans, uncovered, for about 8 minutes. Put the beans in a colander and run cold water through them until they are cool. Trim the ends of the beans so that they are uniform in size and dry them on a towel. Melt 1 tablespoon of the butter in a large frying pan, add the beans and shake them over low heat until they are hot. Season them lightly with salt and pepper and toss them with 1 more teaspoon of butter or margarine. Transfer the beans to a heated serving dish and top them with sour-cream sauce. Sprinkle the sauce with snipped chives or parsley or both.

Preparation and cooking time: approximately 45 minutes.

SOUR-CREAM SAUCE

¼ cup onion, minced
⅓ cup butter or margarine
3 tablespoons flour
2 cups hot milk

Sour cream to taste, approximately ½ to 1 cup
Salt and pepper to taste
Few drops of lemon juice

In a saucepan sauté the onions in the butter or margarine over low heat until they are soft but not colored. Add the flour, cook the roux over low heat for a few minutes and pour in the hot milk, stirring. Cover the sauce with a buttered round of waxed paper until serving time. Just before serving remove the paper and reheat the sauce. Add the sour cream and stir until the sauce is hot, *but do not allow it to boil*. Season with salt and pepper to taste and a few drops of lemon juice.

††LEEKS

SERVES 6

2 dozen leeks, tops, roots and
   outer leaves removed
4 tablespoons olive oil
Salt and pepper to taste
3 to 4 tomatoes, peeled and cut
   into quarters
2 cloves garlic, minced

1 tablespoon fresh dill, minced, or
   1 teaspoon dried dill
1½ teaspoons chopped parsley
¾ cup red wine
2 tablespoons chicken stock
2 tablespoons lemon juice

Cut the trimmed leeks in half lengthwise. In a heavy oval dish heat the oil, add the leeks and sauté until soft but not brown. When the leeks have been cooking for 3 to 4 minutes, salt and pepper them lightly, add the tomatoes, sprinkle with minced garlic, dill and chopped parsley, add the red wine, chicken stock and lemon juice, cover the dish with foil and simmer for 7 to 10 minutes. Serve hot or cold.

Preparation and cooking time: approximately 30 minutes.

††LENTILS

SERVES 6

½ pound lentils
2 onions, chopped fine
2 cloves garlic, chopped fine
2 tablespoons olive oil

One 6-ounce can tomatoes, seeded
  and chopped
1 teaspoon chopped fresh coriander,
  or 1½ teaspoons dried coriander
Salt and pepper to taste

In a large saucepan cook the lentils in water to cover for about 1 hour, or until they are almost tender. Drain and reserve the beans. In a frying pan sauté the onions and garlic in the olive oil until they are tender. Add the tomatoes. Stir in the coriander, salt and pepper, and cook until the mixture forms a fairly thick sauce. Add the sauce to the reserved lentils and cook over low heat for about 10 minutes.

Preparation and cooking time: approximately 1 hour 30 minutes.

†FRIED SNOW PEAS

SERVES 6

10 cloves garlic, crushed
3 tablespoons vegetable oil
3½ ounces lean pork, chopped
  fine
3½ ounces shrimp, shelled,
  deveined and chopped

1 pound snow peas
1 tablespoon fish soy (nam pla)‡
1 teaspoon sugar
Fresh-ground pepper to taste

In a wok brown the crushed garlic in the oil. Add the pork and
sauté it, stirring over moderately high heat until it is lightly browned.
Add the shrimp and snow peas and sauté, stirring, for 3 minutes, or
until the snow peas are cooked but still crisp. Season with fish soy,
sugar and pepper to taste.

Preparation and cooking time: approximately 30 minutes.

††MUSHROOMS IN MADEIRA AND COGNAC

SERVES 2

½ pound firm fresh mushrooms
2 tablespoons butter or margarine
2 tablespoons clarified butter (see
  page 275)
1 tablespoon meat glaze‡
1 teaspoon minced shallots
1 teaspoon minced scallions
2 bay leaves

½ teaspoon thyme
2 tablespoons flour
1 tablespoon tomato paste
3 cups brown stock (see page
  279) or beef broth, heated
1 cup Madeira
1 teaspoon Cognac
Salt and pepper to taste

‡ Fish soy is available at most Chinese or Japanese food shops.
‡ Meat glaze can be bought at most specialty food shops or ordered from
Maison Glass, 52 East 58 Street, New York, New York 10022.

Wipe the mushrooms with a damp cloth. Remove the stems and reserve them for another use. Quarter the caps. In a large, deep frying pan, sauté the mushroom caps in the butter or margarine over moderately high heat until they are browned. Transfer them to a dish and keep warm. Add clarified butter to the pan and in it sauté the meat glaze, shallots, scallions, bay leaves and thyme, until the shallots and scallions are golden. Add the flour and tomato paste and cook over moderately high heat, stirring, for 5 minutes. Remove the pan from the heat and stir in the warm brown stock or beef broth and the Madeira. Bring the liquid to the boil, stirring constantly. Reduce the heat and simmer, stirring occasionally, for 30 minutes, or until the liquid is reduced by half. Strain the sauce over the mushrooms, pressing down on the solids to extract the juices. Return the mushroom mixture to the pan and simmer it until the mushrooms are heated through. Stir in the Cognac and salt and pepper to taste.

Preparation and cooking time: approximately 1 hour 30 minutes.

††MUSHROOMS WITH GRAPE LEAVES

SERVES 4

1 pound large button mushrooms	*1 clove garlic, crushed*
Salt	*1 can grape leaves*
3 tablespoons pitted black olives,	*2 tablespoons olive oil*
chopped	*Salt and pepper to taste*
One 3-ounce can pimentos	

Clean the mushrooms, remove and reserve the stalks. Salt the caps and allow to stand, right side up, for 1 hour to drain off moisture. Chop the mushroom stalks, olives and pimentos; add the garlic and mix well. Place the grape leaves in a flameproof dish, cover with oil and heat, but do not allow the oil to bubble. Arrange the mushroom caps over the grape leaves, upside down, and cook for 20 minutes. Fill the caps with the chopped mixture, season with salt and pepper to taste, and cook for 15 minutes. Serve the mushrooms and grape leaves very hot.

Preparation time: approximately 1 hour for draining mushrooms.
Cooking time: approximately 45 minutes.

†MUSHROOM RICE

SERVES 8

1 pound fresh, firm button mushrooms	*1⅓ cups long-grain rice*
¼ cup butter	*2 tablespoons butter, cut into small pieces*
Salt and pepper to taste	*1 tablespoon parsley, chopped fine*
1 quart rapidly boiling water	

Wash, stem, peel and slice the mushrooms fine. Melt the butter in a frying pan and, as soon as it has stopped foaming, add the mushrooms. Toss and shake the pan over moderate heat and cook mushrooms for 5 minutes. Remove from heat and season to taste with salt and very little fresh-ground pepper. To the boiling water, add the unwashed rice slowly (so that the water does not stop boiling). Boil for exactly 13 minutes. Put the rice into a colander and rinse immediately under cold running water. (The rice may be prepared in advance to this point.) Twenty-five minutes before serving cover the rice with a towel and steam it over boiling water. Fluff with a fork to separate the grains while warming. Add the sautéed mushrooms and mix lightly with 2 forks. When very hot add the butter, place in hot serving dish, sprinkle with chopped parsley and serve at once.

Preparation and cooking time: approximately 30 minutes.

†SPICED MUSHROOMS

SERVES 6

Serve with duck, pork or ham.

1½ pounds small fresh mushrooms
2 tablespoons butter or margarine
1 teaspoon flour
1 tablespoon soft brown sugar

Pinch of fresh-grated
  nutmeg
Pinch of ground ginger
¼ cup dry sherry

Trim and clean the mushrooms. In a saucepan melt the butter or margarine, blend in the flour and cook over very low heat for several minutes. Stir in smoothly the brown sugar, nutmeg and ground ginger. Add the mushrooms and cook over very low heat, turning frequently, for 10 to 12 minutes. Remove the pan from the heat and stir in the sherry.

Preparation and cooking time: approximately 20 minutes.

†GLAZED ONIONS

SERVES 6

24 pearl onions, each peeled and
  seasoned with a pinch of salt
  and sugar

2 tablespoons butter or margarine
1 tablespoon vegetable oil
½ cup chicken stock

In a heavy frying pan, large enough to hold them in one layer, cook the onions in the butter or margarine and the vegetable oil over moderately high heat for 4 to 5 minutes or until they are lightly browned. Add the chicken stock and continue to cook, covered, over low heat for 30 to 40 minutes, or until the onions are tender. Remove the cover and shake the pan to coat the onions with the juice.

Hint: If you keep dipping the onions in a bowl of warm water as you peel them and hold a bit of bread between your teeth, they will not make you cry.

Preparation and cooking time: approximately 1 hour 30 minutes.

☩ONIONS STUFFED WITH PEAS

SERVES 6

6 *fairly large Spanish onions,*
  peeled
3 *tablespoons butter*
1½ *cups frozen green peas*
1¼ *cups chicken stock or*
  chicken broth

½ *teaspoon fresh tarragon or 1*
  teaspoon dried tarragon
Salt and pepper to taste
¼ *cup dry white wine*
2 *tablespoons hollandaise sauce (see*
  page 296)

Preheat oven to 350° F.

Scoop out the centers of the onions, leaving a shell about ¼ inch thick. Chop fine enough of the centers to make ½ cup. Blanch the onion shells in boiling water for about 5 minutes and turn them upside down on a rack to drain. In a saucepan sauté the chopped onion in 2 tablespoons of the butter until tender. Add the green peas, 1 cup of the chicken stock or broth, the tarragon and salt and pepper to taste. Cook the peas for 15 to 20 minutes, or until they are tender. Season the onion shells lightly with salt and pepper and fill them with the pea mixture. Arrange them in a buttered shallow flameproof gratin dish just large enough to hold them and dot onions with the remaining butter. Combine the remaining chicken stock or broth with the wine and pour it around the onions. Bring the liquid to the boil on top of the stove, then transfer to the preheated oven, and bake the onions, basting them a few times with the liquid, for about 30 minutes, or until they are glazed. Top each onion with hollandaise sauce and put the dish under the broiler for about 3 minutes, or until the sauce is lightly browned. Transfer the onions to a serving dish. Reduce the juices by at least half and pour them around the onions.

Preparation and cooking time: approximately 2 hours 30 minutes.

†FRIED PARSLEY

SERVES 6
Good with fish.

1 large bunch of parsley
Vegetable oil, for deep-fat frying
Salt to taste
Soy sauce to taste

1 small clove garlic, minced
¼ teaspoon superfine granu-
lated sugar

Wash and drain the parsley and divide it into small bunches. Trim the stems short and dry the bunches thoroughly. Put them in a deep-frying basket, a few at a time, and plunge them into very hot deep vegetable oil (390° F.) for 30 to 40 seconds, or until they are crisp. Drain on paper towels and sprinkle lightly with salt. Warm the soy sauce, minced garlic and sugar together, and serve this as an accompaniment to the parsley.

Preparation and cooking time: 15 minutes.

†DEVILED PARSNIPS

SERVES 6

2 pounds parsnips, peeled and sliced
5 tablespoons melted butter
2 tablespoons brown sugar
2 tablespoons red-wine vinegar
1 teaspoon dry mustard

1 teaspoon minced chives
1 teaspoon chopped fresh
basil
Salt and pepper to taste
Hungarian sweet paprika

Brown the sliced parsnips on both sides in the melted butter over moderate heat, turning them occasionally. Stir in the brown sugar, red-wine vinegar, dry mustard, minced chives and chopped basil, with salt and pepper to taste. Cover the pan and cook the parsnips over moderate heat for about 10 minutes, or until they are tender. Serve sprinkled with paprika.

Preparation and cooking time: approximately 20 minutes.

†PARSNIPS IN ROSEMARY

SERVES 6

2 pounds parsnips, peeled	*½ teaspoon dried rosemary*
2 eggs, well beaten	*Salt and pepper to taste*
1 tablespoon dry bread crumbs	*¼ cup butter or margarine*

Cook the parsnips in boiling water for 10 minutes. Drain them and cut into slices ½ inch thick. Dip the slices into the beaten eggs, and roll them in a mixture of the bread crumbs, dried rosemary and salt and pepper. Brown the slices on both sides in the butter over moderate heat.

Preparation and cooking time: approximately 30 minutes.

††PARSNIPS WITH MADEIRA

SERVES 10
Good with game, fowl or roast pork.

5 to 6 pounds parsnips	*¼ teaspoon nutmeg*
½ cup melted butter	*Salt to taste*
½ cup Madeira	*1 cup walnuts, chopped fine*
½ cup heavy cream	*½ cup butter*

Preheat oven to 375° F.

Wash and trim the parsnips and put into a large pan of boiling salted water to cover. Boil for 10 to 12 minutes or until the parsnips can be easily pierced with a fork. Drain them and allow to cool until they can be handled. Peel and cut into pieces 3 to 4 inches long. Put the pieces through a food mill and combine the purée with the melted butter, Madeira, heavy cream, nutmeg and salt to taste. Beat the purée well, adding more butter or cream if necessary. Spoon into a baking dish, sprinkle with fine-chopped walnuts and top with pieces of butter. Heat in the preheated oven for about 20 minutes, or until heated through. Serve very hot.

Preparation and cooking time: 1 hour 30 minutes.

†SWEET AND SOUR PARSNIPS

SERVES 6

2 pounds parsnips, peeled
  and sliced thin
¼ cup melted butter or margarine
2 tablespoons chopped parsley
2 tablespoons lemon juice
1 teaspoon brown sugar

½ teaspoon grated lemon
  rind
Salt and pepper to taste
4 slices crisp lean bacon,
  cooked and crumbled

Sauté the sliced parsnips in the butter or margarine over moderate heat for about 10 minutes, or until they are tender. Stir them from time to time. In a saucepan blend all the rest of the ingredients except the bacon and cook slowly until heated through. Arrange the parsnips and sauce on a dish and sprinkle with the bacon bits.

Preparation and cooking time: approximately 15 minutes.

†PEAS WITH MUSHROOMS AND CELERY

SERVES 4 to 5

2 stalks of celery with their
leaves, chopped
¼ cup butter
2 cups frozen green peas
½ cup chicken stock or broth

½ teaspoon chervil
Salt and pepper to taste
1½ teaspoons arrowroot
1 tablespoon water
1 cup mushrooms, sliced thin

In a saucepan sauté the celery in 2 tablespoons of the butter for 3 minutes. Stir in the peas, chicken stock or broth, chervil and salt and pepper to taste. Simmer, covered, for 10 to 20 minutes, or until the vegetables are tender. Mix the arrowroot with the water, stir it into the pea mixture and cook it, stirring, until thickened. In a frying pan sauté the sliced mushrooms in the remaining butter for about 2 minutes, or until they are well coated. Season with salt and pepper to taste and cook for 5 minutes longer. Stir the mushrooms into the pea mixture and serve.

Preparation and cooking time: approximately 45 minutes.

†PEAS WITH PROSCIUTTO

SERVES 6

½ cup scallions, chopped fine
½ cup butter
2 cups shredded Boston lettuce
4 cups frozen green peas
1 teaspoon each of basil and salt
¼ teaspoon pepper

¼ cup water
1 cup prosciutto, cut into julienne strips
3 to 4 tablespoons grated Parmesan cheese
Salt and pepper to taste

In a saucepan sauté the scallions in 6 tablespoons of the butter for 2 minutes. Stir in the lettuce, peas, basil, salt, pepper and water.

Cover the pan tightly and cook over low heat for 10 to 20 minutes, or until the peas are tender. Sauté the prosciutto in a frying pan with the remaining butter until heated through. Mix the prosciutto with the peas and stir in the grated Parmesan cheese. Season with salt and pepper to taste.

Preparation and cooking time: approximately 30 minutes.

††HUNGARIAN MIXED PEPPERS

SERVES 6 to 8

4 large carrots
2 red peppers, seeded
2 green peppers, seeded
2 cucumbers, peeled lengthwise, with 4½-inch strips left unpeeled
7½ pints water

Bouquet garni (1 celery stalk, 4 sprigs parsley, 1 bay leaf, 1 sprig thyme)
2 tablespoons cider vinegar
2 tablespoons salt
¾ cup butter
2 cloves garlic, crushed
2 tablespoons lemon juice
Salt and white pepper to taste

Soak the carrots, red and green peppers and cucumbers for 10 minutes in iced water. Cut the peppers into large squares, cut the carrots and cucumbers into 1-inch rounds, and seed the cucumbers. In a large casserole combine the water, the bouquet garni and the cider vinegar and salt. Bring the liquid to the boil, add the carrots and cook for 10 minutes. Add the peppers and cucumbers and cook for 10 minutes longer, or until the vegetables are tender but still crisp. Drain and reserve the vegetables. Melt the butter with the garlic. Strain the butter and toss it with the cooked vegetables. Add the lemon juice and salt and white pepper to taste.

Preparation and cooking time: approximately 45 minutes.

††BAKED POTATOES WITH EGGS

SERVES 6

6 baking potatoes, cooked	*Worcestershire sauce to taste*
⅓ cup butter or margarine	*6 eggs, poached or shirred*
1 cup light cream, scalded	*6 tablespoons butter*
Salt and pepper to taste	*Chopped parsley or chives*
Nutmeg to taste	

Cut a ½-inch slice from the top of each baked potato, scoop out the pulp and reserve the deep shells. Purée the potato pulp with the butter, scalded cream, salt, pepper and nutmeg to taste. Fill the reserved potato shells one-quarter full with the purée, then shake in the Worcestershire sauce to taste and drop an egg into each potato. Divide the remaining potato mixture over the eggs and dot it with butter. Put the potatoes under the broiler for 3 to 5 minutes, or until they are browned, and sprinkle them with chopped parsley or chives.

Preparation and cooking time: approximately 1 hour 30 minutes.

†CARAWAY POTATOES

SERVES 6 TO 8

2 pounds red-skinned or new potatoes, peeled
2 teaspoons caraway seed
¼ cup butter, melted

In a large saucepan boil the potatoes with the caraway seed in enough salted water to cover for 15 to 20 minutes, or until they are just tender. Drain and toss with the melted butter.

Preparation and cooking time: approximately 45 minutes.

††POTATOES WITH TRUFFLES

SERVES 6

Marvelous with beef, lamb or game.

1½ pounds potatoes
¼ cup butter, margarine or pork fat
½ pound fresh truffles, sliced thin
Salt and fresh-ground pepper
    to taste

Chopped parsley
Additional chopped truffles
    (optional)

Peel the potatoes, cut them into thin uniform slices and spread them out on a dish towel. In a heavy saucepan heat the butter, margarine or pork fat until the foam subsides. Add the potatoes and sauté over brisk heat, turning frequently with a wooden spatula to color them on all sides for approximately 5 minutes or until they are about two-thirds cooked. Blend in the truffles and add more fat to the pan if necessary. Continue to cook the potatoes, turning them occasionally, for 2 to 3 minutes more or until they are tender. Season with salt and pepper to taste, transfer to a heated dish and sprinkle lightly with chopped parsley or additional chopped truffles.

Preparation and cooking time: approximately 1 hour.

†††SOUFFLÉ POTATOES

SERVES 6 TO 8

2 pounds peeled potatoes
2½ cups cooking oil, approximately
Salt to taste

Cut the potatoes into oval shapes, each about 2 inches long. With a mandoline or other slicer, cut the ovals lengthwise into ¾-inch-thick slices and chill in a bowl of iced water for 15 minutes. Drain and dry thoroughly. In a deep fryer heat 3 inches of cooking oil to 280° F., and drop in the potato slices one at a time. Fry for 6 minutes and drain on paper towels. Heat the oil to 375° F., and add the drained potato slices, a few at a time, shaking the pan slightly. Fry the potatoes until they puff up, remove from the oil and drain on paper towels. (At this point they will depuff. They may be kept for several hours or finished immediately.) For final frying, heat the oil to 400° F., add the potatoes a few at a time and cook for about 1 minute or until lightly golden and puffed. Remove and drain on paper towels. Salt lightly and serve.

Preparation and cooking time: approximately 1 hour.

††STUFFED POTATOES WITH DUXELLES AND CHICKEN LIVERS

SERVES 6

6 baking potatoes, cooked
1 cup light cream
Salt and pepper to taste
Duxelles (see page 344)

½ pound chicken livers, sautéed and diced
6 tablespoons bread crumbs
2 tablespoons butter

Preheat broiler.

Halve the cooked potatoes, scoop out the pulp and reserve the shells. Purée the pulp and add the cream and salt and pepper to taste. Blend in the duxelles and chicken livers. Heap the mixture into the reserved potato shells, sprinkle them with bread crumbs and dot with butter. Brown the potatoes under the broiler for 3 to 5 minutes.

Preparation and cooking time: 1 hour 30 minutes.

†SALSIFY BUTTERED WITH GARLIC AND HERBS

SERVES 6

2 pounds salsify
1 tablespoon lemon juice or vinegar
2 tablespoons lemon juice
1 teaspoon salt
3 tablespoons butter or margarine
3 tablespoons vegetable oil
½ teaspoon fresh-ground
   black pepper

2 tablespoons chopped
   parsley
2 tablespoons chopped chives
1 or 2 cloves garlic (according to taste), chopped fine
4 tablespoons butter

Peel the salsify, cut it into 2½-to-3-inch lengths and put it into cold water with the vinegar or lemon juice to keep it from turning dark until cooking time. Drain the salsify and put it in a 1½-pint saucepan with cold water barely to cover, the lemon juice and salt. Bring the liquid to a boil, simmer the salsify until it can be pierced with a fork and drain it. In a saucepan heat the salsify in the butter or margarine and oil, shaking the pan well, until it is hot, adding more oil and butter if needed. Add the pepper and transfer the salsify to a serving dish. Pour the pan juices over the salsify and sprinkle with the parsley, chives and garlic. Toss with the butter.

Preparation and cooking time: approximately 30 minutes.

†SPINACH WITH ROSEMARY AND PINE NUTS

SERVES 6

3 pounds fresh spinach, washed
    and drained
2 cloves garlic, chopped fine
3 sprigs parsley, chopped
⅓ teaspoon fresh rosemary or
    generous pinch dried rosemary

¼ cup melted butter or
    vegetable oil
Salt and pepper to taste
1½ ounces pine nuts

Trim the thick stems from the spinach. In a large saucepan cook the chopped garlic, parsley and rosemary in the melted butter or oil for a minute or two. Pile the spinach into the pan, toss it in the herb mixture and cook, covered, for about 5 minutes, or until limp. Season with salt and pepper to taste and sprinkle with pine nuts.

Preparation and cooking time: approximately 30 minutes.

†SPINACH WITH SORREL

SERVES 4

½ pound sorrel
2 pounds spinach
⅓ cup butter or margarine

Salt to taste
Few grains of nutmeg

Cook the sorrel and the spinach separately, each well washed and immediately steamed over low heat, in the water that clings to the leaves. Drain well and chop. Combine the vegetables, and add the butter or margarine, salt to taste and a few grains of nutmeg. Toss the mixture well over low heat and serve at once.

Preparation and cooking time: 15 minutes.

†BAKED TOMATOES WITH SESAME SEEDS

SERVES 6

  3 tablespoons fresh bread crumbs
  2 tablespoons melted butter
  Several sprigs parsley, chopped fine
  1 teaspoon basil

  Salt to taste
  6 medium tomatoes, cored
    and halved horizontally
  Sesame seeds

Preheat oven to 350° F.

In a bowl mix together the bread crumbs, melted butter, parsley, basil and salt. Spread the mixture on the tops of the tomato halves and sprinkle with a generous coating of sesame seeds. Arrange the tomatoes in a baking pan and cook in the preheated oven for about 15 minutes, or until they are tender but still hold their shape.

Preparation and cooking time: approximately 30 minutes.

††BROILED DEVILED TOMATOES

SERVES 6

  ⅓ cup butter or margarine
  5 teaspoons Worcestershire sauce
  1½ teaspoons Tabasco sauce,
    or to taste
  1 teaspoon dry mustard

  2 teaspoons minced parsley
  1 teaspoon grated onion
  Salt to taste
  3 large ripe tomatoes, peeled
    and halved horizontally

Preheat broiler.

In a bowl cream together the butter, Worcestershire sauce, Tabasco sauce, dry mustard, half the parsley, the onion and salt. Sprinkle the tomatoes with salt and arrange them in a shallow baking dish just large enough to hold them in 1 layer. Spread the butter mixture over the tomatoes and broil them under a preheated broiler 4 inches from the heat, basting them every 2 minutes with the pan juices, for 8 minutes, or until they are soft and the tops are browned. Serve hot, sprinkled with the remaining parsley.

Preparation and cooking time: approximately 30 minutes.

††TOMATOES WITH CHORON SAUCE

SERVES 6

1 ¼ *cups Choron sauce (see*   3 *sprigs chervil, chopped fine*
    page 295)   6 *firm tomatoes, halved*
Salt to taste   3 *tablespoons melted butter*
Cayenne to taste   2 *tablespoons bread crumbs*
3 *sprigs tarragon, chopped*   ½ *pound lean bacon, cut very thin*
    fine   *and fried*

Preheat broiler.

Prepare Choron sauce and season it with salt and cayenne to taste. Strain through a fine sieve and add the tarragon and chervil. Brush the tomato halves with melted butter and sprinkle lightly with bread crumbs and broil for 2 or 3 minutes or until lightly browned. Cover with the Choron sauce and serve very hot with fried lean bacon.

Preparation and cooking time: approximately 45 minutes.

††TURNIPS WITH MUSHROOMS

SERVES 6

To be served with duck or game, or roasted, broiled or braised meats.

    2 *pounds medium turnips*   ½ *teaspoon fresh-ground black*
    ½ *pound mushrooms*   *pepper*
    ½ *cup butter or margarine*   ½ *teaspoon salt*
                             Chopped parsley

Peel the turnips and cut them into ¼-inch-thick rounds. Slice the mushrooms ¼ inch thick. In a heavy saucepan cook the turnips in boiling salted water over fairly brisk heat, watching carefully, for about 8 to 12 minutes or until they are tender but still crisp. Drain them well and add 3 tablespoons of the butter or margarine and ¼ teaspoon of the pepper. While the turnips are cooking, quickly sauté the mushrooms in the remaining butter or margarine, seasoning them with the salt and the remaining pepper. Combine the turnips with the mushrooms and cook, shaking the pan gently to mix them, for 2 minutes. Transfer the vegetables to a heated serving dish and sprinkle with chopped parsley.

Preparation and cooking time: approximately 15 minutes.

††VEGETABLES WITH AÏOLI SAUCE

SERVES 6

1 cup sliced string beans
1 cup shelled lima beans
½ cup shelled green peas
½ cup sliced zucchini
6 artichoke hearts (fresh or canned)

½ cup canned chickpeas, drained
½ cup frozen or canned flageolets, drained
1 cup aïoli sauce (see page 212)

Preheat oven to 200° F.

Cook separately in boiling salted water until tender the string beans, lima beans, green peas, zucchini and artichoke hearts, if fresh. Combine these vegetables with the chickpeas and flageolets and mix gently. Turn the vegetables into a buttered baking dish and heat in the preheated oven for about 15 minutes. Meanwhile, make the aïoli sauce. Carefully mix the sauce into the cooked vegetables and serve.

Preparation time: 30 minutes. Cooking time: 45 minutes.

AÏOLI SAUCE

MAKES I CUP

1 thick slice of white bread,	*2 egg yolks*
crusts removed	*1 cup olive oil*
3 tablespoons milk	*Juice of 1 lemon*
4 to 6 cloves garlic	*Salt and fresh-ground black pepper*
¼ teaspoon salt	*to taste*

Crumble the bread into a bowl, stir in the milk and let the bread soak for 10 minutes, then squeeze out the milk. Crush the garlic cloves thoroughly in a mortar and pound in the salt. In a bowl blend the garlic and salt with the egg yolks. Add a few drops of the olive oil, beating vigorously with a whisk or an electric mixer at low speed. Continue adding oil, a little at a time, until about 2 tablespoons have been added. Add the rest of the oil in a thin, steady stream, beating constantly. If the mixture seems too thick, beat in ½ table-spoon or more of water. Finish the sauce with the lemon juice and season it with salt and fresh-ground black pepper to taste. If the sauce separates, rebind the emulsion by beating it again while adding 1 egg yolk.

TWO RELIABLE WAYS TO COOK
LONG-GRAIN RICE

1 cup raw long-grain rice
2 cups cold water
1 tablespoon cooking oil or 1 tablespoon butter
1 teaspoon salt
1 slice of lemon

Combine all ingredients in a large, heavy saucepan, turn the heat to very high until the water begins to boil. Reduce the heat almost to low and stir the rice once with a fork (important: use only a fork to stir rice). Cover the pan tightly and simmer for 12 to 15 minutes, or until all the liquid is absorbed and the rice is almost done. Then transfer the rice to a covered colander set over boiling water and steam for 15 minutes. This should make over 1 pound of fluffy rice.

> 2½ cups cold water
> 1 teaspoon salt
> 1 tablespoon olive oil or 1 tablespoon butter
> 1 cup raw long-grain rice

Bring the water to a rapid boil. Add the salt and oil or butter. Add the rice and bring the water back to the boil. Cover the pan tightly and cook over low heat for 20 to 25 minutes, or until the water has been completely absorbed. Transfer the rice to a colander set over boiling water and steam, covered, for 15 minutes.

Whichever of the above methods you use, add 1 to 2 tablespoons of oil or butter to the cooked rice and toss with a fork until all the grains are well coated. Then add seasoning or herbs as desired. Allow approximately ⅓ cup of raw rice per person.

†HERBED RICE

SERVES 8 TO 10

Toss 2 to 3 tablespoons fine-chopped parsley and 1 to 2 tablespoons fine-cut chives with 1 pound of hot cooked rice. Fresh or dried tarragon or 2 tablespoons fine-chopped chervil may also be added.

†MOROCCAN RICE

SERVES 16 TO 20

Good with braised lamb.

Butter 2 pounds of hot cooked rice and toss it with ⅔ cup white raisins plumped in Madeira, sherry or Cognac. Sprinkle the top with ⅔ cup of roasted sliced almonds, toasted, sliced or coarse-chopped hazelnuts and 1⅓ cups very crisp fried onions. Add about 2 tablespoons of chopped parsley.

†PARSLEYED RICE

SERVES 8 TO 10

Good with roast beef or steak.

In a frying pan sauté 6 to 8 chopped shallots very lightly in 2 tablespoons olive oil or 2 tablespoons butter. With a fork, toss the shallots and butter into 1 pound of hot cooked rice with 2 to 3 tablespoons chopped parsley.

†PESTO WITH RICE

SERVES 8 TO 10

Toss 4 to 5 tablespoons of pesto (see page 262) with 1 pound of hot cooked rice. The pesto turns the rice light green and adds delicious flavoring.

†RICE AND PEAS

SERVES 8 TO 10

Good with veal dishes or broiled chicken.

Butter 1 pound hot cooked rice and toss it with 1 pound hot cooked green peas. Add 1 to 2 tablespoons chopped fresh tarragon or 1 teaspoon or more of dried tarragon, and 2 tablespoons chopped parsley.

†SPICED RICE

SERVES 8 TO 10

2 teaspoons peppercorns	Salt to taste
2 teaspoons cardamom seed	3 tablespoons lemon juice
1½ teaspoons whole cloves	Cashew nuts
1 pound long-grain rice	Grated coconut
¼ cup peanut oil	Minced coriander leaves
3¾ cups boiling water	

Preheat oven to 250° F.

Spread the peppercorns, cardamom seed and whole cloves on a baking sheet and roast in the preheated oven, shaking the pan frequently, for 1 hour. Remove from the oven and raise the heat to 350° F. Transfer the spices to a blender and pulverize. In an ovenproof saucepan sauté the rice with the spice mixture in the peanut oil until the rice is almost dry. Stir in the boiling water and salt to taste, and cook the rice for 5 minutes, or until most of the water is absorbed. Transfer the pan to the preheated oven and cook, covered, for 15 minutes, or until the rice is tender. Add the lemon juice, toss the rice with a fork and top it with the cashew nuts, coconut and minced coriander leaves.

Preparation and cooking time: approximately 2 hours.

To Steam Wild Rice

In a sieve rinse wild rice under cold running water for 2 minutes and drain it thoroughly. In a large saucepan, over moderately high heat, bring to the boil enough lightly salted water to cover the rice by 3 inches. Pour in the rice and cook it for 30 minutes, or until it is tender but not mushy. Drain the rice in a sieve and put the sieve over a saucepan containing 1 inch of boiling water. Steam the rice, covered with a folded tea towel and the lid, for 10 to 15 minutes, or until it is dry. The rice will triple in bulk while it is cooking.

††ALMOND WILD RICE PILAF

SERVES 4

1 cup wild rice
6 tablespoons softened butter
½ pound mushrooms, sliced
2 teaspoons chives, minced

2½ cups chicken stock or broth
Salt and pepper to taste
½ cup almonds, blanched, slivered
* and toasted*

Preheat oven to 325° F.

In a sieve rinse the wild rice under cold running water for 2 minutes and drain it thoroughly. In a flameproof dish or an oven-proof frying pan, sauté the rice in 4 tablespoons of the butter for 3 minutes. Add the mushrooms and chives and sauté until the mushrooms are golden. Remove the pan from the heat and stir in the chicken stock or broth. Bring the liquid to the boil, cover the pan tightly and bake in the preheated oven for 40 to 45 minutes or until the liquid is absorbed. Season the rice with salt and pepper to taste and toss it with the almonds and the remaining butter.

Preparation and cooking time: 1 hour 15 minutes.

DESSERTS

---

†*MOUSSE AU CHOCOLAT

SERVES 8

½ pound semisweet chocolate
¼ cup water
5 egg yolks
1 teaspoon vanilla extract
1½ tablespoons rum or Cognac

¼ cup chopped blanched
  almonds
5 egg whites, beaten until stiff
⅛ cup ground almonds

Chop the chocolate into small pieces, keeping a small handful in reserve. Over simmering water melt the chocolate in the top of a double boiler with the ¼ cup water. Stir the melting chocolate until it is smooth, and set aside to cool. Beat the egg yolks with the vanilla extract, adding either rum or Cognac, according to taste. Add this mixture to the melted chocolate. Transfer to a bowl, add reserved chocolate bits and the chopped almonds. Carefully but thoroughly fold in the egg whites and pour into an 8-inch soufflé dish. Sprinkle the ground almonds on top and chill for at least 2 hours.

Preparation and cooking time: approximately 30 minutes. Chilling time: 2 to 3 hours.

††MOCHA POTS DE CRÈME

SERVES 4

1 cup milk	*5 egg yolks*
1 cup heavy cream	*1 whole egg*
5 ounces semisweet chocolate,	*½ cup superfine granulated sugar*
grated	*½ teaspoon vanilla extract*
2 tablespoons instant coffee	*Praline powder (see below)*

Preheat oven to 325° F.

In a saucepan combine the milk, heavy cream and grated chocolate. Bring the mixture to the boiling point over low heat, stirring, and continue to stir until the chocolate has dissolved and is smooth. Stir in the instant coffee, remove the pan from the heat and cool. In a bowl beat the egg yolks, whole egg, sugar and vanilla until the eggs are frothy. Stir in the mocha mixture in a stream and skim the froth from the surface. Fill individual pots de crème or ramekins with the mixture and cover them with their lids or with foil. Put them in a shallow baking pan, fill the pan with hot water to reach halfway up the sides of the dishes and bake in the middle of the preheated oven for 45 minutes, or until they are set. Allow them to cool completely, uncovered, and chill. Serve with a sprinkling of praline powder.

Preparation and cooking time: 1 hour. Chilling time: 3 to 4 hours.

PRALINE POWDER

MAKES APPROXIMATELY 2 CUPS

1 cup unblanched almonds
1 cup superfine granulated sugar
¼ cup water
Pinch of cream of tartar

Preheat oven to 350° F.

Spread the almonds in a baking pan and roast them in pre-heated oven for 10 to 15 minutes, or until they are lightly colored. In a heavy frying pan cook the sugar with the water and cream of tartar over moderately high heat, washing down any undissolved sugar crystals clinging to the sides of the pan with a brush dipped in cold water, until the mixture is a light caramel in color. Add the almonds, pour onto a buttered piece of aluminum foil and let it cool until it is hard. Transfer to a board and chop it into coarse pieces. In a blender pulverize the pieces, a few at a time. Store the praline powder in an airtight container at room temperature.

†MOCHA PARFAIT

SERVES 4

½ to 1 pint coffee ice cream
¼ pound chocolate coffee-bean candies

4 tablespoons crème de cacao
Praline powder (see page 218)

In a bowl combine the coffee ice cream, softened slightly, with the chocolate coffee-bean candies. Put 1 tablespoon of the crème de cacao in each of 4 parfait glasses, divide the ice-cream mixture among the glasses and sprinkle with praline powder.

Preparation time: 15 minutes.

†††*FROZEN ORANGE MOUSSE

SERVES 6 TO 8

Genoise batter (see page 221)
1 cup superfine granulated sugar
⅓ cup water
2 tablespoons grated orange rind
6 egg yolks
¼ cup orange-flavored
   liqueur (make your own—
   see page 351)

2 cups heavy cream
Sweet almond oil
Glacé orange sections
Sweetened whipped cream
   flavored with orange-flavored
   liqueur

Prepare the Genoise batter. In a heavy saucepan bring the sugar, water and grated orange rind to the boil over moderately high heat, washing down any undissolved sugar crystals clinging to the sides of the pan with a brush dipped in cold water. Increase the heat and cook the syrup until a candy thermometer registers 220° F. In a bowl beat the egg yolks until they are thick and form a ribbon when the beater is lifted. Pour the syrup in a stream over the egg yolks and beat the mixture until it is thick and cool. Beat in the orange-flavored liqueur. In a chilled bowl beat the heavy cream until it is lightly whipped and fold it gently but thoroughly into the egg-yolk mixture. Fit an 8-inch soufflé dish with a 6-inch-deep band of waxed paper, doubled and oiled with sweet almond oil, to form a standing collar extending 2 inches above the rim, and tie it with string. Spoon a 2-inch layer of the mousse into the soufflé dish and top it with half the prepared cake cubes. Cover the cubes with another layer of mousse, add the remaining cake cubes and top them with the remaining mousse. Freeze the mousse for at least 6 hours. Remove the collar and decorate with glacé orange sections and sweetened whipped cream flavored with orange-flavored liqueur.

Preparation time: approximately 1 hour. Cooking time: 45 minutes. Chilling time: 6 hours.

GENOISE BATTER

2 eggs
¼ cup superfine granulated sugar
½ cup flour
1½ tablespoons clarified butter
  (see page 275)
½ teaspoon kirsch

1 tablespoon orange juice
1 tablespoon grated orange
  rind
⅓ cup orange-flavored liqueur
  (see page 351)

Preheat oven to 350° F.

In the bowl of an electric mixer, combine the eggs with the sugar. Set the bowl over a saucepan containing 2 inches of hot but *not* boiling water, and heat the mixture over low heat, stirring, until it is lukewarm. Transfer the bowl to the mixer and beat at high speed for 7 minutes, or until it has tripled in volume. Sift in the flour, a little at a time, folding in each part gently and thoroughly. Combine the clarified butter, melted and cooled, the kirsch, orange juice and grated orange rind, and fold into the batter, 1 tablespoon at a time. Butter and flour a 9-inch round cake pan and fill it with the batter. Bake in a moderate oven for 30 minutes, or until the cake is well puffed and browned and the sides come easily away from the pan. Turn the cake onto a rack to cool. Cut into 1-inch cubes and sprinkle with orange-flavored liqueur.

††*FROZEN LIME SOUFFLÉ

SERVES 6

4 to 5 large limes
1 tablespoon gelatine
6 egg yolks
1¼ cup superfine granulated sugar
1 cup scalded milk

1 to 2 drops green food coloring (optional)
2 egg whites
Pinch of salt
¾ cup heavy cream
Sweet almond oil

Grate and reserve the lime rind. Squeeze the juice and strain it into a small bowl and, if necessary, add enough additional juice to measure 1 cup. Sprinkle the gelatine over the juice to soften it. In a bowl beat the egg yolks with the sugar until the mixture makes a ribbon when the beater is lifted. Add the milk in a stream, stirring constantly. Transfer the custard to a heavy saucepan and cook over moderately low heat, stirring constantly with a wooden spoon, until it thickens and begins to coat the spoon. Do not allow the custard to reach the boiling point. Remove the pan from the heat and add the gelatine mixture and the food coloring, if desired. Stir the custard into a bowl and add all but 1 teaspoon of the grated lime rind. Put the bowl of custard in a bowl of ice and stir it occasionally until it is completely cool and thick but not set. In a bowl beat the egg whites with a pinch of salt until they hold soft peaks. In another bowl whip the cream until it holds soft peaks, fold it lightly into the egg whites and fold the mixture into the custard. Fit a 2-pint soufflé dish or metal mold with a 6-inch-deep band of waxed paper, doubled and oiled with sweet almond oil, to form a standing collar extending 2 inches above the rim, and tie with a string. Fill the dish with the soufflé mixture and freeze for at least 6 hours or until it is firm. Remove the collar carefully and sprinkle the top with the reserved lime rind.

Preparation time: approximately 1 hour. Chilling time: 6 hours.

†*RED-CURRANT MOUSSE

SERVES 6

2 cups red currants	Pinch of salt
¾ cup superfine granulated sugar	1 cup heavy cream, whipped
1 teaspoon vanilla extract	until it holds a peak

Stem the currants, wash them and crush them with a fork. Work the fruit through a sieve and mix the purée with the sugar, vanilla and a pinch of salt. Lightly fold in the whipped cream and place either in a small soufflé dish or in a refrigerator tray in the freezing compartment for at least 8 hours or until the mousse is firm. Serve in iced glasses.

Preparation time: approximately 30 minutes. Chilling time: 8 hours.

†ICED CRANBERRY SOUFFLÉ

SERVES 4

½ pound cranberries
1 cup superfine granulated sugar
2 tablespoons orange-flavored
   liqueur (see page 351)

1 cup heavy cream, whipped
   until stiff
2 egg whites
Pinch of salt
Grated orange rind

In a saucepan combine the cranberries with the sugar, cover the pan and cook over low heat, stirring once or twice, for 10 minutes. Remove the lid and cook for 5 minutes more. Add the orange-flavored liqueur and allow the mixture to cool. Fold in the whipped cream. Beat the egg whites with a pinch of salt until they are stiff, and fold them into the mixture. Pour into an 8-inch soufflé dish, cover with foil and freeze until firm. Sprinkle grated orange rind on top and serve.

Preparation time: approximately 45 minutes. Chilling time: 6 hours.

†*MADAME SERGIO CORRÊA DE COSTA'S PISTACHIO SOUFFLÉ

SERVES 10

ICE CREAM

3½ cups heavy cream
1 pound superfine granulated
sugar

3 teaspoons pistachio extract
5 eggs
2 drops green food coloring

SAUCE

¾ cup crystallized cherries
½ cup sugar
4 tablespoons water

1 teaspoon pistachio extract
¼ cup butter

Whip the cream with 1½ cups of the sugar until very firm. Add the pistachio extract. Beat the eggs with the remaining sugar until very firm (use a blender or beat over heat in a double boiler). Allow to cool and blend well with the whipped cream. Add the green food coloring. Chill an 8-inch soufflé dish in the freezer for 30 minutes before filling with the ice-cream mixture, then return to the freezer for 6 to 8 hours. Mix the cherries, sugar and water in a blender. Add the pistachio extract and butter and heat in double boiler. Serve the sauce hot with the ice cream.

Preparation time: approximately 30 minutes. Chilling time: 6 to 8 hours.

†††APRICOT AND ALMOND SOUFFLÉ

SERVES 6

1 cup apricot purée (see below)
¼ cup superfine granulated sugar
2 tablespoons lemon juice
½ teaspoon grated lemon rind
4 egg yolks

½ cup chopped, roasted
  almonds
5 egg whites, beaten until stiff
  with a pinch of salt

Preheat oven to 350° F.

Prepare the apricot purée and, while it is still warm, stir in the sugar, lemon juice, lemon rind and egg yolks. Add the chopped almonds and fold the mixture into the egg whites. Turn the mixture into a buttered and sugared soufflé dish and bake in the preheated oven for about 35 minutes. Serve with whipped cream or, better still, sour cream.

APRICOT PURÉE

Cover 1 pound dried apricots with hot water and allow them to stand for about 2 hours. Put apricots and liquid in a saucepan, bring to the boil and simmer gently, covered, for about 25 minutes or until the apricots are tender. Drain the apricots and force the fruit through a fine sieve, or purée them in a blender with a little of the juice. There should be about 1 cup of purée.

Preparation time: approximately 2 hours 30 minutes. Cooking time: approximately 1 hour.

†††GRAND MARNIER SOUFFLÉ

SERVES 6

3 lady fingers	Pinch of salt
⅔ cup Grand Marnier	5 egg yolks
8 egg whites	⅔ cup superfine granulated sugar

Preheat oven to 350° F.

Soak the lady fingers in half the Grand Marnier for 1 hour, and cover the dish so that the liqueur does not evaporate. Beat the egg whites with a pinch of salt until stiff. Beat the egg yolks, add the soaked lady fingers and beat together. Fold the egg whites into the yolk mixture. Finally add the sugar and the rest of the Grand Marnier so that the whites do not become too soft. Pour the mixture into a buttered and sugared soufflé dish and bake in the preheated oven for about 35 minutes. Serve immediately.

Preparation time: approximately 1 hour 30 minutes. Cooking time: approximately 35 minutes.

††MRS. ANTHONY LEWIS'S GINGER SOUFFLÉ

SERVES 6

3 tablespoons butter	1 tablespoon Cognac
3 tablespoons flour	Pinch of powdered ginger
1¼ cups milk	¼ cup preserved, crystallized ginger,
¼ cup sugar	chopped
Pinch of salt	4 eggs, separated

Preheat oven to 375° F.

In a saucepan melt the butter, add the flour and stir with a wire whisk until blended. Meanwhile, bring the milk to the boil and add all at once to the butter-and-flour mixture, stirring vigorously. Add the sugar, salt, Cognac and powdered and crystallized ginger. Remove from the heat. Beat in the egg yolks one at a time. Cool. Beat the whites until they stand in peaks, and fold into the yolk mixture. Transfer to an 8-inch buttered-and-sugared soufflé dish and bake at 375° for 35 to 40 minutes. Serve immediately.

Preparation and cooking time: approximately 1 hour.

††CHESTNUT SOUFFLÉ

SERVES 6

*1 pound chestnuts, shelled and
  peeled (see page 137)*
Milk, to cover
¾ cup superfine granulated sugar
¼ cup heavy cream

3 egg yolks, well beaten
*1 teaspoon vanilla extract or
  coffee extract*
3 egg whites, beaten until stiff
Confectioners' sugar

Preheat oven to 350° F.

Put the peeled chestnuts in a saucepan with just enough milk to cover and bring them just to the boil. Simmer for about 30 minutes, or until the chestnuts are soft. Drain and force them through a fine sieve or purée them in a blender. In a saucepan combine the purée with the sugar and cream. Cook slowly, stirring constantly, until the mixture is smooth and thick. Remove the pan from the heat and stir in the egg yolks and vanilla extract or coffee extract. Fold in the egg whites, put the mixture in a buttered and sugared 1½-quart soufflé dish and bake in the preheated oven for 30 to 40 minutes, or until it is firm. Sprinkle with confectioners' sugar and serve at once.

Preparation time: 1 hour (for peeling chestnuts). Cooking time: approximately 1 hour 15 minutes.

††*BASIC DESSERT CRÊPES

MAKES APPROXIMATELY 12 CRÊPES

4 tablespoons flour   *2 teaspoons sugar*
⅔ cup milk   *2 tablespoons butter, melted and cooled*
¼ cup water   *Clarified butter (see page 275)*
3 eggs

In a blender combine the flour, milk, water, eggs and sugar and blend for 30 seconds, scraping the batter down from the sides of the container. Add the melted butter and blend for a few seconds more. Transfer the batter to a bowl and let it stand, covered, for at least 1 hour.

Preheat oven to 350° F. Heat a 6-to-7-inch crêpe pan and brush it lightly with clarified butter. Half fill a soup ladle with the batter and pour into the pan, quickly tilting and rotating the pan so that the batter covers the bottom in a thin layer. Return all excess batter to the bowl. Cook the crêpe over moderately high heat until the underside is browned, turn it and brown the other side. Transfer the crêpe to a plate. Make crêpes with the remaining batter in the same manner; stack them on a plate and cover them with a dampened tea towel. If the crêpes are made in advance, they should be covered with a round of foil and reheated in a preheated 300° F. oven before serving. They also freeze very well, if stored in an airtight freezing container with a round of aluminum foil separating each crêpe. Defrost at room temperature before reheating.

Preparation time: approximately 1 hour 10 minutes. Cooking time: 30 minutes.

††LEMON CRÊPES

SERVES 4

8 basic dessert crêpes
  (see page 228)
¾ cup superfine granulated sugar
2 teaspoons grated lemon peel
¾ cup butter
¼ cup Cognac

¼ cup orange-flavored liqueur
  (see page 351)
2 tablespoons lemon juice
1½ ounces blanched, sliced
  almonds

Fold the crêpes in half and arrange them, in 1 layer, overlapping slightly, in a buttered shallow flameproof dish. Sprinkle the crêpes with the sugar and grated lemon peel, mixed, and dot them with 2 tablespoons of the butter. Broil the crêpes about 5 inches from the heat until the sugar is melted and bubbling. In a saucepan melt the remaining butter, add the Cognac, orange-flavored liqueur and lemon juice and heat, stirring, until blended. Sprinkle the almonds over the crêpes and serve with the sauce.

Preparation time (including cooking the crêpes): 1 hour 40 minutes.

††HAZELNUT CRÊPES WITH STRAWBERRY BUTTER

SERVES 6

2 eggs
¾ cup milk
¼ cup flour
Pinch of salt
3 tablespoons lightly toasted
  ground hazelnuts
Clarified butter (see page 275)
⅓ cup butter

3 tablespoons superfine granulated
  sugar
¾ cups strawberries
½ teaspoon lemon juice
1 cup whipped cream
12 strawberries, sliced and dusted
  with sugar
Handful slivered, lightly toasted
  hazelnuts

Put the eggs in the container of a blender with the milk, flour, salt and ground hazelnuts and blend the mixture at high speed for a few seconds. With a rubber spatula push down any flour clinging to the sides of the container. Blend the batter for a few seconds more, pour it into a bowl and allow to stand for 1 hour. Brush a 6-inch crêpe pan with clarified butter. Heat the pan until it is hot and pour in 2 tablespoons of the batter. Quickly tilt and rotate the pan so that the batter covers the bottom in a thin layer, and return any excess to the bowl. Cook the crêpe until it is lightly browned on the bottom, turn it and cook it until the other side is browned. Slip the crêpe onto a plate. Continue making crêpes in this manner until all the batter is used. Keep the crêpes warm, covered lightly with foil in 300° F. oven. These crêpes may also be made in advance and heated just before using, or they may be frozen.

In a bowl cream together the butter and sugar. In another bowl mash the strawberries with the lemon juice. Incorporate the strawberries into the butter mixture, a portion at a time, until well blended. Spread each crêpe with 1 tablespoon of the strawberry butter and fold the crêpes in half. Serve them on heated plates with whipped cream, sliced sweetened strawberries and hazelnuts.

Preparation time (cooking crêpes): approximately 1 hour 40 minutes.
Added preparation time: approximately 45 minutes.

†††MADAME SERGIO CORRÊA DA COSTA'S CRÊPES COPACABANA

SERVES 10

To save time, you may, if you prefer substitute commercial ice cream. The crêpes and the praline filling can be made in advance, or even frozen, so that only the sauce has to be made at the last minute.

COFFEE ICE CREAM

¼ cup superfine granulated sugar
2 egg yolks
4 tablespoons strong coffee
1¼ cups heavy cream, lightly
  whipped
Preparation and chilling time: approximately 7 hours.

*PRALINE FILLING

½ cup superfine granulated sugar
6 tablespoons water
¾ cup shelled hazelnuts
6 ounces semisweet chocolate,
  melted
Preparation and cooking time: approximately 30 minutes.

*CRÊPES

1½ cups flour
1 teaspoon salt
2 eggs
2½ cups milk
Preparation and cooking time:
approximately 1 hour 40 minutes.

LIQUEUR SAUCE

1½ cups superfine granulated
  sugar
12 tablespoons water
1¼ cups strong coffee
2 tablespoons each Cognac,
  Tia Maria and rum
Preparation and cooking time:
approximately 30 minutes.

To make the ice cream, put the sugar, egg yolks and coffee into a bowl over a pan of simmering water and whisk the mixture until thick and foamy. Remove from the heat and continue to whisk until cool. Fold in the cream, turn into a ¾-quart shallow plastic container, cover and freeze for at least 6 hours.

In an 8-inch pan, make 20 thick crêpes according to the directions on page 228. Put the crêpes to one side on greaseproof paper until needed.

To make the praline filling, boil the sugar and water until the mixture becomes a light caramel color. Add the nuts and turn onto oiled greaseproof paper on a wooden board to cool. Mince the cooled nut mixture into coarse bits, and blend with the melted chocolate. Spread each crêpe with the filling and fold them in half, then in half again, making a fan. Arrange the folded crêpes in a row down the center of a shallow flameproof dish and put to one side.

To make the sauce, slowly dissolve the sugar in the water over low heat, then boil to a pale caramel color. Add the coffee and other ingredients, bring to the boil, pour over the crêpes and cover. Reheat

on top of the stove for a few minutes, then serve 2 crêpes and 1 scoop
of coffee ice cream to each person.

††WALNUT CRÊPES WITH CHOCOLATE SAUCE

SERVES 8

*THE CRÊPES

2 eggs   1 teaspoon olive oil
2 cups milk   Pinch of salt
1 cup sifted flour   Clarified butter (see page 275)
1 teaspoon Cognac

THE FILLING

1¼ cups ground walnuts   ⅓ cup milk
3 tablespoons superfine   1 tablespoon rum
   granulated sugar

THE CHOCOLATE SAUCE

6 squares semisweet chocolate,   1 egg yolk
   broken into pieces   ¼ cup milk
¼ cup water   ½ teaspoon flour
1 to 2 tablespoons superfine
   granulated sugar

In a blender combine all the ingredients except the clarified butter.
Cover the container and blend at high speed for a few seconds. With
a rubber spatula push down any flour that clings to the sides of the
container and blend for a few seconds more. Pour the batter into a
bowl and allow it to stand, covered, for at least 1 hour. Brush a 7-by-
8-inch pan lightly with clarified butter. Heat the pan until hot and
pour in just enough batter to make a thin layer. Cook until lightly
browned on the bottom, turn and cook until the other side is
browned. Continue making crêpes until all the batter is used.

To make the walnut filling, combine the walnuts and sugar in a small saucepan. Stir in the milk, bring the mixture to the boil, stirring, and cook for 2 minutes over medium heat. Remove from the heat and stir in the rum. Spread each crêpe with 1 tablespoon of the filling, roll it up and put in a buttered shallow baking dish. Keep the crêpes warm while you prepare the sauce.

In the top of a double boiler, combine the chocolate with the water and sugar. Heat the mixture, stirring, until the chocolate has melted and the mixture is smooth. In a small bowl beat the egg yolk with the milk and flour. Stir into the chocolate mixture and heat the sauce, stirring, until thickened, but do not allow it to boil. Pour the sauce over the crêpes and serve at once. Do not reheat the sauce.

Preparation time: 1 hour 10 minutes. Cooking time: approximately 1 hour.

†*FRESH STRAWBERRY SORBET

SERVES 6

¾ cup superfine granulated
   sugar
1 cup water
1 pint fresh strawberries, puréed

Juice of ½ lemon
Juice of ½ orange
Pinch of salt

In a saucepan combine the sugar, water and strawberries. Bring to the boil, boil for 6 minutes and allow to cool slightly. Stir in the lemon and orange juices and the salt. Pour the mixture into a refrigerator tray and freeze it until it is mushy. Transfer to a chilled bowl and beat with a fork, wire whisk or rotary beater to break up the ice crystals. Return the sorbet to the refrigerator tray and freeze it until it is frozen but not solid. Serve in chilled glasses.

Preparation and cooking time: approximately 30 minutes. Chilling time: approximately 6 to 8 hours.

†*BLACKBERRY SORBET

SERVES 6

¾ cup superfine granulated sugar   Juice of ½ lemon
1 cup water   Pinch of salt
1 pint fresh blackberries, puréed,
    and worked through a sieve

Combine the sugar and water in a saucepan; bring the mixture to the
boil and boil it for 6 minutes. Remove the pan from the heat and
allow the syrup to cool. Stir in the blackberry purée, lemon juice and
salt. Pour into a refrigerator tray and freeze until mushy. Transfer
the sorbet to a chilled bowl and beat it with a fork, wire whisk or
rotary beater to break up the ice crystals. Return the sorbet to the
refrigerator tray and freeze until it is frozen but not solid. Serve it in
chilled glasses.

*Preparation and cooking time: approximately 30 minutes. Chilling
time: approximately 6 to 8 hours.*

†*LIME SORBET

SERVES 6

¾ cup superfine granulated sugar   Few drops of green food color-
2 cups water   ing
¾ cup lime juice   Pinch of salt
1 teaspoon grated lime rind   6 lime shells, chilled

In a saucepan combine the sugar and water and boil for 6 minutes.
Remove the pan from the heat and allow the syrup to cool. Stir in
the lime juice, grated lime rind, food coloring and salt. Pour the
mixture into a refrigerator tray and freeze until it is mushy. Transfer
the sorbet to a chilled bowl and beat with a fork, wire whisk, or
rotary beater to break up the ice crystals. Return the sorbet to the

refrigerator tray and freeze until it is frozen but not solid. Serve it in chilled lime shells.

Preparation and cooking time: approximately 20 minutes. Chilling time: 6 to 8 hours.

†*PEACH OR NECTARINE SORBET

SERVES 6

¼ cup superfine granulated sugar
1 cup water
1¼ cups fresh peaches or nectarines, peeled and sliced

Juice of ½ lemon
Pinch of salt

In a saucepan combine the sugar and water, bring the mixture to the boil and boil for 6 minutes. Remove the pan from the heat and allow the syrup to cool. Work the sliced peaches or nectarines through a sieve, or purée them in a blender. Stir the purée into the syrup and add the lemon juice and salt. Pour the mixture into a refrigerator tray and freeze it until mushy. Transfer the sorbet to a chilled bowl and beat it with a fork, wire whisk or rotary beater to break up the ice crystals. Return the sorbet to the refrigerator tray and freeze until it is frozen but not solid. Serve it in chilled glasses.

Preparation and cooking time: approximately 30 minutes. Chilling time: 6 to 8 hours.

†*PEACH ICE CREAM

SERVES 6

10 ripe peaches
2 cups sour cream
¾ cup confectioners' sugar
¼ cup lime juice

Peel, crush and pit the peaches and press the pulp through a fine sieve, or purée it in a blender. Stir the purée into the sour cream and flavor it with the sugar and lime juice. Freeze the cream in a refrigerator tray in the coldest part of the refrigerator or in the freezer. Beat it with an egg beater when it reaches the mushy stage and again before it solidifies. Cover the tray with plastic wrap and store the ice cream at freezing temperature for several hours before serving.

Preparation time: approximately 25 minutes. Chilling time: 4 to 6 hours.

††*LADY VICTORIA WAYMOUTH'S BURNT ICE CREAM

SERVES 6

1¼ cups heavy cream
1 vanilla bean
8 tablespoons superfine granulated sugar
3 eggs, beaten

Scald the heavy cream with the vanilla bean in it and sweeten with 6 tablespoons of the sugar. Allow to cool. Make a custard by stirring the cream into the beaten eggs. Heat the mixture in a double boiler, stirring continually until it thickens. Set aside to cool. Put the remaining 2 tablespoons of sugar into a small, heavy pan and heat until it first liquefies and then turns honey color to mahogany. At the point where it starts to bubble and to give off the scent of caramel, tip the sugar into the cooled custard. Stir well, then freeze for at least 4 to 6 hours before serving.

Preparation time: approximately 1 hour 30 minutes. Chilling time: 4 to 6 hours.

†*LEMON AND PARSLEY ICE

SERVES 6

Juice and rind of 1 lemon
1½ cups water
3 tablespoons superfine granulated sugar
1 bunch parsley

Put the lemon rind in a saucepan with the water and sugar. Bring the mixture to the boil, cover the pan, remove from the heat and steep for 5 minutes. Add the lemon juice, strain and cool. Cook the parsley in water to cover for 5 to 10 minutes. Drain well and rub through a fine sieve. Add the sieved parsley to the lemon mixture and freeze in a refrigerator tray for 6 to 8 hours.

Preparation and cooking time: 1 hour 30 minutes. Freezing time: 6 to 8 hours.

††COEUR À LA CRÈME WITH RASPBERRIES

SERVES 6 TO 8

¾ pound creamed cottage cheese (not low-fat)
½ pound cream cheese
Pinch of salt
1 tablespoon confectioners' sugar
1 cup heavy cream

Line a 5-to-6-inch metal or porcelain heart-shaped coeur à la crème mold, or 3 small ones, with a square of cheesecloth wrung out in cold water. Using a fork, mix the cottage cheese, cream cheese, salt and confectioners' sugar together in a bowl. Moisten with the cream and with a wooden spoon, press the mixture through a fine sieve. Fill the mold or molds with the cheese mixture, pressing down well, and fold the corners of the cheesecloth over the top. Place in the refrigerator on a dish to drain overnight. When ready to serve, turn back the corners of the cheesecloth carefully so as not to spoil the heart shape and unmold. Surround the crème with raspberries, or any other fresh berries, and serve with heavy cream and sugar.

Preparation time: 12 hours.

†RASPBERRIES AND HONEY CREAM

SERVES 6

1 pound raspberries, rinsed and   *¼ cup clear honey*
*   thoroughly drained*   *2 teaspoons grated orange rind*
1 cup sour cream   *½ cup heavy cream, whipped*

Put raspberries in a glass bowl, and chill. In a bowl mix together the sour cream, honey and orange rind. Fold in the whipped cream. Chill the mixture for 2 hours and pour it over the raspberries.

Preparation time: 10 minutes. Chilling time: 2 hours.

†PEACHES WITH RASPBERRY SYRUP

SERVES 6

6 ripe peaches, washed   *1 cup superfine granulated sugar*
2 cups water, simmering   *2 tablespoons kirsch*
1 pound raspberries

Poach the peaches in the simmering water for 5 minutes. Peel the peaches and arrange them in a glass bowl. In the same water simmer the raspberries with the sugar for 10 minutes. Strain the syrup, discarding the pips. Return the syrup to the pan and cook it for another 5 minutes, or until it is thickened and slightly reduced. Cool to lukewarm, add the kirsch and pour over the peaches. Serve slightly warm or at room temperature.

Preparation and cooking time: approximately 1 hour.

†FRUIT-STUFFED CANTALOUPE

SERVES 6 TO 8

2 ripe cantaloupes	*Handful of white almonds*
1 lemon	*1 banana*
1 pound cherries	*2 peaches*
1 pound white grapes	*A little kirsch, dry maraschino or Grand Marnier*

Cut off the tops of the melons, scoop out the seeds and rub the cut surfaces with lemon. Cut up the cherries, grapes, almonds, banana and peaches. Soak them in the liqueur and mound the soaked fruit plus a little of the liqueur into the melons. Chill thoroughly in the refrigerator before serving.

Preparation time: approximately 15 minutes. Chilling time: approximately 4 hours.

†GREEN GRAPES IN COGNAC

SERVES 6

1¼ pounds seedless green grapes	*1½ teaspoons lemon juice*
6 tablespoons honey	*1 cup sour cream*
3 tablespoons Cognac	

Wash the grapes and drain them thoroughly. Remove the stems and toss the grapes gently in a mixture of the honey, Cognac and lemon juice. Chill for at least 5 hours, stirring occasionally, and serve in a chilled bowl with sour cream piled on top of the grapes.

Preparation time: 15 minutes. Chilling time: 5 hours.

†WILD STRAWBERRIES CARCASSONNE
___

SERVES 6

1 pound wild strawberries or small cultivated ones

2 tablespoons superfine granulated sugar

Fresh-ground pepper

¼ cup Armagnac

Put the strawberries into a deep bowl and add the sugar. Grind a bit of pepper over the berries and add the Armagnac. Shake the bowl to distribute the flavorings and serve.

Preparation time: 15 minutes.

†MRS. JEANETTE DE ROTHSCHILD'S MELON AND BLACKBERRIES
___

SERVES 6

1 pound blackberries, washed

3 tablespoons superfine granulated sugar

1¼ cup port wine

3 honeydew melons or 3 cantaloupes, halved

Put the blackberries in a bowl, add the sugar and port, turn the fruit until it is completely covered with the mixture and let stand for 1 hour. Then mound the blackberries and juice into the hollow centers of the melons. Chill until ready to serve.

Preparation time: approximately 1 hour 15 minutes. Chilling time: approximately 1 hour.

†STRAWBERRIES À L'ORANGE

SERVES 6

2 pounds ripe strawberries
Sherry
Superfine granulated sugar

¾ cup fresh-squeezed orange juice
¼ cup orange-flavored liqueur (see page 351)
Juice of ½ lemon

Wash the strawberries in sherry, hull and drain them. Put the berries in a glass bowl with sugar to taste. Add the orange juice and orange-flavored liqueur. Just before serving add the lemon juice. Serve the strawberries very cold.

Preparation time: approximately 15 minutes.

††BAKED BANANAS IN ORANGE

SERVES 6

6 firm, ripe bananas, peeled
¼ cup butter or margarine
1 cup orange juice
½ cup light-brown sugar
2 teaspoons dark rum
½ teaspoon Angostura bitters

½ teaspoon ground allspice
½ teaspoon grated orange rind
⅓ cup slivered, blanched almonds, lightly toasted
1 orange

Preheat oven to 350° F.

Halve the bananas lengthwise. In a frying pan sauté the bananas in 2 batches, in butter or margarine, until they are golden and transfer to a buttered shallow baking dish just large enough to hold them in 1 layer. In a bowl combine the orange juice, brown sugar, rum, Angostura bitters, allspice and grated orange rind. Pour the orange-juice mixture over the bananas and top with almonds. Bake in preheated oven for 10 minutes. Arrange six ¼-inch-thick orange slices, seeded and halved, over the bananas and bake for 5 minutes more, or until the oranges are heated through. Serve warm.

Preparation and cooking time: approximately 30 minutes.

†*THE LADY PLUNKET'S GINGERSNAP PUDDING

SERVES 8

> *1½ sixteen-ounce boxes gingersnaps*
> *⅔ cup Cognac*
> *2½ cups heavy cream, lightly whipped*

Dip each gingersnap into the brandy, but do not allow it to become too soft. Sandwich the biscuits together with cream and stand them in rows in a 7-inch soufflé dish. Fill the dish, then coat all over with the remaining whipped cream, making sure that all the empty spaces between the piles of biscuits are filled and the top covered. Refrigerate for 24 hours before serving.

Preparation time: approximately 30 minutes. Chilling time: 24 hours.

††CHILLED ZABAGLIONE

SERVES 6

6 egg-yolks	½ teaspoon vanilla extract
¾ cup Marsala	½-inch piece stick cinnamon
¼ cup superfine granulated sugar	1 tablespoon maraschino liqueur
	1 tablespoon light rum
Rind of ½ lemon, grated	Glacé chestnuts (marrons glacés)

In a large bowl combine the egg yolks, Marsala and sugar, and beat with a whisk until frothy. Stir in the lemon rind, vanilla and cinnamon stick. Set the bowl over a pan of simmering water and beat the mixture with a whisk until it is thick and has tripled in bulk. Remove from the heat, discard the cinnamon and stir in the maraschino liqueur and light rum. Beat for 1 minute longer, then spoon the zabaglione into dessert glasses and chill for 1 hour. Top with chopped glacé chestnuts.

Preparation time: approximately 45 minutes. Chilling time: 1 hour.

†††OLD ENGLISH PLUM PUDDING
(*Without Sugar*)

MAKES 5 PLUM PUDDINGS

1 pound citron or sliced lemon	1 teaspoon cinnamon
½ pound crystallized lemon peel	¼ teaspoon cloves
½ pound crystallized orange peel	¼ teaspoon ground ginger
½ pound pitted dates	¼ teaspoon nutmeg
1 cup blanched almonds	¼ teaspoon mace
1 pound dried currants	1 pound minced beef suet
1 pound seedless raisins	3 ounces fine dry bread crumbs
1 pound sultanas	1 teaspoon salt
2½ cups Cognac	4 eggs
2 cups flour	4 ounces red-currant jelly

Chop the citron or sliced lemon, lemon peel, orange peel, dates and almonds fine. Combine with the dried currants, raisins and sultanas and pour the Cognac over the mixture. Soak for 24 hours, stirring several times. Sift the flour with the cinnamon, cloves, ginger, nutmeg and mace. Mix the spiced flour with the minced beef suet, bread crumbs and salt and blend in the brandy-steeped fruits. Beat the eggs until light and stir them thoroughly into the mixture. Add the red-currant jelly gradually and carefully. Fill five well-buttered two-pint pudding basins three-quarters full with the batter and adjust the covers tightly. Tie each pudding basin in a towel wrung out in cold water and dusted with flour. Boil the puddings gently in enough water to reach the tops of the pudding basins for about 8 hours, adding more boiling water as necessary. The pudding basins should not be submerged. Unmold the puddings, wrap them in several layers of cheesecloth well moistened with brandy and store them in tightly covered containers. Allow the puddings to ripen for 3 to 4 weeks, keeping the wrappings moist with brandy. Before serving, steam the puddings for 3 hours, then, just before serving, pour brandy over the pudding and light it. Serve with brandy butter (see below).

Preparation and cooking time: approximately 2 days.

BRANDY BUTTER

Cream ½ cup unsalted butter well and gradually beat in 1½ cups confectioners' sugar and ¼ cup Cognac, or to taste. Beat the butter until it is light and perfectly mixed. Add a small amount of salt and chill.

††BREAD PUDDING WITH BOURBON SAUCE

SERVES 6 TO 8

*1½ long, thin loaves day-old
    French bread, broken into pieces
3¼ cups milk
2 eggs, lightly beaten
1½ cups superfine granulated
    sugar*

*½ cup raisins
3 tablespoons butter, softened
1½ tablespoons vanilla extract
Bourbon sauce (see below)*

Preheat oven to 325° F.

In a bowl soak the bread in the milk until it is softened and combine the mixture until it is fairly smooth. Stir in the eggs, sugar, raisins, butter and vanilla. Pour the mixture into a buttered baking dish, 12 inches by 9 inches, and bake it in a preheated oven for 2 hours, or until it is well browned. Serve with bourbon sauce.

BOURBON SAUCE

MAKES APPROXIMATELY 1¾ CUPS

*1 cup superfine granulated sugar
3 tablespoons water
½ cup butter, melted*

*1 egg, well beaten
⅓ cup bourbon whiskey*

In a saucepan cook the sugar and water over moderately high heat, washing down any undissolved sugar clinging to the sides of the pan with a brush dipped in cold water, until the sugar is completely dissolved. Stir in the melted butter, quickly beat in the egg and cook the sauce over low heat, stirring, for 4 minutes, or until it is well combined and slightly thickened. Do not allow it to boil. Remove from the heat and stir in the bourbon.

Preparation time: approximately 30 minutes. Cooking time: approximately 2 hours.

†DATE AND NUT PUDDING

SERVES 6 TO 8

3 eggs
1 cup superfine granulated sugar
½ cup butter, softened
1 cup milk
3 teaspoons flour
½ teaspoon salt

½ teaspoon baking powder
½ teaspoon cinnamon
1 cup chopped dates
1 cup chopped walnuts
½ pint cream, whipped
½ cup vanilla-flavored sugar

Preheat oven to 350° F.

In a bowl beat the eggs with the sugar until light. Beat in the butter until well combined. Gradually beat in the milk. Sift the flour with the salt, baking powder and cinnamon and add to the egg mixture. Stir in the dates and nuts (the batter may separate during the combining, but it will amalgamate during the baking). Butter a 9-inch-square baking pan and line the bottom with buttered waxed paper. Turn the batter into the pan and bake in the preheated oven for 1 hour, or until a knife inserted in the center comes out clean. Allow the cake to cool in the pan on a wire rack for 5 minutes before turning out. Wrap tightly in plastic and let stand at room temperature for a day. To serve, rewrap in foil and reheat. Serve in squares, with whipped cream and vanilla-flavored sugar.

Preparation time: approximately 2 hours. Allow to stand for 24 hours.

††ICED BRIE

SERVES 4

½ pound Brie cheese
6 tablespoons dry white wine
¾ cup heavy cream
1¼ teaspoons salt

Pinch of cayenne
3 tablespoons white bread crumbs
⅓ cup fresh-grated Parmesan
   cheese

Force the Brie through a fine sieve, with a wooden spoon (the skin may be left on if the cheese is not too ripe). Gradually add the white wine and heavy cream until mixture is almost liquid; add the salt, cayenne and bread crumbs. Pour the mixture into an ice tray and freeze for about 2 hours, or until set firm. Cut into 1½-inch squares, sprinkle with Parmesan and transfer to a serving plate. Serve while still very cold.

Preparation time: approximately 30 minutes. Chilling time: 2 hours.

††PINEAPPLE AND BLUEBERRY TRIFLE

SERVES 6

1¼ cups heavy cream

2 tablespoons confectioners' sugar

1 teaspoon vanilla extract

4 tablespoons dark rum

4 tablespoons water

2 tablespoons superfine granulated
  sugar

12 lady fingers

⅔ cup cubed fresh pineapple

¼ pound fresh blueberries

4 tablespoons blackberry jam,
  melted

In a bowl beat the heavy cream until it forms soft peaks. Add the confectioners' sugar and vanilla and beat until stiff. In a saucepan boil together the rum, water and sugar for 5 minutes and allow the syrup to cool. Halve the lady fingers and moisten with the syrup (or use a sponge-cake layer, split). Spread a third of the whipped cream in the bottom of an 8-inch soufflé dish. Sprinkle with half the pineapple and 1½ ounces of the blueberries. Spread the fruit with half the melted blackberry jam. Top the jam with a layer of half the lady fingers or sponge cake. Continue making layers, using another third of the whipped cream, the remaining pineapple, another 1½ ounces of blueberries, the remaining melted jam and lady fingers. Finish with the last of the whipped cream and sprinkle with the remaining blueberries.

Preparation and cooking time: approximately 1 hour 30 minutes.

††MRS. RALPH F. COLIN'S LEMON
MERINGUE PIE

SERVES 8 TO 10

BASIC PIE PASTRY
2¼ cups flour
2 teaspoons superfine granulated
   sugar
½ teaspoon salt
½ cup cold butter, cut into bits
⅓ cup cold vegetable fat
Iced water
Raw rice, for pau
1 egg white
2 tablespoons sugar

THE FILLING AND
MERINGUE
5 egg yolks
1 cup superfine granulated
   sugar
Juice and grated rind of 2
   lemons
5 egg whites, beaten
⅔ cup confectioners' sugar

Into a bowl sift together the flour, sugar and salt. Add the butter
and fat and blend the mixture until it resembles meal. Add 5 to 6
tablespoons iced water, or just enough to form a dough. Toss the
mixture until the water is incorporated, and form the dough into
a ball. Wrap it in waxed paper and chill for at least 1 hour.

Preheat oven to 400° F.

Roll out basic pie pastry into a circle about 12 inches in diameter
on a lightly floured surface. Lift the dough lightly over a rolling
pin and transfer it to a 9-inch plate, draping the excess dough loosely
over the sides. Allow to set for 10 minutes, then press the dough
firmly into the plate and trim the excess, leaving a 1-inch overhang.
Crimp the overhanging dough to form a decorative rim and chill
for 30 minutes. Line the chilled shell with a buttered round of
aluminum foil, fill the foil with raw rice and bake in the lower
third of the preheated oven for 10 minutes. Remove the foil and rice
carefully. In a bowl beat the egg white with the 2 tablespoons of
sugar until it is frothy and brush the shell with the glaze. Reduce

the heat to 350° F. and bake the shell for 15 minutes more, or until it is golden.

Beat the egg yolks until light. Add the superfine sugar, lemon juice and rind to the yolks. Place in a double boiler and cook, stirring constantly until thick and smooth. Allow to cool and fold in half of the beaten egg whites. When both the filling and pie crust are cold, fill the crust and place it in oven for a few minutes, then allow to cool. Fold the confectioners' sugar into the remaining egg whites. Top the cooled lemon pie with the meringue mixture and put in oven at 350° F. for 5 to 10 minutes or until brown.

Preparation and cooking time: approximately 2 hours.

††BLUEBERRY SOUR-CREAM PIE

SERVES 6 TO 8

1 basic pie shell (see page 248)	*Pinch of nutmeg*
½ cup superfine granulated sugar	*3 cups blueberries*
¼ teaspoon cinnamon	*3 eggs*
	1 cup sour cream
⅛ teaspoon salt	*⅓ cup honey*

Make a pie shell as described for lemon meringue pie.

Preheat oven to 325° F.

In a dish combine ¼ cup of the sugar, the cinnamon, salt and nutmeg. In a large bowl toss the blueberries with the sugar mixture. In a small bowl beat the eggs with the sour cream, honey and the remaining sugar. Add the custard mixture to the berries and blend gently. Pour the filling into the prepared shell and bake the pie in the preheated oven for 1 hour. Serve the pie warm.

Preparation and cooking time: approximately 3 hours 30 minutes.

LUNCHEON OR SUPPER DISHES

††THE COUNTESS OF DROGHEDA'S EGGPLANT WITH CRAB MEAT

SERVES 4

2 good-sized eggplant
Salt
¼ cup vegetable oil
2 medium-sized onions, sliced
2 tablespoons butter
1 tablespoon paprika
½ pound ripe tomatoes, skinned, seeds removed and sliced
1 tablespoon tomato paste
½ teaspoon oregano

Pinch of cayenne or drop of Tabasco
Salt and pepper to taste
6 to 7 ounces lump crab meat
2 tablespoons grated Parmesan and Gruyère cheese, mixed
2 tablespoons butter, melted

Preheat oven to 350° F.

Split the eggplant lengthwise, sprinkle each half with salt and leave for 30 minutes. Wipe the eggplant, then score them and brown the cut surfaces in the hot oil. Remove with a slotted spoon, set on a baking sheet and put in the oven for about 10 minutes, or just until tender. Put the sliced onions in a frying pan with the butter and sauté until soft, add the paprika and, after a few seconds, the tomatoes, tomato paste, oregano and cayenne (or Tabasco). Season with salt and pepper and cook to a thick mixture. Scoop out the pulp from the cooked eggplant, reserving the shells. Add it, stirring, to the tomato mixture and cook, stirring occasionally for 3 minutes. Then flake the crab meat with a fork, add to the pan and simmer for 1 minute. Fill the reserved eggplant shells with the mixture, sprinkle well with cheese and melted butter and bake in a 425° F. oven for 6 to 7 minutes, or until the tops are browned.

Preparation and cooking time: approximately 1 hour.

✝✝BROWN BEANS AND BACON

SERVES 6 TO 8

1 pound red kidney beans, rinsed and soaked overnight in a bowl with water to cover by 2 inches
Brown stock (see page 279) or beef broth to cover the beans

One 1-pound piece of bacon, rind removed, cut into 1/4- by-1/2-inch pieces
3 large onions, sliced into thick rings
Salt and pepper to taste

Preheat oven to 400° F.

Drain the soaked beans, transfer them to a saucepan and add brown stock or beef broth to cover. Bring the liquid to the boil, stirring, and cook the beans, covered, over low heat for 45 minutes to 1 hour, or until they are tender. Drain the beans of any remaining liquid and transfer them to a heatproof dish. Brown the bacon pieces in a frying pan, and transfer them with a slotted spoon to a dish. To the fat in the frying pan add the onion rings, sauté for 5 minutes, or until they are browned, and transfer to a bowl. Toss the bacon and ¼ cup of the bacon fat with the beans and add salt and pepper to taste. Arrange the onion rings on top of the beans and place the dish in the preheated oven for 10 minutes, or until the beans are heated through. Serve with hot mustard and boiled potatoes.

Soaking: 12 hours. Preparation and cooking time: approximately 1 hour 30 minutes.

††*MRS. MARK LITTMAN'S HAM JAMBALAYA

SERVES 8

10 ounces cooked ham, diced
1 large green pepper, chopped
2 onions, diced
2 cups celery leaves, chopped
1 cup parsley, chopped
1 clove garlic, chopped fine
Several drops Tabasco sauce

Salt and pepper to taste
One 13-ounce can of tomatoes or
*   10 fresh tomatoes, peeled*
One 5-ounce can tomato paste
2 cups white long-grain rice
2 pounds medium-sized shrimp

Brown the ham in an iron skillet until the fat is rendered. Add the green pepper, onions, celery, parsley and garlic and cook until soft, stirring constantly. Add several drops of Tabasco sauce and salt and pepper to taste. Add the tomatoes and tomato paste and stir well. Pour into a heavy pot in which you have put the well-washed rice. Stir again, cover and place over a high flame. When the mixture boils, turn the flame very low. After 30 minutes remove the lid and stir carefully to prevent sticking. Recover and continue to cook very slowly for 15 minutes longer. Then remove lid and allow to stand for at least 7 minutes with the flame turned off. Add the shrimp at the last minute, otherwise they will be overcooked. The more shrimp you use the better, since this is what makes the jambalaya worth the trouble and worth eating.

Preparation and cooking time: approximately 2 hours.

†††PAELLA

SERVES 6 TO 8

½ cup olive oil
One 2½-pound chicken, cut into
  12 pieces
½ pound chorizo or other garlic
  sausage, or ½ pound lean diced
  pork
1 medium-sized onion, sliced
3 cloves garlic, crushed
½ teaspoon salt
½ teaspoon powdered saffron
1½ cups long-grain rice
2 cups clam juice or fish stock

1¼ cups chicken stock, strained
½ cup Amontillado sherry
1 can artichoke hearts
¾ pound shelled, deveined
  shrimp
1 large can whole clams and
  juice (or 12 mussels in their
  shells)
2½ ounces canned pimentos,
  cut into strips
3 tablespoons minced parsley

Preheat oven to 350° F.

Heat the oil in a large skillet, heavy pot or paella pan. Quickly brown the chicken pieces. Remove and set aside. Add the sausage or pork to the pan. Brown quickly, remove and reserve. Drain off all but 2 tablespoons of fat, add the onion, garlic, salt and saffron and cook until the onion is soft. Add the rice, stirring to coat with oil. This part of the preparation may be done several hours in advance. Half an hour before serving add all the remaining ingredients, including the strained chicken stock and sherry. Place the browned chicken and sausage on the top, simmer for 20 to 25 minutes, then put in the preheated oven for 10 minutes. If dinner is delayed, the paella may be left covered in the turned-off oven for an additional 15 to 20 minutes without spoiling.

Preparation and cooking time: approximately 1 hour 30 minutes.

††*SAUSAGES WITH LIMA BEANS AND DILL

SERVES 6

¼ pound salt pork, cut into small dice
2 tablespoons butter or lard
½ cup scallions, sliced fine
1 clove garlic, minced
¾ cup dry white wine

1 pound chorizo or other smoked sausage, cut into ⅓-inch slices
1 bay leaf
Salt and pepper to taste
4 cups frozen lima beans
2 tablespoons chopped dill

In a heavy casserole cook the salt pork in the butter or lard until brown. Remove with a slotted spoon and reserve. To the fat remaining in the casserole add the scallions and garlic and cook for 5 minutes. Pour in the white wine and add the chorizo or smoked sausage, the salt pork, bay leaf and salt and pepper to taste. Simmer, partly covered, for about 20 minutes. Add the lima beans and dill and simmer, uncovered, for about 10 minutes longer, or until thoroughly heated. Add more salt and pepper to the casserole if necessary.

Preparation and cooking time: approximately 1 hour 15 minutes.

††*SCRAPPLE

MAKES 3 LOAF PANS

½ pig's head, cut in half, eyes, teeth, tongue and brain removed
Pig's liver, heart and sweetbreads or
4 pig's feet, thoroughly scraped

5 tablespoons sage
3 sachets bouquet garni
1 teaspoon cayenne pepper
Salt and pepper to taste
2 to 4 pounds corn meal
1 bunch scallions, chopped
Flour, for dredging

Wash the head and put it in a large saucepan with cold water to cover. Add the liver, heart and sweetbreads, or the pig's feet, and bring the liquid to the boil, skim the surface, cover the saucepan and simmer gently for 2 to 3 hours, or until the head meat falls away easily from the bones. Remove the meat, chop it and discard the bones. Skim the broth and season it with the sage, the bouquets garnis, cayenne and salt and pepper. Weigh the meat. For every 3 pounds, set aside 2 pounds of corn meal. Return the meat to the broth, bring it to the boil and sift in the meal, stirring constantly, to make a soft mush. Cook the mixture over low heat for 1 hour, stirring it frequently to prevent scorching. Adjust the seasoning, add the chopped scallions, and pour into bread pans rinsed with cold water. Set the pans in a cool place until the scrapple is firm. To serve, slice the scrapple thin, dip in flour and fry the slices in hot butter or drippings until they are crisp and brown.

Preparation and cooking time: approximatley 5 hours.

†*BASIC ENTRÉE CRÊPES

MAKES 18 TO 25 CRÊPES

4 eggs	1¼ cups water
1 cup flour	1 tablespoon melted butter
½ teaspoon salt	Clarified butter (see page 275)
1¼ cups milk	

In a bowl beat the eggs with a wire whisk. Add the flour sifted with the salt, and beat until smooth. Gradually add the milk, water and melted butter, stirring the batter until it is well blended and has the consistency of heavy cream. Allow to stand for at least 30 minutes before using and, if necessary, thin it again with a spoonful of water or milk. Heat a small iron or aluminum frying pan until it is very hot and brush it with clarified butter. Pour in about 3 tablespoons of the batter, tilting and rotating the pan to distribute it evenly. Cook the crêpe until it is lightly browned on the underside. Lift one edge with the fingers or with the aid of a spatula and flip the crêpe over to brown the other side. Continue making crêpes in this manner, stacking them to keep them moist, until the batter is used. The crêpes can be made in advance and frozen, separated by pieces of foil or waxed paper and wrapped in foil.

Preparation time: approximately 45 minutes. Cooking time: approximately 30 minutes.

††*BASIC ENTRÉE CRÊPES STUFFED WITH SPINACH

SERVES 6 TO 8

12 entrée crêpes (see page 255)	*Salt and pepper to taste*
2 pounds tender young spinach (or frozen spinach)	*2 tablespoons Parmesan cheese, grated fine*
5 cups boiling water	*2 tablespoons chopped parsley*
1 tablespoon salt	*2 egg yolks, lightly beaten*
1 clove garlic, chopped very fine or mashed	*1¼ cups tomato sauce (see page 61)*
1 tablespoon butter	

Preheat oven to 350° F.

Wash the spinach thoroughly. Bring the water to the boil with the salt, drop in the spinach and cook for 3 to 4 minutes. Drain the spinach in a colander, squeezing out as much water as possible, and chop it fine. In a saucepan cook the garlic in the butter until soft. Add the spinach and cook it, stirring, to evaporate any excess moisture. Season the spinach with salt and pepper to taste and stir in the Parmesan cheese and chopped parsley. Mix in the egg yolks. Spread some of the spinach mixture in the center of a crêpe. Fold the crêpe over and roll it up. Prepare the remaining crêpes in the same manner and arrange them in a lightly buttered baking dish. Spoon the tomato sauce over them, and put the dish in preheated oven until the crêpes are hot and the sauce bubbling.

Preparation and cooking time: approximately 45 minutes (if crêpes are already made).

††SPINACH OMELETTE

SERVES 6

1 clove garlic, peeled
1 small onion, chopped fine
2 tablespoons vegetable oil
6 eggs, lightly beaten
1 cup toasted, coarse bread crumbs
3 tablespoons parsley, chopped
   fine

5 ounces frozen chopped
   spinach
Pinch of marjoram
Pinch of nutmeg
Salt and pepper to taste
1 teaspoon dry vermouth
¾ cup grated Parmesan cheese

In a heavy frying pan sauté the garlic and onion in the oil until golden. Discard the garlic. Into the beaten eggs stir all the rest of the ingredients except the Parmesan. Blend well and pour into the frying pan. Cover the pan with aluminum foil and cook over low heat until the sides of the omelette shrink away from the pan and the bottom is lightly browned. Put the pan under the broiler for a few minutes until the top is set. Cut the omelette into wedges and serve with grated Parmesan cheese.

Preparation and cooking time: approximately 30 minutes.

†*VEGETABLE CURRY

SERVES 6

3 onions, chopped
2 cloves garlic, minced
3 tablespoons butter or margarine
2 teaspoons curry powder
1 teaspoon ground cumin
1 teaspoon ground coriander
1 teaspoon salt

1 small head cauliflower, sepa-
    rated into small flowerets
6 small carrots, sliced
½ pound small lima beans
1 cup chicken stock or chicken
    broth
1 tablespoon lemon juice

In a large casserole cook the onions and garlic in the butter or margarine, covered, over low heat for 2 minutes or until they are soft. Sprinkle them with the curry powder, cumin, coriander and salt and stir until well blended. Add all the rest of the ingredients except the lemon juice and simmer, covered, stirring occasionally, for 12 to 15 minutes or until the vegetables are tender but still crisp. Sprinkle the lemon juice over the curry and serve.

Preparation and cooking time: approximately 30 minutes.

††*VEGETABLE STEW

SERVES 6

3 tablespoons sesame seeds
2 eggplant, cut crosswise in
    ⅓-inch slices
Salt
3 onions, sliced
2 cloves garlic, minced
⅓ cup olive oil

1½ cups tomatoes, peeled, seeded and
    diced
1½ cups chopped spinach
6 tablespoons chopped celery leaves
3 tablespoons chopped chives
1½ teaspoons oregano
¾ teaspoon pepper

Preheat oven to 350° F.

Spread the sesame seeds in 1 layer on a baking sheet and toast them in the oven, stirring occasionally, for 10 minutes, or until they are lightly browned. Arrange the eggplant slices on paper towels, sprinkle with salt and allow them to drain. In a large, heavy frying pan, cook the onions and garlic in the oil at a bare simmer for about 2 minutes, or until the onions have softened. Transfer the onions and garlic with a slotted spoon to a large bowl and combine with all the rest of the ingredients except the sesame seeds and eggplant. Wipe the eggplant slices, removing most of the salt but leaving enough to season. Add the slices to the frying pan and sauté them in batches, adding more oil if necessary, until they are browned on both sides and tender. Arrange a third of the eggplant slices in the frying pan and top them with a third of the vegetable mixture. Continue to make layers in the same manner until all the ingredients are used, ending with a layer of vegetable mixture. Simmer, covered, for 10 minutes, or until the vegetables are cooked through and the flavors are well blended. Sprinkle the top of the stew with the toasted sesame seeds and serve hot.

Preparation and cooking time: approximately 1 hour 30 minutes.

†LADY VICTORIA WAYMOUTH'S CHEESE PUDDING

SERVES 4 TO 6

1 regular-size loaf Pepperidge Farm white bread
Butter, to grease the pan
½ pound grated Cheddar cheese

2 eggs
2 cups milk
Pepper, salt and nutmeg

Preheat oven to 375° F.

Butter each slice of bread and cut off the crusts. Cut the bread into ½-inch squares and arrange in a buttered ovenproof dish. Cover with the grated Cheddar cheese. Beat the eggs with the milk, season to taste and pour over the cheese. Refrigerate for 2 to 3 hours, then cook in the preheated oven for 45 minutes. To make this a main supper dish, add ham, shrimp or crab to the mixture. Or serve it as a side dish instead of potatoes.

Preparation time: 3 hours 30 minutes. Cooking time: 45 minutes.

††CHEESE SOUFFLÉ

SERVES 6

1 cup grated Emmentaler cheese and	*Pinch of paprika*
1 cup Parmesan cheese, mixed	*Salt and pepper to taste*
¼ cup butter	*6 egg whites, beaten stiff*
4 tablespoons flour	*but not dry*
1¼ cups milk, scalded	*5 egg yolks, beaten*
Pinch of nutmeg	

Preheat oven to 350° F.

Butter an 8-inch soufflé dish and sprinkle ⅓ cup of the mixed grated cheese on the bottom and around the sides. In a saucepan melt the butter slowly—do not allow it to brown. Then add the flour, stirring constantly, until it becomes a smooth paste. Remove the pan from the heat and add the milk, stirring constantly. Return to the heat and stir constantly for about 1 minute, or until the sauce becomes smooth and thick. Remove the pan from the heat and add the nutmeg, paprika, salt and pepper. Return the pan to the heat and stir in the remaining cheese. When the mixture is smooth take the pan off the heat and allow it to cool. Beat the egg whites stiff but not dry. Add beaten egg yolks to the cheese mixture, a little at a time, stirring constantly. When the mixture is smooth carefully but thoroughly fold in a third of the egg whites with a metal spoon, then fold in the rest. Pour the batter into the prepared soufflé dish and place in the preheated oven for 40 to 45 minutes, or until it is puffed high and delicately brown. Serve immediately.

Preparation and cooking time: approximately 1 hour 10 minutes.

†SWISS CHEESE FONDUE

SERVES 4

1 clove garlic
¾ pound diced Gruyère cheese and
  ¾ pound diced Emmentaler
1¼ cups dry white wine

1½ teaspoons cornstarch
Salt and pepper to taste
Dash of nutmeg
⅓ cup kirsch

Rub an earthenware flameproof casserole with the garlic. Place over low heat, add the cheese and wine, continually stirring, allowing cheese to melt and blend with the wine. When the mixture is creamy add the cornstarch and blend with the cheese. Season with salt, pepper and a little nutmeg. As the mixture starts to boil, add the kirsch. Serve in the casserole placed over a spirit lamp at the table. The dish is traditionally accompanied by small pieces of French bread, which each person puts on a fondue fork and dunks into the cheese mixture. If the fondue becomes too thick, thin with more kirsch.

Preparation and cooking time: approximately 30 minutes.

†WELSH RAREBIT

SERVES 4

2 tablespoons butter
10 ounces grated sharp Cheddar cheese
½ cup beer or pale ale
¾ teaspoon dry mustard
¾ teaspoon Worcestershire sauce

¼ teaspoon salt
1 egg, lightly beaten
Pinch of cayenne
8 slices cold toast

In a small saucepan melt the butter over moderate heat. Add the grated cheese and stir until the cheese is melted. Slowly add the beer or ale, the mustard, Worcestershire sauce and salt. Remove the pan from the heat and stir in the beaten egg. Add a pinch of cayenne and serve immediately over cold toast.

Preparation and cooking time: approximately 30 minutes.

††FETTUCCINE WITH PESTO

SERVES 8

   10 cups water   *¼ cup butter, softened and cut into slices*
   4 teaspoons salt   *Grated Parmesan cheese*
   2 pounds fettuccine

FOR THE PESTO:

   3 cups coarse-chopped   *1 cup fresh-grated Parmesan cheese*
     fresh basil leaves   *½ cup olive oil*
   1 cup pine nuts   *Salt and pepper to taste*
   1 cup coarse-chopped
     Italian parsley

In a large saucepan bring the water and salt to the boil over high heat. Drop the fettuccine into the water, reduce the heat to moderate and cook the fettuccine for 5 to 7 minutes, until it is *al dente* or just tender. Put all the ingredients for the pesto into a blender and blend for a few seconds. Scrape down the sides of the blender and blend again until the pesto is smooth. On a heated serving dish toss the fettuccine, cooked and drained, with the butter. Top the pasta with the pesto and toss it. Serve fresh-grated Parmesan cheese separately.

Preparation and cooking time: approximately 30 minutes.

††WILD RICE WITH MUSHROOMS IN CREAM

SERVES 6

1 cup wild rice (see page 216)
1 clove garlic, minced
1 cup onion, minced
½ cup butter, plus extra for
  the mold
¼ pound chicken livers
½ teaspoon commercial
  poultry seasoning

Salt and pepper to taste
1½ pounds button mushrooms,
  stems trimmed
3 tablespoons Madeira
1½ cups heavy cream
Few drops of lemon juice

Preheat oven to 350° F.

Steam the wild rice with the minced garlic. Transfer the rice to a large bowl. In a saucepan sauté the onion in ¼ cup of the butter until it is softened. Add the chicken livers and sauté until they are browned on the outside but still pink on the inside. Transfer the livers with a slotted spoon to a board, dice them and add them, with the onion mixture, to the rice. Season the rice mixture with the poultry seasoning and salt and pepper to taste. Butter an 8-inch ring mold and fill it with the rice mixture. Put the mold in a baking pan, fill the pan with hot water to reach two-thirds of the way up the sides of the mold, and bake the rice ring in the preheated oven for 20 minutes. While the rice ring is baking, in a large frying pan sauté the mushrooms in the remaining ¼ cup of butter for 7 minutes, or until they are tender and browned. Add the Madeira and reduce the liquid over high heat to 1 tablespoon. Pour in the cream, ½ cup at a time, allowing each addition to reduce for 1 minute before adding the next. Simmer the mixture for 3 to 5 minutes, or until the sauce is thickened. Remove the pan from the heat and season the dish with a few drops of lemon juice and salt and pepper to taste. Turn out the rice ring onto a heated dish and fill the center with the mushrooms in cream.

Preparation and cooking time: approximately 1 hour.

SALADS

†MUSHROOM SALAD WITH GREEN SAUCE

SERVES 6

*1½ pounds large mushrooms,
trimmed, cleaned, with stems
removed and chopped fine*
*1 large onion, peeled and
chopped fine*

Salt and pepper to taste
Water
*1 bunch of arugola or 1 head
Cos lettuce*
Green sauce (see page 265)

Put the chopped mushroom stems in a bowl with the chopped onion,
a sprinkling of salt and pepper and enough water to moisten. Put
the mushroom caps in a large saucepan and pour the chopped-stems
mixture over them. Cover the pan and cook over moderate heat for
5 to 6 minutes. Chill the mushroom mixture, drain off all the liquid
and serve the salad with green sauce on a bed of arugola, if available,
or Cos lettuce.

Preparation time: approximately 20 minutes. Chilling time: approximately 1 to 2 hours.

GREEN SAUCE

In a bowl combine ½ cup each of watercress leaves and parsley, chopped fine, 1 garlic clove, minced, 3 tablespoons olive oil, stirred in drop by drop, 1 tablespoon lemon juice and salt and pepper to taste.

†YOGURT AND SPINACH SALAD

SERVES 4

1½ pounds fresh spinach
1 onion, chopped
Juice of 1 large lemon
½ teaspoon salt
Several grinds of pepper

1 cup plain yogurt, well beaten
Salt to taste
¼ cup slightly toasted walnuts
1 teaspoon crushed dried mint leaves or
1 tablespoon chopped fresh mint

Wash the spinach in cold water and remove and coarse stems and wilted leaves. In a saucepan simmer the spinach with the chopped onion, covered, for 10 minutes in the water that clings to the leaves. Drain the spinach well in a colander, transfer it to a wooden bowl and chop it into coarse pieces. Sprinkle the spinach with the lemon juice, salt and pepper. Stir in the yogurt, add salt to taste and transfer the mixture to a salad bowl. Sprinkle with the walnuts and mint.

Preparation time: approximately 45 minutes.

†SPINACH AND MUSHROOM SALAD WITH BACON DRESSING

SERVES 4

1 pound fresh spinach
4 slices lean bacon, diced
2 tablespoons tarragon vinegar

1½ cups mushrooms, sliced thin
2 tablespoons lemon juice
Salt and pepper to taste

Wash and dry the spinach, removing the tough stems. In a frying pan fry the bacon bits until they are crisp. Transfer with a slotted spoon to a paper towel to drain, then keep them warm. Stir the vinegar into the bacon fat and keep it warm. Put the spinach leaves in a salad bowl. Add the mushrooms combined with the lemon juice and toss the salad with the vinegar mixture, reserved bacon bits and salt and pepper to taste.

Preparation and cooking time: approximately 1 hour.

†CUCUMBER AND YOGURT SALAD

SERVES 4

4 cucumbers	1 tablespoon shallots, minced
Salt	1 tablespoon lemon juice
½ cup plain yogurt	1½ teaspoons tarragon
¼ cup sour cream	Salt and pepper to taste
2 tablespoons minced fresh dill	Chopped fresh mint

Peel the cucumbers, halve them lengthwise and scoop out the seeds. Slice thin and sprinkle with salt. Put the cucumber slices in a colander, weighing them down with a plate, and let them drain for 30 minutes. In a bowl combine the yogurt, sour cream, dill, shallots, lemon juice, tarragon and salt and pepper to taste. Pat the cucumbers dry and put them in a bowl. Toss with the yogurt dressing and chill for at least 3 hours. Serve the salad with chopped mint sprinkled on top. This is particularly good with hot curries or hot Spanish dishes as a cool contrast.

Preparation time: approximately 40 minutes. Chilling time: 3 to 4 hours.

†CHICKPEA SALAD

SERVES 6

One 1-pound 4-ounce can chickpeas, well drained
1 cup frozen shrimp
¼ cup mayonnaise

2 tablespoons chopped parsley
2 scallions, chopped
Salt to taste

In a bowl combine all the ingredients, toss well and serve immediately.

Preparation time: approximately 10 minutes.

†DILLED ASPARAGUS VINAIGRETTE

SERVES 4 TO 6

THE SALAD

2½ pounds fresh asparagus
2½ cups boiling water
3 tablespoons snipped dill
3 tablespoons minced shallots

2 tablespoons minced parsley
2 teaspoons grated lemon rind
Salt and pepper to taste

THE FRENCH DRESSING

⅔ cup safflower oil
⅓ cup lemon juice (or more, to taste)

1 teaspoon Dijon mustard
Dill to taste

Scrape and trim the asparagus. Tie it in bunches and place upright in the boiling water in the bottom half of a double boiler. Cover with the top half of the boiler set upside down. Steam for about 10 minutes, depending on the thickness of the asparagus—it should remain crisp. Transfer to a shallow dish and remove the strings. Combine all the ingredients for the dressing. While the asparagus is still warm, sprinkle it with the dill, shallots, parsley, lemon rind, salt and pepper to taste, and pour on the French dressing. Toss gently and allow to stand, covered, for 1 hour. Serve at room temperature.

Preparation time: approximately 30 minutes. Standing time: approximately 1 hour.

†BEAN-SPROUT SALAD

SERVES 4

1 pound fresh bean sprouts	*1 tablespoon wine vinegar*
2 tablespoons soy sauce	*1 tablespoon chopped scallions*
2 tablespoons sesame oil	*1 tablespoon vodka*

Put the bean sprouts in a colander and blanch them by pouring boiling water over them. Refresh the bean sprouts under cold running water, drain them thoroughly, and put them in a bowl. Toss the sprouts with all the rest of the ingredients and let the salad marinate for 1 hour, then chill it for at least 3 hours.

Preparation time: 15 minutes. Marinating time: 1 hour. Chilling time: 3 to 4 hours.

†LENTIL AND SAUSAGE SALAD

SERVES 6

1½ cups water	*¾ cup garlic French dressing*
1 cup lentils, rinsed and picked over	*3 hard-boiled eggs, sliced*
2 cups sliced smoked sausage	*1 large cooked beet, sliced*
⅓ cup minced scallions	*Minced parsley*
⅓ cup minced green pepper	

In a large saucepan combine the water and lentils and bring to the boil over high heat. Reduce the heat and simmer the lentils for 30 minutes, or until they are tender. Drain the lentils and combine them in a bowl, with the sausage, scallions and green pepper. Prepare a garlic French dressing, using the recipe on page 267, but substituting tarragon for the dill and adding 2 cloves of garlic, pressed. Pour this over the lentil-and-sausage mixture and toss well. Mound the salad in a salad bowl and top with the egg and beet slices and the minced parsley.

Preparation and cooking time: approximately 40 minutes.

††HERBED OMELETTE SALAD

SERVES 2

THE OMELETTE

4 eggs	4 teaspoons minced fresh dill
Salt and pepper to taste	4 tablespoons minced fresh parsley
2 tablespoons softened butter	4 tablespoons minced fresh chives

THE DRESSING

½ cup cucumber, peeled, seeded and coarse-grated	2 teaspoons yogurt
	Salt and pepper
	1 cooked beet, sliced
⅓ cup chopped radishes	1 large tomato, sliced
⅛ teaspoon salt	Watercress
¼ cup sour cream	

In a bowl lightly beat the eggs with salt and pepper to taste. Heat an 8-to-9-inch omelette pan over moderately high heat, add the butter and heat it until the foam subsides, tilting the pan to coat it with butter. Pour the eggs into the pan, allow them to set for a few seconds, then stir them with a fork, shaking the pan gently. Move the set eggs towards the center of the pan, tilting the pan to let any uncooked egg run to the bottom and the edge. Shake the pan again to loosen the eggs and remove it from the heat. Slide the omelette onto a plate, sprinkle it with the dill, parsley and chives and roll it up tightly. Chill the omelette.

In a colander toss the cucumber with the salt and let it drain for 30 minutes. Transfer the cucumber to a bowl and combine it with the radishes, sour cream, yogurt and salt and pepper to taste. Arrange beet and tomato slices alternately on 2 plates lined with watercress. Slice the omelette into ½-inch rounds and arrange on the beet and tomato slices. Put 1 teaspoon of the dressing on each round of omelette.

Preparation time: approximately 1 hour 15 minutes. Chilling time: 1 hour.

††MARINATED SWEET RED PEPPER AND MUSHROOM SALAD

SERVES 6

1½ cups water
⅓ cup olive oil
¼ cup white-wine vinegar
¾ teaspoon salt
Spice bag made from 3 scallions cut into pieces, 1 small stalk celery cut into pieces, 5 sprigs parsley, 2 cloves garlic, unpeeled, ¼ teaspoon thyme,

¼ teaspoon coriander seed,
¼ teaspoon peppercorns
¾ pound mushrooms, sliced thick
4 large sweet red peppers
Pepper to taste
12 black oil-cured olives, stoned and sliced

Preheat broiler.

In a heavy saucepan combine the water, olive oil, vinegar, salt and the spice bag. Simmer the marinade for 10 minutes, add the mushrooms and simmer them, covered, for 4 minutes. Transfer the mushrooms with a slotted spoon to a serving dish. Remove the spice bag, pressing out the juices into the pan. Reduce the marinade over high heat to ½ cup and reserve it. Broil the sweet red peppers under a preheated broiler 4 to 5 inches from the heat for 3 to 4 minutes on each side and both ends, or until the skins are charred. While the peppers are still warm, pull out and discard the stems. With a sharp knife peel off the skins, halve the peppers and scrape off the seeds and ribs. Quarter each pepper-half lengthwise. Add the peppers to the mushrooms, pour the reserved marinade over all and sprinkle with pepper. Chill the salad for at least 6 hours. Top it with the olive slices and serve at room temperature.

Preparation time: approximately 30 minutes. Chilling time: 6 hours.

†MEDITERRANEAN SHELLFISH SALAD

SERVES 4

½ pound cooked shrimp, shelled, deveined and cut in ½-inch pieces
1½ pounds cooked lobster meat, cut into ½-inch pieces
2 hard-boiled eggs, coarse-chopped
2 tomatoes, peeled, seeded and cut into ½-inch cubes

½ cup onion, chopped fine
½ cup mayonnaise for shellfish (see page 272)
1 head Boston lettuce
Strips of pimento
Chopped chives

In a large bowl combine the shrimp and lobster meat with the eggs, tomatoes and onion, and squeeze the mixture in cheesecloth to remove the moisture. Toss the mixture gently with the mayonnaise for shellfish until it is well blended, and add salt and pepper to taste. Transfer to a serving bowl lined with lettuce leaves and top with strips of pimento sprinkled with chives. Serve any remaining mayonnaise separately.

Preparation and cooking time: approximately 45 minutes.

MAYONNAISE FOR SHELLFISH

2 egg yolks
2 teaspoons white-wine vinegar
1 teaspoon Dijon mustard
Pinch of salt
½ cup olive oil

½ cup vegetable oil
3 tablespoons lemon juice
1 teaspoon Worcestershire sauce
Salt and pepper to taste

Put the egg yolks into the bowl of an electric mixer with the vinegar and mustard, all at room temperature, and a pinch of salt. Mix the ingredients for 2 minutes, then add the olive oil and vegetable oil in a thin stream, beating constantly. Season the mayonnaise with the lemon juice, Worcestershire sauce and salt and pepper to taste. Thin, if necessary, with 1 to 2 teaspoons warm water.

Preparation time: approximately 15 minutes.

††SALAD MUGETTE

SERVES 4 TO 6

7 large heads Belgian endive,
　cut into ¼-inch rounds
8 to 10 radishes, sliced paper-thin
1 cup mixed parsley or chervil,
　minced fine
6 small tomatoes, peeled, seeded
　and sliced thin

6 apples, peeled, cored and
　sliced thin
3 celery hearts, scraped and cut
　into matchsticks
2 cups walnuts
½ teaspoon chervil
1 teaspoon red-wine vinegar

FOR THE DRESSING:

2 small egg yolks
1 teaspoon vinegar
½ teaspoon salt
Pinch of pepper
¾ cup olive oil

2 drops Worcestershire sauce
1 drop Tabasco sauce
Dash of Dijon mustard
Pinch of sugar
⅓ cup whipped cream

This salad must be prepared just before serving or made at the table. Cover the bottom of a wide salad bowl with a layer of endive slices.

Cover the endive with a layer of radish slices. In the center of the radishes, place the parsley and chervil. Around this arrange alternately mounds of tomato, apple, celery and walnuts. Combine the chervil with the vinegar and sprinkle over the salad. Serve with the dressing poured over it at the table. In a small bowl combine the egg yolks, vinegar, salt and pepper. Stirring constantly, add ½ cup of the olive oil, drop by drop. Add the rest of the oil in a very thin stream. Still stirring, add the rest of the seasonings. Stir the sauce until thick and smooth, and fold in the cream.

Preparation time: approximately 45 minutes.

†RICE SALAD

SERVES 6
2 cups raw rice
4 cups chicken stock
¼ cup each: cooked peas, blanched almonds, walnuts, currants,
*   chopped green pepper, chopped cucumber*
French dressing (see page 267)
2 cloves garlic, pressed
1 tablespoon chives, snipped

Cook the rice in the chicken stock until it is quite dry (see page 276). Combine the cooked rice with the peas, almonds, walnuts, currants, pepper and cucumber. Prepare the French dressing, adding the garlic and chives. Pour this over the rice mixture, toss well and serve.

Preparation and cooking time: approximately 45 minutes.

†DEREK HART'S SALAD

SERVES 6

1 pound raw mushrooms, sliced (not too thin)

3 heads of purple cauliflower, divided into flowerets

FOR THE DRESSING:

½ cup olive or sesame oil

2 tablespoons vinegar

Salt and fresh-ground pepper, to taste

Combine all the ingredients for the dressing, add the vegetables and toss well.

SAUCES

To Clarify Butter

In a heavy saucepan melt butter over low heat. Allow the butter to rest for 2 to 3 minutes away from the heat and skim the froth off the top. Pour the clear butter carefully through a cheesecloth-lined sieve into a small bowl, leaving the milky solids in the bottom of the saucepan. One cup butter yields about ¾ cup clarified butter.

To Clarify Stock

For each 3¼ cups of stock, use 1 egg white, slightly beaten, and 1 egg shell, crushed. Skim all fat from the stock, add the beaten whites and crushed shells, and bring the liquid to the boil, stirring constantly. Simmer the stock for 15 minutes, remove it from the heat and allow it to stand for 5 minutes. Skim off the froth and strain the stock through several thicknesses of cheesecloth or a linen napkin. The liquid should be a good strong color and absolutely clear.

†*WHITE OR CHICKEN STOCK FOR SAUCES

MAKES 6 CUPS

1 pound veal bones	2 onions, peeled and quartered
1 pound chicken bones	2 leeks, cut into chunks
2 quarts water	Bouquet garni (4 sprigs of parsley, 1
1 teaspoon salt	stalk of celery with leaves, 1 sprig of
1 carrot, cut into chunks	thyme, bay leaf)

Parboil the bones for a few minutes, just long enough for the first scum to rise to the surface. Drain the bones, cover them with the 2 quarts of water and add the rest of the ingredients. Bring the water to the boil, skim off the fat and simmer the stock for 3 hours. Remove the fat and strain the stock. It can be stored in the refrigerator for up to 1 week or frozen indefinitely. The best method for freezing is to pour the stock into ice cube trays with the dividers in. Then freeze the stock in cubes. One ice cube tray usually holds 1 cup of stock.

†*FISH STOCK

MAKES 3 CUPS

1 pound bones and trimmings from any white fish, chopped	½ teaspoon salt
	Butter
1 cup sliced onions	3½ cups water
6 sprigs parsley	½ cup dry white wine
2 tablespoons lemon juice	

Put the fish bones and trimmings, onions, parsley, lemon juice and salt in a heavy, well-buttered saucepan and steam, covered, over moderately high heat for 5 minutes. Add the water and white wine and bring the liquid to the boil. Reduce the heat and skim the froth that rises to the surface. Simmer the stock for 25 minutes and strain it, pressing the solids so as to obtain all the liquid. Allow the stock to cool and chill it. This stock may also be frozen, using same method as for white stock (see above).

†††WHITE WINE SAUCE FOR FISH

MAKES 2 CUPS

½ cup dry white wine
½ cup fish stock (see page 276)
1 cup velouté sauce, made with
  fish stock (see below)

Salt and pepper to taste
Heavy cream
2 tablespoons butter
Few drops lemon juice

In a saucepan combine the white wine and fish stock and cook the mixture over high heat until it is reduced by half. Add the velouté sauce and salt and pepper to taste. Thin the mixture to desired consistency with cream, add the butter and lemon juice and strain the sauce.

††VELOUTÉ SAUCE

MAKES 2 CUPS

1 tablespoon minced onion
3 tablespoons butter
2 tablespoons flour

2 cups white or chicken stock (see
  page 276), or fish stock (see page
  276), scalded
¼ teaspoon salt
White pepper to taste

In a saucepan sauté the onion in the butter until it is soft. Add flour, mixing well, and cook the roux, stirring, over low heat for 3 minutes. Remove the pan from the heat and pour in the stock, stirring vigorously with a whisk until the mixture is thick and smooth. Add

salt and pepper to taste and simmer the sauce for 10 minutes. Strain
it through a fine sieve and cover it until needed with a buttered
round of waxed paper.

†*BASIC COURT BOUILLON

MAKES 6 CUPS

½ cup onions, chopped   *½ cup dry white wine*
½ cup carrots, chopped   *1 tablespoon salt*
½ cup celery, chopped   *½ teaspoon white pepper*
2 tablespoons butter   *Bouquet garni (sprigs of parsley, 1*
8 cups water   *bay leaf, 1 sprig of thyme)*
½ cup white-wine vinegar

In a saucepan cook the onions, carrots and celery in the butter,
covered, until the vegetables have softened. Add the rest of the ingredients and bring the liquid to the boil. Reduce the heat, simmer
the mixture for 25 minutes and allow it to cool.

††BASIC WHITE OR BÉCHAMEL SAUCE

MAKES APPROXIMATELY 2 CUPS

1 tablespoon onion, chopped fine   *¼ teaspoon salt*
2 tablespoons butter   *3 white peppercorns*
2 tablespoons flour   *Sprig of parsley*
3 cups milk, scalded   *Pinch of nutmeg*

In a saucepan sauté the onion in the butter until it is soft. Add the
flour, mix well and cook the roux slowly, stirring constantly, until it
just starts to turn golden. Add the milk gradually and cook the mixture, stirring vigorously with a wire whisk, until it is thick and

smooth. Add the salt, peppercorns, parsley and nutmeg. Cook the sauce slowly, stirring frequently, for about 30 minutes, or until it is reduced by one-third. Strain the béchamel through a fine sieve.

The following brown sauces and stocks will keep refrigerated for several days and last longer if they are brought to the boil every 3 days, cooled and stored in airtight jars. They also freeze well for up to 3 months.

†*BROWN STOCK

MAKES APPROXIMATELY 8 CUPS

2 pounds meaty beef bones, cracked into small pieces

2 pounds meaty veal bones, cracked into small pieces

2 onions, cubed

1 carrot, cubed

3 quarts water

1½ teaspoons salt

Pinch of thyme

Bouquet garni (4 sprigs parsley, 2 stalks celery, 1 small bay leaf)

Preheat oven to 375° F.

In a flat pan spread out the meat bones, onions and carrot. Brown the bones and vegetables well on all sides in the preheated oven. Transfer them to a large saucepan and add the water, salt, thyme and bouquet garni. Bring the water slowly to the boil, skimming the fat from the surface when necessary. Cook the stock slowly for at least 4 hours or until it is reduced by about half. Strain through a fine sieve or cheesecloth.

†*PHEASANT STOCK

MAKES APPROXIMATELY 6 CUPS

Giblets, trimmings and feet of　　*2 stalks celery*
　2 or 3 small pheasant　　　　*1 medium onion stuck with a few*
1½ teaspoons salt　　　　　　　*cloves*
A few whole peppercorns　　　　*½ bay leaf*
8 cups water　　　　　　　　　*Pinch of thyme*
3 small leeks

Blanch and skin the pheasant feet. Add them, along with the other pheasant parts and the salt and peppercorns, to the water. Bring to a boil and simmer for 1 hour, skimming frequently. Add the leeks, celery, onion, bay leaf and thyme and continue to simmer the stock for 1 hour or longer. Strain through a fine sieve and cool.

†*GAME STOCK

MAKES APPROXIMATELY 8 TO 10 CUPS

Bones and any remaining meat　　*1 teaspoon salt*
　from roast venison, pheasant,　*Few grinds black pepper*
　partridge or rabbit　　　　　*Bouquet garni (6 sprigs of*
1¼ cups onions, coarse-chopped　　*parsley, 1 bay leaf, 1 clove, ½*
1 cup celery, coarse-chopped　　　*teaspoon berries)*
1 cup carrots, coarse-chopped　　*12 cups water*
¼ pound salt pork, blanched
　and cut into pieces

Put all the ingredients into a large soup kettle. Bring the stock to the boil over high heat. Lower the heat, simmer the stock for 2½ hours, skimming the surface every 15 minutes, and strain it.

††*SAUCE ESPAGNOLE OR BROWN SAUCE

MAKES APPROXIMATELY 4 CUPS

This is used as a base for various sauces, so you should always try to keep a quantity in the freezer.

½ cup beef, veal or pork drippings
2 medium-sized onions,
  coarse-chopped
1 small carrot, coarse-chopped
½ cup flour
9 cups hot brown stock (see
  page 279)
3 sprigs parsley

1 stalk celery
1 small bay leaf
1 clove garlic, crushed
Pinch of thyme
5 tablespoons tomato sauce
  (see page 61) or tomato
  paste

Melt the drippings in a heavy saucepan. Add the onions and carrot and cook until the onions start to turn golden, shaking the pan to ensure even cooking. Add the flour and cook the mixture, stirring, until the flour, carrot and onions are a rich brown. Add 3 cups hot brown stock, the parsley, celery, bay leaf, garlic and thyme, and cook the mixture, stirring frequently, until it thickens. Add 3 cups more stock and simmer the sauce slowly, stirring occasionally, for 1 to 1½ hours, or until it is reduced to about 3 cups. As it cooks, skim off the fat that rises to the surface. Add the tomato sauce or paste, cook for a few minutes more and strain through a fine sieve. Add 3 more cups stock and continue to cook the sauce slowly for about 1 hour, skimming the surface from time to time, until it is reduced to about 4 cups. Strain the sauce and let it cool.

†SAUCE DIABLE

MAKES APPROXIMATELY 1½ CUPS

Serve with broiled poultry and meat.

*4 tablespoons very dry white wine
  or vinegar
2 shallots, chopped
8 peppercorns, crushed*

*1 cup brown sauce (see page
  281)
1 teaspoon Worcestershire
  sauce
½ teaspoon chopped parsley*

In a saucepan cook the wine or vinegar, shallots and peppercorns until the mixture is reduced to a thick paste. Add the brown sauce, Worcestershire sauce and parsley.

†SAUCE PIQUANTE

MAKES APPROXIMATELY 1½ CUPS

Serve with pork and other meats.

*3 tablespoons dry white wine
1½ tablespoons vinegar
Generous teaspoon minced shallots
1 cup brown sauce (see page 281)
1½ tablespoons sour
  gherkins, chopped fine*

*1 tablespoon chives, chopped
  fine
1 tablespoon parsley,
  chopped fine
Generous pinch tarragon,
  chopped fine*

In a saucepan cook the wine, vinegar and shallots over high heat until the mixture is reduced by half. Stir in the brown sauce and allow it to boil up twice. Remove the sauce from the heat and stir in the gherkins, chives, parsley and tarragon.

†FINES HERBES SAUCE

MAKES APPROXIMATELY 1½ CUPS
Serve with poultry and eggs.

½ cup dry white wine
1 tablespoon shallots, chopped
1 tablespoon parsley, chopped
1 tablespoon tarragon, chopped
1 tablespoon chives, chopped

1 cup brown sauce (see page 281)
Lemon juice to taste
Salt and pepper to taste
¼ cup butter, cut into nut-size
   pieces

In a saucepan combine the wine, shallots, parsley, tarragon and
chives, reserving a few of the chopped herbs. Boil the mixture until
it is reduced by half. Strain the liquid, add the brown sauce and heat
thoroughly. Add lemon juice, salt and pepper to taste, swirl in the
butter and sprinkle the sauce with the reserved chopped herbs.

†*CHINESE DUCK SAUCE

MAKES APPROXIMATELY 4 CUPS
1 pound plums, halved and pitted
1 pound apricots, halved and pitted
2½ cups cider vinegar
¾ cup water
1 cup soft brown sugar
1 cup sugar
½ cup lemon juice
¼ cup fresh ginger root,
   peeled and chopped
1 small onion, sliced

1 fresh hot green chili
   pepper, seeded and
   chopped
2 small cloves garlic, sliced
4 teaspoons salt
1 tablespoon mustard seed,
   toasted
1 cinnamon stick
One 7-ounce jar pimentos,
   rinsed and chopped

In an enamel saucepan combine the plums and apricots, half the
cider vinegar and the water, and cook the fruit, covered, over

moderate heat for 5 minutes. Reduce the heat and simmer, uncovered, for 15 minutes, or until the fruit is soft. In a large enamel saucepan combine the rest of the cider vinegar, the brown and white sugars and the lemon juice, and boil the mixture for 10 minutes. Add the fruit mixture, the ginger root, onion, green chili pepper, garlic, salt, mustard seed and cinnamon stick and simmer over low heat for 45 minutes. Add the pimentos and simmer, stirring frequently, for 45 minutes longer. Remove and discard the cinnamon and purée the mixture through the coarse disk of a food mill into a bowl. Return the puréed mixture to the saucepan and simmer it until it is thick. Transfer the sauce to sterilized preserving jars, cap the jars loosely and allow the sauce to cool. Tighten the caps and allow the sauce to stand in a dark place for at least 2 weeks.

†MADEIRA MUSHROOM SAUCE

MAKES 2 CUPS
Serve with steak.

4 tablepoons butter	*1 shallot, chopped fine*
1 pound mushroom caps, cleaned,	*⅓ cup Madeira or dry sherry*
dried and cut into thick slices	*1 cup brown sauce (see page*
½ teaspoon salt	*281)*
Pepper to taste	*½ teaspoon chopped parsley*

In a saucepan melt the butter and add the mushrooms, salt and a little pepper. Cook the mushrooms, shaking the pan frequently, until they are golden brown. Add the shallot, Madeira or dry sherry and the brown sauce. Simmer the sauce for 5 to 6 minutes and add the chopped parsley.

†CUMBERLAND SAUCE

MAKES APPROXIMATELY 2½ CUPS
Serve with roast lamb and hot ham.

1 thick-skinned orange
5 tablespoons red wine
1 pound 4 ounces red-currant jelly
4 tablespoons orange juice

2 to 3 tablespoons lemon juice
2 teaspoons dry mustard
Salt to taste

Remove zest from the orange and cut into fine julienne strips. Put the strips into a saucepan with 3 tablespoons of the red wine, bring to a rolling boil and allow to cool. Add the red-currant jelly and stir the orange and lemon juices into the wine mixture. In a dish mix the mustard with the remaining red wine to form a smooth paste and stir it into the currant mixture. Season with salt to taste.

†MINT BASTING SAUCE

MAKES APPROXIMATELY 1 CUP
Use to baste lamb roasts, or steaks or chops grilled over charcoal.

⅓ cup red wine
⅓ cup red-wine vinegar
⅓ cup water
2 cloves garlic, minced
1 small onion, minced

15 fresh mint leaves, chopped
2 to 3 sprigs fresh rosemary, chopped
4 peppercorns
Salt to taste

In a bowl combine the red wine, vinegar and water. Add all the rest of the ingredients and allow the mixture to stand for several hours or overnight at room temperature.

†HOT BARBECUE SAUCE

MAKES ENOUGH FOR 10 POUNDS MEAT

Two 22½-ounce bottles tomato
  ketchup
1 cup vinegar
1 cup butter
¾ cup Worcestershire sauce
1 clove garlic, minced

Juice of 8 lemons
2 tablespoons dry mustard
2 tablespoons Tabasco sauce
1 tablespoon onion salt
1 teaspoon pepper

In a large saucepan combine all the ingredients. Heat the sauce over low heat until the butter is melted. Raise the heat, bring the sauce to the boil and cook it for 1 minute. Stir the sauce well, and use it to baste any meat suitable for barbecuing.

††*PEPPER SAUCE

MAKES 2½ CUPS
Suitable for all game.

1 cup chopped onion
1 cup chopped carrots
¼ cup butter
2 tablespoons vegetable oil
1 pound stewing beef, cubed, or
  1 pound poultry giblets
3 tablespoons flour

1½ cups brown stock (see page
  279)
1 tablespoon tomato paste
Bouquet garni (4 sprigs parsley,
  ½ bay leaf, ¼ teaspoon thyme,
  2 bruised juniper berries)
4 peppercorns, crushed

In a deep, heavy saucepan sauté the onions and carrots in the butter and oil until they are lightly browned. Remove the vegetables with a slotted spoon and reserve them. In the fat in the pan, brown the stewing beef or giblets. Remove the meat cubes or giblets with a slotted spoon and reserve them. Add the flour to the fat remaining in the pan and cook the roux over low heat, stirring until it is lightly browned. Add the hot brown stock and cook the sauce, stirring, for approximately 5 minutes or until it is thickened. Return the vegetables and meat or giblets to the saucepan and add the tomato paste and bouquet garni. Simmer the sauce, covered, skimming it occasionally, for 3 to 4 hours. Add the peppercorns, cook the sauce for 10 minutes more, strain and discard solids.

††CHESTNUT SAUCE

MAKES 2 CUPS
Suitable for game.

2 tablespoons fat from the pan juices of a roast game bird
2 tablespoon minced onions
½ teaspoon sage
¼ teaspoon thyme
2 tablespoons flour

1½ cups chicken stock or broth, heated
⅔ cup peeled, braised, drained and chopped chestnuts (see page 137)
1 tablespoon port

To the pan juices add the onions, sage and thyme and cook over moderate heat until the onions have softened. Add the flour and cook the roux, stirring, for 3 minutes. Remove the pan from the heat, pour in the heated chicken stock or broth, stirring in the brown bits clinging to the bottom and sides of the pan, and simmer until the sauce is thickened. Stir in the chestnuts and port and simmer, covered, for 5 minutes.

††*FRUITED CURRY SAUCE WITH PINE NUTS

MAKES 2 CUPS

For game birds.

¼ cup raisins

2 tablespoons Madeira

⅔ cup dried apricots

¼ cup water

2 tablespoons sugar

Strip of lemon peel

¼ cup pine nuts

1 tablespoon clarified butter (see page 275)

2 tablespoons fat from the pan juices of a roast pheasant or duck

2 tablespoons minced onion

1 tablespoon curry powder

1 cup chicken stock or chicken broth, heated

Salt to taste

In a bowl soak the raisins in the Madeira for 30 minutes. In a covered saucepan stew the apricots with the water, sugar and lemon peel for 25 minutes. Drain the apricots, discarding the syrup, and mince them. In a frying pan brown the pine nuts in clarified butter over moderately high heat, stirring constantly. Remove the frying pan from the heat and reserve the nuts. To the pan-juice fat, add the minced onion and cook over moderate heat, stirring until softened. Add the curry powder and cook, stirring, for 1 minute more. Pour in the chicken broth or stock, stirring in the brown bits clinging to the sides and bottom of the pan. Add the apricots, the raisin mixture, the reserved nuts and salt to taste. Bring to the boil and simmer for 5 minutes.

†SPICED MUSTARD SAUCE

MAKES APPROXIMATELY 1½ CUPS

Serve on hamburgers, hot dogs, hot and cold roasts or on cottage cheese.

1 cup sour cream
2 tablespoons Dijon mustard
1 tablespoon soy sauce
1 tablespoon Worcestershire sauce

1 teaspoon grated onion
1 clove garlic, crushed
Salt and pepper to taste

Combine all the ingredients. Stored in a tight-capped jar, the sauce will keep in the refrigerator for weeks.

†GRUNE SAUCE

MAKES 1½ CUPS

Serve with boiled potatoes or sliced cold meats.

1 bunch parsley, minced
½ small onion, minced
½ cup sorrel or spinach, minced
5 borage or mint leaves, minced
1 teaspoon capers, minced
2 stalks celery, chopped fine

Olive oil to taste
Lemon juice to taste
Salt and pepper to taste
2 hard-boiled eggs, chopped
1 teaspoon whole capers

Combine the minced parsley, onion, sorrel or spinach, borage or mint leaves, minced capers and celery. Add olive oil and lemon juice in equal parts, or to taste, to make a thick sauce. Season with salt and pepper. Stir in the hard-boiled eggs and whole capers.

†CORIANDER SAUCE

MAKES APPROXIMATELY 2 CUPS
Serve with cold chicken or turkey.

2 tablespoons butter	1 teaspoon basil
2 tablespoons flour	1 teaspoon seasoned salt
1 cup heavy cream	1 teaspoon tarragon
½ cup sour cream, or plain yogurt	1 teaspoon onion powder
	1 teaspoon powdered coriander
¼ cup walnuts	½ teaspoon garlic salt
4 teaspoons dill	¼ teaspoon cayenne

In a frying pan melt the butter, blend in the flour and cook the roux over low heat, stirring, for 1 minute. Remove the pan from the heat and blend in the heavy cream and sour cream. Return the pan to the heat and bring the mixture to the boil, stirring constantly. Allow it to simmer for a few minutes, stirring often. Add the rest of the ingredients, taste the sauce and adjust the seasonings.

†HONEY AVOCADO CREAM

MAKES 1 CUP
Serve with cold meat.

1 large avocado, peeled and pitted	¼ cup honey
¼ cup lime juice	½ teaspoon crushed dried mint leaves
	Salt to taste

Cut the avocado pulp into chunks. Put it into the container of a blender with the lime juice and blend until smooth. Stir in the honey, mint leaves and salt to taste. Chill the mixture, covered, for several hours.

†CURRIED HONEY SAUCE

MAKES APPROXIMATELY 3 CUPS
Serve with crudités.

2 cups mayonnaise	1 tablespoon curry powder
3 tablespoons tomato paste	1 tablespoon lemon juice
3 tablespoons honey	2 to 3 drops Tabasco sauce
3 tablespoons chopped onion	Salt to taste

Put the mayonnaise into the container of a blender with the tomato paste, the honey, chopped onion and curry powder and blend the mixture until it is smooth. Stir in the lemon juice, Tabasco sauce and salt to taste. Chill, covered, overnight.

†SPICED GINGER SOY SAUCE

MAKES 1 CUP
Use to flavor soups, sauces and dressings.

1 tablespoon fresh ginger root, peeled and minced	½ teaspoon whole cloves
1 teaspoon whole allspice	¾ cup dry white wine
1 teaspoon whole peppercorns	⅓ cup white-wine vinegar
½ teaspoon mustard seed	2 tablespoons soy sauce

In a mortar combine the fresh ginger root, allspice, peppercorns, mustard seed and whole cloves and pound the spices lightly to bruise them. Transfer to a small saucepan, add the wine and vinegar and simmer for 8 minutes. Strain the mixture into a bowl, discarding the spices, and add soy sauce. Pour into a hot sterilized jar and cap it. This sauce will keep almost indefinitely.

†BACON TOMATO SAUCE

MAKES APPROXIMATELY 2 CUPS
Serve with pasta.

1 tablespoon butter
½ pound lean bacon, diced
½ pound mushrooms, sliced
1 clove garlic, chopped fine

6 tomatoes, peeled and sliced
3 to 4 fresh basil leaves
Salt and pepper to taste

In a heavy frying pan melt the butter and sauté the diced bacon until it is very crisp. Remove the bacon and keep it warm. In the same pan sauté the mushrooms and garlic for 3 minutes. Add the tomatoes, basil leaves and salt and pepper to taste. Cook the sauce for 4 to 5 minutes, or until it is slightly thick and the tomatoes are soft. Stir in the reserved bacon.

†APPLE SAUCE WITH ORANGE

MAKES APPROXIMATELY 2 CUPS
Particularly good with pork.

2 pounds unpeeled cooking apples,
*   cored and quartered*
½ cup orange juice
2 tablespoons lemon juice

⅓ cup light-brown sugar
1½ tablespoons grated
*   orange rind*

Put the apples in a saucepan with the orange and lemon juice and cook, covered, for about 20 minutes, or until the apples are tender. Stir in the sugar and put the mixture through a sieve or through the fine disk of a food mill. Stir in the orange rind.

††SAUSAGE SAUCE

MAKES APPROXIMATELY 4 CUPS
Serve with pasta.

½ pound mild Italian sausage
½ pound hot Italian sausage
2 tablespoons water
2 tablespoons butter
2 cups onion, minced
1½ cups celery, minced
1 clove garlic, minced
One 1-pound can Italian plum
   tomatoes
1 small can tomato paste

1 cup red wine
1 tablespoon chopped parsley
1 tablespoon oregano
2 teaspoons salt
1 teaspoon sugar
¼ teaspoon ground cumin
¼ teaspoon cayenne
¼ teaspoon black pepper
1 bay leaf

In a large, deep frying pan, cook the sausages in the water, turning them, until the water has evaporated and the sausages have browned on all sides. Remove the sausages with a slotted spoon and cut them into thirds. Melt the butter in the same frying pan, add the onion, celery and garlic, and sauté them until soft. In a bowl combine all the rest of the ingredients and add them to the frying pan with the reserved sausages. Simmer the sauce, uncovered, for 2 hours. Serve hot.

††BÉARNAISE SAUCE

MAKES APPROXIMATELY 1½ CUPS
Delicious with steak or eggs.

1 cup butter
3 sprigs tarragon, chopped fine
2 teaspoons chervil, chopped fine
2 shallots, chopped fine
4 crushed peppercorns
4 tablespoons tarragon vinegar
4 tablespoons white wine

1 tablespoon cold water
3 egg yolks
Salt and cayenne to taste
1 teaspoon tarragon, chopped fine
1 teaspoon chervil, chopped fine

Have the butter, divided into 12 parts, at room temperature. In a small, heavy saucepan combine the tarragon, chervil and shallots, the peppercorns, vinegar and white wine. Cook the mixture over high heat until all but 1 tablespoon of liquid has evaporated. Add the cold water and strain if desired. Add the egg yolks and stir the mixture briskly with a wire whisk until it is thick and creamy. Set the pan over low heat and beat in the butter, one part at a time, lifting the pan occasionally to cool the mixture. Make sure that each part of the butter is completely melted before adding more. Continue to beat the sauce until it is thick and firm. Season it with salt and cayenne to taste and add the remaining tarragon and chervil.

†QUICK BÉARNAISE SAUCE

MAKES APPROXIMATELY 1½ CUPS
If you are short of time.

2 tablespoons white wine
1 tablespoon tarragon vinegar
2 teaspoons chopped shallots
2 teaspoons fresh tarragon, chopped,
  or 1 teaspoon dried

¼ teaspoon pepper
1½ cups hollandaise sauce
  (see page 296)

In a saucepan combine the white wine, vinegar, shallots, tarragon and pepper and cook over high heat until all but 1 tablespoon of the liquid has evaporated. Pour the mixture into the hollandaise sauce and put into the container of a blender. Cover and blend at high speed for 4 seconds.

†CHORON SAUCE
Serve with broiled meats and fish.
To 1 cup béarnaise sauce add 4 tablespoons thick tomato paste.

†MAYONNAISE

MAKES APPROXIMATELY 2 CUPS

4 egg yolks	*1 teaspoon salt*
2 teaspoons warm water	*Pinch of pepper*
1 teaspoon Dijon mustard	*1 teaspoon vinegar*
Juice of 1 lemon	*1½ cups olive oil*

Combine all the ingredients except the oil. Add the oil, a few drops at a time, beating constantly with a whisk until the sauce begins to thicken. Then continue adding oil in a thin stream, beating steadily, until all is absorbed.

†GREEN MAYONNAISE
Serve with salmon.
To 2 cups stiff mayonnaise add 2 tablespoons fine-chopped parsley, 1 tablespoon each of chopped chives and tarragon and 1 teaspoon each of chopped dill and chervil. Mix the sauce well, and let it stand for at least 2 hours before serving.

†HOLLANDAISE SAUCE

MAKES APPROXIMATELY 2 CUPS
Serve with fish, vegetables, eggs.

1 cup butter
2 tablespoons white-wine vinegar
2 tablespoons water
¼ teaspoon salt
Fresh-ground white pepper

1 tablespoon cold water
3 egg yolks
Lemon juice to taste
Salt to taste
Cayenne to taste

Have the butter, divided into 12 parts, at room temperature. In a small, heavy saucepan combine the white-wine vinegar and the 2 tablespoons water with the salt and few grinds of pepper and cook over high heat until reduced to one tablespoon. Remove the pan from the heat and add the 1 tablespoon of cold water. Add the egg yolks and stir briskly with a wire whisk until thick and creamy. Set the pan over low heat and beat in the butter, one part at a time, lifting the pan occasionally to cool the mixture. Make sure that each part of the butter is completely melted before adding more. Continue to beat the sauce until it is thick and firm. Add lemon juice, salt and cayenne to taste. (Note: If a thicker sauce is desired, use 4 egg yolks. If a thinner sauce is desired, use 2 egg yolks, or thin it by adding 1 or 2 tablespoons cream or hot water.) Keep the sauce warm in a shallow pan of warm water until needed. It may be refrigerated for a few days and reheated over hot water, beating constantly. Add a few teaspoons cream while reheating if the sauce is too thick.

†QUICK HOLLANDAISE SAUCE

MAKES APPROXIMATELY 1¼ CUPS
To make if you are short of time.

½ cup butter
3 egg yolks
2 teaspoons lemon juice

¼ teaspoon salt
Few grains of cayenne

In a saucepan heat the butter until it begins to bubble. Put the egg yolks in the container of a blender with the lemon juice, salt and a few grains of cayenne. Cover the container and turn the blender on and immediately off. Put the blender on high speed, remove the cover and gradually pour the hot butter into the mixture. Turn off the blender. If the hollandaise is to be served at once, pour it into a small, heavy pan or bowl and set it in a pan of barely warm water. If the sauce must be reheated, set it in a pan of hot water and beat it constantly with a whisk until warm and fluffy.

†MOUSSELINE SAUCE

MAKES 1¼ CUPS

Into 1 cup hollandaise sauce fold 2 to 4 tablespoons whipped cream. Serve at once with vegetables, eggs or poached fish. Or spread over a fish or asparagus dish and put under a broiler to brown.

†MALTESE SAUCE

MAKES 1¼ CUPS

To 1 cup hollandaise sauce add 2 to 3 tablespoons orange juice and fine-grated orange zest to taste. Use a blood orange or add 1 to 2 drops red food coloring. Serve with asparagus and broccoli.

†SAUCE GRIBICHE

MAKES APPROXIMATELY 2½ CUPS
Serve with hot fish, cold meats and cold vegetables.

3 hard-boiled eggs	*½ cup vinegar*
½ teaspoon salt	*4 tablespoons sour pickles*
1 teaspoon dry English mustard	*1 tablespoon chopped parsley,*
Dash of pepper	*chervil, tarragon and chives,*
1½ cups olive oil	*mixed*

Mash the egg yolks in a bowl and add the salt, mustard and pepper. Add the olive oil and vinegar alternately, little by little, beating vigorously after each addition and adding the vinegar whenever the mixture begins to get too thick. Add the hard-boiled egg whites, chopped fine, the pickle and herbs.

†CHEESE SAUCE

MAKES APPROXIMATELY 2 CUPS

1 tablespoon cornstarch	*8 ounces Emmentaler cheese, grated*
1 cup light cream	*Salt, pepper and nutmeg to taste*
3 eggs, well beaten	

In a bowl dissolve the cornstarch in a few tablespoons of the cream. Add the remaining cream and the eggs. Stir in the grated cheese, the salt, pepper and nutmeg. Pour over puréed potatoes or spinach in a shallow dish and bake until the sauce is puffy.

†CHEESE AND WINE SAUCE

MAKES APPROXIMATELY 1 CUP

¼ cup white wine	*¼ teaspoon salt*
¼ cup light cream	*Pinch of pepper*
¼ cup butter	*½ teaspoon cornstarch mixed*
1½ ounces grated Gruyère cheese	*with 1½ teaspoons water*

In a saucepan combine the white wine, light cream and butter and heat the mixture until the butter is melted. Add the grated cheese, salt, pepper and cornstarch mixed with water. Cook the sauce, stirring, until it is hot. Serve it over poached chicken breasts, skinned and boned.

†CHEESE AND MUSSEL SAUCE

MAKES APPROXIMATELY I CUP

½ pound grated Cheddar cheese
¼ cup milk
I teaspoon butter

Pinch each of salt and cayenne
I egg, lightly beaten
3½ ounces shelled steamed mussels

In the top of a double boiler, over boiling water, combine the grated cheese, milk, butter, salt and cayenne. Heat the mixture, stirring, until the cheese is melted. Remove the pan from the heat and add the beaten egg and mussels. Serve the sauce over toast.

†PORTUGUESE CUCUMBER SAUCE

MAKES APPROXIMATELY 2 CUPS
Serve with broiled or boiled fish.

I medium cucumber, peeled and chopped fine
2 thick slices Spanish onion, chopped fine
I clove garlic, chopped fine
½ teaspoon lemon juice

3 tablespoons sour cream
2 tablespoons Worcestershire sauce
I teaspoon mayonnaise
Salt and pepper to taste

Blend the cucumber, onion and garlic into the lemon juice. Put the mixture in a piece of cheesecloth and squeeze out the moisture. In a bowl combine this mixture with the rest of the ingredients and chill the sauce by putting the bowl over crushed ice.

†CHIVE SOUR-CREAM SAUCE

MAKES APPROXIMATELY 1½ CUPS
Serve with cold fish dishes.

1 cup sour cream   *Pinch of sugar*
2 tablespoons lime juice   *Salt and pepper to taste*
2 teaspoons minced chives

Combine all the ingredients thoroughly and chill the sauce. Beat well before serving.

†*BRANDIED CHOCOLATE SAUCE

MAKES APPROXIMATELY 2 CUPS

¾ cup superfine granulated   *2 ounces semisweet chocolate,*
  sugar   *broken into bits*
½ cup heavy cream   *3 tablespoons Cognac*
2 tablespoons butter   *½ teaspoon vanilla extract*

In a saucepan combine the sugar, cream, butter and chocolate, and cook over low heat, stirring, until the butter and chocolate are melted. Increase the heat to moderate, bring the mixture to a simmer, stirring, and simmer it for 5 minutes. Remove the pan from the heat and add the Cognac and vanilla, stirring. Allow the sauce to cool for 5 minutes and serve it warm.

BAKING: BREAD, BISCUITS, COOKIES AND CAKE

A Note on Dough

If dough is set in a properly warm place (85 to 90° F.), it will usually double in size in 1 to 2 hours on the first rising. Subsequent risings generally take less time. To test, touch the surface lightly with a finger. If a dent remains, the dough has risen enough. If the depression fills in quickly, the dough needs to rise more. Excessive rising may give the bread a sour taste. Insufficient rising makes it tough or soggy and lumpy.

††*CUMIN BREAD

⅓ cup softened butter
¼ cup brown sugar
6 tablespoons honey
2 teaspoons salt
2 cups scalded milk
5 tablespoons orange juice
1½ tablespoons active dried yeast
3 tablespoons lukewarm water

Pinch of sugar
1 egg, beaten
1 pound 2 ounces whole-wheat
  flour
3 cups sifted flour
1 tablespoon ground cumin
2 tablespoons butter

Preheat oven to 425° F.

In a bowl combine the softened butter with the brown sugar and 4 tablespoons of the honey, and add the salt. Add the scalded milk and let the mixture cool to lukewarm. Add the orange juice. Dissolve the yeast in the lukewarm water and a pinch of sugar for 5 minutes and add it to the milk mixture. Add the egg and combine the mixture well. Beat in the whole-wheat flour, 2 cups of the sifted flour and the cumin. Turn dough onto a well-floured board and knead in the remaining flour or enough to make a smooth dough. Put the dough in a well-buttered bowl and turn to coat it on all sides with the butter. Cover the dough with a linen towel and let it rise in a warm place for 1 hour, or until it has doubled in bulk. Punch the dough down and knead it on a floured board for 1 minute. Butter the bowl again, add the dough and turn to coat it on all sides with the butter. Cover the dough and let it rise for 30 minutes. Punch the dough down and divide it in half. Shape each half into a loaf and put each loaf into a well-buttered loaf pan, 9 inches by 5 inches. Cover the loaves and let them rise in a warm place until they have doubled in bulk. Bake the loaves in the preheated oven for 10 minutes. Lower the heat to moderate (350° F.), and bake for 25 to 30 minutes more, or until the bread is golden and sounds hollow when tapped. Let the loaves cool. Turn them out of the pans, and brush the tops with a mixture of 2 tablespoons of softened butter and the remaining 2 tablespoons honey.

††*DILL BREAD

1 tablespoon active dried yeast *1 teaspoon salt*
3 tablespoons warm water *¼ teaspoon baking powder*
1 cup creamed cottage cheese *1 egg*
2 tablespoons sugar *2¼ cups flour*
1 tablespoon butter *Melted butter*
1 tablespoon chopped onion *Salt*
2 teaspoons dill seed

Preheat oven to 350° F.

Dissolve the yeast in the warm water. In a large bowl combine the cheese with the sugar, butter, chopped onion, dill seed, salt, baking powder, egg and the yeast mixture. Gradually add the flour, beating well after each addition. Cover the bowl with a light towel and let the dough rise in a warm place (85 to 90° F.), for 50 to 60 minutes, or until it has doubled in size. Punch down the dough, turn into a well-buttered 10-cup round casserole and let it rise for 30 to 40 minutes in the same warm temperature (85 to 90° F.), or until it is light. Bake in the preheated oven for 40 to 50 minutes. Brush with butter, sprinkle with salt and allow to cool on a wire rack.

††*RAISIN BREAD

1½ tablespoons active dried yeast
¼ cup hot water
2½ cups flour
½ cup sugar
⅔ cup scalded milk
⅓ cup butter, softened
  and cut into bits
½ teaspoon ground cardamom
½ teaspoon salt
2 egg yolks

Grated rind of 1 lemon and
  1 orange
Melted butter
1⅓ cups raisins
Egg wash made from 1 egg
  yolk, lightly beaten and combined with 1 teaspoon water
⅓ cup sliced blanched almonds
3 to 4 tablespoons coarse sugar
  crystals

Preheat oven to 350° F.

In a small bowl dissolve the yeast in ¼ cup hot water with 2 tablespoons of the flour and 3 tablespoons of the sugar for 10 minutes. In a large bowl combine the scalded milk, the remaining sugar, the butter, cardamom and salt, stir the mixture until the butter is melted and allow it to cool to lukewarm. Add the egg yolks, grated lemon and orange rinds, the yeast mixture and 2 cups of the flour, 4 tablespoons at a time, and beat the mixture for 1 minute or until it is smooth. Turn the dough out onto a lightly floured surface and knead in the remaining flour, or just enough to make a very soft dough. Put the dough in a buttered bowl, brush the top with melted butter and allow it to rise, covered, in a warm place for 1 hour, or until it has doubled in bulk. Punch down the dough and knead in the raisins. Cut off one-third of the dough. Divide the larger piece into thirds and roll each piece into an 18-inch strip. Braid the strips, lay the braid diagonally on a buttered baking sheet and flatten it slightly. Brush the dough with egg wash. Braid the remaining dough in the same manner and arrange the braid on top of the larger braid, tucking the ends underneath. Brush the dough with the remaining egg wash and sprinkle it with the almonds and coarse sugar crystals. Allow the dough to rise in a warm place for 20 minutes and bake in the preheated oven for

30 minutes. Cover the bread lightly with a sheet of foil, bake it for 20 minutes more and transfer it to a rack.

††*WHOLE-WHEAT HONEY BREAD

1½ tablespoons active dried yeast
4 tablespoons hot water
1¼ cups hot water
4 tablespoons honey

2 tablespoons vegetable
   shortening
1¼ teaspoons salt
1½ cups whole-wheat flour
2¾ cups sifted flour

Preheat oven to 375° F.

Sprinkle the yeast over the 4 tablespoons of hot water to soften. In a large bowl combine the 1¼ cups of hot water with the honey, shortening and salt. Stir until the honey and shortening are melted and allow to cool to lukewarm. Add the yeast, sift in the whole-wheat flour and 1 cup of the sifted flour and beat the mixture until it is well combined. Add the rest of the sifted flour, or enough to make a moderately stiff dough. Turn the dough out on a well-floured board and knead for 10 minutes, or until it is very smooth and elastic. Transfer the dough to a well-greased bowl, turn it once and let it stand, covered, in a warm place away from draft for about 1½ hours, or until it has doubled in bulk. Punch the dough down, turn it out onto a floured board and form it into a ball. Let the dough stand, covered, for 10 minutes. Shape the dough into a loaf and put it into a well-greased loaf pan, 9 by 5 by 3 inches. Let the dough stand again, covered and away from drafts, until it has doubled in bulk. Bake in the preheated oven for 40 to 45 minutes, or until it is golden brown and sounds hollow when tapped. Turn the loaf out onto a wire rack and cool.

††*HOT CROSS BUNS

MAKES APPROXIMATELY 18

1 tablespoon active dried yeast
¼ cup hot water
1 teaspoon sugar
¼ cup butter, softened
  and cut into bits
4 tablespoons superfine granulated
  sugar
1 teaspoon cinnamon
½ teaspoon salt

1 cup scalded milk
2 eggs, lightly beaten
3½ cups flour
½ cup currants
1 egg white, lightly beaten
9 tablespoons confectioners'
  sugar, sifted
1½ tablespoons milk
¼ teaspoon vanilla

Preheat oven to 350° F.

In a small bowl soften the active dried yeast in the hot water and 1 teaspoon sugar for 10 minutes. In a large bowl combine the softened butter, 4 tablespoons superfine sugar, the cinnamon and the salt. Stir the scalded milk into the butter mixture and let cool to lukewarm. Add the yeast mixture and the eggs. Gradually beat in enough flour to make a soft dough and add the currants. Butter the top of the dough lightly and set it to rise, covered, in a warm place for 1½ hours, or until it has doubled in bulk. Punch down the dough and cut off pieces large enough to shape into balls about 2 inches in diameter. Arrange the balls on a buttered baking sheet so that they touch one another, and let them rise, covered, in a warm place for about 45 minutes or until they have doubled in bulk. With the blunt edge of a knife, mark each bun with a cross and brush the buns with beaten egg white. Bake in the preheated oven for 20 to 25 minutes, or until they are golden, and transfer them to a rack. In a small bowl combine the confectioners' sugar, milk and vanilla and dribble the glaze over the buns, forming a cross, while they are still warm.

††*SAUSAGE BREAD

1½ tablespoons active dried yeast
4 tablespoons hot water
1 cup sugar
1½ cups hot milk
¼ cup butter
1 teaspoon salt

3 eggs, well beaten
3 cups sifted flour
1 pound sausage meat, cut into
   1-inch cubes, parboiled and
   sautéed until cooked
Melted butter

Preheat oven to 300° F.

Dissolve the yeast in the hot water. Mix together the sugar, hot milk, butter and salt, and stir until the butter is melted. Cool the mixture to lukewarm and beat in the eggs, then the yeast mixture. Gradually beat in the flour, blending the dough until smooth. Turn onto a well-floured board and sprinkle with flour. Knead for 15 to 20 minutes or until it is very smooth and small blisters appear on the surface, adding more flour to the board if necessary. Transfer the dough to a buttered bowl, cover with a damp towel and let it rise in a warm place for about 2 hours, or until doubled in size. Punch the dough down and work in the sausage meat. Shape the dough into 2 long loaves, transfer to buttered loaf pans, 24 by 6, and flatten to shape of the pans. Let the dough rise in a warm place for about 1 hour or until doubled in size. Bake in the preheated oven for about 20 minutes or until it is golden brown and skewer inserted in the center comes out clean. Brush with a little melted butter and cool on a wire rack.

††*WALNUT BREAD

2½ cups flour
2 tablespoons sugar
1 tablespoon salt
1½ tablespoons active dried yeast
1½ cups hot milk

½ cup butter, melted and
   cooled
1 small onion, chopped fine
½ cup chopped walnuts

Preheat oven to 400° F.

Into a bowl sift together the flour, sugar and salt. In a small bowl dissolve the yeast in ½ cup of the hot milk. Make a well in the flour and pour in the dissolved yeast, the remaining milk and the melted butter. Knead the dough for about 10 minutes, or until it forms a ball and is smooth. Cover the bowl and let the dough rise in a warm place for 2 hours. Punch down the dough and add the onion and chopped walnuts. Shape the dough into 4 rounds, put them on 2 buttered baking sheets and let them rise for 45 minutes. Bake the loaves in the preheated oven for 45 minutes. Cool on a wire rack.

††*WHOLE-MEAL BROWN BREAD

2 tablespoons fresh yeast or   1 teaspoon salt
  1½ tablespoons dried yeast   3 pounds whole-meal flour
2 tablespoons brown sugar   2 tablespoons lard
3 tablespoons slightly warmed milk

Preheat oven to 375 to 400° F.

Put the yeast in a bowl with the brown sugar and the milk. Leave in a warm place to activate for an hour. Mix the salt with the flour in a large bowl and rub in the fat. Make a well in the middle of the flour mixture, pour the yeast into it and mix together for a couple of minutes. Sprinkle the top of the dough with flour and put in a warm place to rise for 1 hour, or until it has doubled in size. Flour a board and work the dough lightly with the fingertips, folding it over and over. Leave in a warm place to rise for 30 minutes, then repeat the kneading process. Leave for 45 minutes. Bake in deep, buttered 10-inch loaf pan for 45 minutes. The bread is done when a skewer inserted in the center comes out clean.

†*APPLE TEA BREAD

½ cup butter
1¼ cups brown sugar
2 eggs
2 tablespoons sour cream
1 large cooking apple, chopped
2 cups flour

2 tablespoons baking powder
1 teaspoon baking soda
1 teaspoon salt
¼ teaspoon each ginger,
   cinnamon and nutmeg
1 cup chopped walnuts

Preheat oven to 350° F.

Cream the butter and gradually beat in the brown sugar. Cream the mixture until very light. Add the eggs, 1 at a time, beating well after each addition. Stir in the sour cream and chopped apple. Sift the flour, baking powder, baking soda and salt together with the spices. Toss the walnuts into the flour mixture and add to the apple batter, mixing well. Spread the batter evenly in a buttered 9-inch loaf pan and allow to stand for 20 minutes. Bake in the preheated oven for about 1¼ hours or until a skewer inserted in the center comes out clean.

†*MRS. GORDON DOUGLAS III'S APRICOT NUT BREAD

1 cup boiling water
1 pound dried apricots
2 tablespoons butter
1 teaspoon salt
1½ cups sugar

2 eggs, well beaten
1⅓ cups whole-meal flour
3 cups flour
2 teaspoons baking powder
1¼ cups walnuts

Preheat oven to 350° F.

Pour the boiling water over the cut-up apricots. Stir in the butter, salt and sugar, and cool. Add the eggs, then sift the flours together with the baking powder and add to the apricot mixture. Add walnuts and pour into two 9-inch bread tins. Bake for 1 hour or until a skewer inserted in the center comes out clean.

†*AVOCADO BREAD

1⅓ cups sifted flour	1 egg, lightly beaten
¾ cup superfine granulated sugar	1 small avocado, mashed
1 teaspoon baking powder	¾ cup buttermilk or sour milk
¼ teaspoon salt	¾ cup chopped pecan nuts

Preheat oven to 350° F.

Sift the flour together with the sugar, baking powder and salt. In a separate bowl combine the beaten egg, mashed avocado, buttermilk and pecans. Add the avocado mixture to the dry ingredients, mixing only until all the flour is moistened. Pour the batter into a buttered loaf pan, 9 by 5 by 3 inches, and bake in the preheated oven for about 1 hour or until a skewer inserted in the center comes out clean. Serve sliced thin and spread with whipped cream cheese.

†*CRACKLING CORN BREAD

1 cup diced pork	1½ teaspoons baking powder
1 cup corn meal	½ teaspoon salt
¼ cup flour	1 cup buttermilk or sour milk
2 teaspoons sugar	1 egg, lightly beaten

Preheat oven to 400° F.

In a heavy frying pan render the diced pork fat over low heat until the crackling has browned, and transfer the cracklings with a slotted spoon to paper towels. Into a bowl sift together the corn meal, flour, sugar, baking powder and salt and stir in the buttermilk, beaten egg and the cracklings. Heat a 9-inch round cake tin in the preheated oven for 10 minutes, then grease it with bacon fat. Pour in the batter and bake it for 25 minutes, or until it is golden and a skewer inserted in the center comes out clean. Cut the bread into wedges.

†*GINGER BANANA BREAD

¾ cup sugar	3 teaspoons baking powder
⅓ cup vegetable fat	½ teaspoon salt
2 eggs	2 ripe bananas
1½ cups flour	4 tablespoons ginger marmalade

Preheat oven to 350° F.

In the bowl of an electric mixer, cream the sugar and vegetable fat. Add the eggs and beat the mixture until it is light and fluffy. Sift the flour with the baking powder and salt. Mash the bananas and blend them with the ginger marmalade. Add the dry ingredients to the sugar mixture alternately with the banana mixture and blend the batter well. Spoon it into an 8-by-11-inch loaf pan, greased and lined with waxed paper. Bake in the preheated oven for about 70 minutes or until it is lightly browned on top and a skewer inserted in the center comes out clean. Allow the bread to cool in the pan for 20 minutes, transfer it to a plate and slice while it is still warm.

†*IRISH BROWN BREAD

5 cups whole-meal flour	1 teaspoon salt
2½ cups flour	½ pound butter
⅓ cup sugar	2 eggs
2 teaspoons baking powder	2¼ cups buttermilk or sour milk

Preheat oven to 400° F.

Mix both flours together with the sugar, baking powder and salt. Work in the butter until the mixture resembles fine bread crumbs. In a separate bowl beat the eggs until frothy and stir in the sour milk. Make a well in the center of the dry ingredients and gradually add the egg mixture until you have formed a stiff dough. Turn the dough out onto a floured board and knead. Divide the dough in half and shape into rounds. Flatten the tops slightly and cut a cross about ½ inch deep with a pointed knife. Put the loaves on a greased baking sheet and bake in the preheated oven for 1 hour.

†*JASMINE TEA BREAD

1 cup superfine granulated sugar	*1 teaspoon baking powder*
¼ cup melted butter	*1 teaspoon baking soda*
1 egg, lightly beaten	*½ teaspoon salt*
1 tablespoon grated orange rind	*¼ teaspoon cinnamon*
1 teaspoon grated lemon rind	*¾ cup orange juice*
1 teaspoon grated lime rind	*½ cup jasmine tea*
3 cups flour	*½ cup chopped pecan nuts*

Preheat oven to 350° F.

In a bowl combine the sugar and melted butter until light. Add the egg, and the orange, lemon and lime rinds. Into a bowl sift together the flour, baking powder, baking soda, salt and cinnamon. Add the flour mixture to the butter mixture alternately with the orange juice and jasmine tea combined, beating well after each addition. Add the nuts and combine the batter well. Turn into a well-buttered loaf pan, 9 by 5 by 3 inches, and let stand for 20 minutes. Bake the loaf in the preheated oven for 45 minutes or until a skewer inserted in the center comes out clean. Allow the bread to cool in the pan for 10 minutes, then turn it out on a wire rack to cool completely.

†*ORANGE OATMEAL LOAF

1 orange
2 tablespoons superfine granulated sugar
1½ cups flour
¾ cup superfine granulated sugar
4½ teaspoons baking powder
½ teaspoon salt

¼ teaspoon baking soda
1 cup rolled oats
2 lightly beaten eggs
2 tablespoons melted
  butter
⅔ cup water

Preheat oven to 350° F.

Grate the rind of 1 orange and reserve it. Remove the white membrane, slice the orange thin, and discard the seeds. Cut each slice into small pieces, mix with the 2 tablespoons of sugar and reserve. In a bowl sift together the flour, ¾ cup sugar, the baking powder, salt and baking soda. Stir in the rolled oats. In a separate bowl mix the lightly beaten eggs with the melted butter, reserved orange mixture, grated orange rind and water. Stir the orange mixture into the dry ingredients until blended. Pour the batter into an oiled loaf pan, 9 by 5 by 3 inches, and bake in the preheated oven for about 1 hour, or until a skewer inserted in the center comes out clean. Or, alternatively, pour the batter into 6 small oiled bread pans, 4 by 2 inches, and bake for 35 to 40 minutes, or until done. Serve with unsalted butter.

†*SOMERSET SPICED BREAD

2 cups sifted flour
¾ cup white raisins
½ cup light-brown sugar
½ cup chopped mixed
  candied fruit
1 teaspoon ground ginger
½ teaspoon ground cloves

½ teaspoon cinnamon
5 tablespoons milk
1 egg, beaten
1 teaspoon baking soda
8 tablespoons molasses
4 teaspoons black treacle

Preheat oven to 300° F.

In a bowl combine the flour with the raisins, brown sugar, candied fruit, ginger, cloves and cinnamon. In another bowl combine the milk with the egg and baking soda. In a saucepan warm the molasses and black treacle. Remove the pan from the heat and stir in the milk mixture. Add this to the flour mixture, stir the batter well and pour it into a well-buttered loaf pan, 9 by 5 by 3 inches. Bake the bread in the preheated oven for 1½ hours or until a skewer inserted in the center comes out clean. Allow to cool on a wire rack and serve with fresh butter.

†*SPICE BREAD

1¼ cups boiling water	*1 teaspoon ground aniseed*
1 cup sugar	*1 teaspoon cinnamon*
1 cup clear honey	*4 cups sifted flour*
2½ teaspoons baking powder	*3 tablespoons blanched almonds*
Pinch of salt	*2 tablespoons chopped citron*
3 tablespoons rum	*½ teaspoon grated orange rind*

Preheat oven to 450° F.

Stir together the boiling water, sugar, honey, baking powder and salt until the sugar is dissolved. Thoroughly mix in the rum, aniseed and cinnamon. Stir the mixture slowly into the flour to make a smooth batter. Add the blanched almonds, citron and orange rind. Pour the batter into a buttered loaf pan, 9 by 5 by 3 inches, and bake in the preheated oven for 10 minutes. Reduce the temperature to moderate (350° F.) and bake for about 1¼ hours more or until a skewer inserted in the center comes out clean.

††*SPICED HONEY LOAVES

MAKES 2 LOAVES

*1 cup buckwheat honey or
    dark, clear flower honey*
1 teaspoon cinnamon
½ teaspoon ground ginger
½ teaspoon ground nutmeg
¼ teaspoon ground cloves
1¼ teaspoons baking soda
6 tablespoons butter
*½ cup firmly packed dark-brown
    sugar*
4 egg yolks

2¼ cups flour
1¼ teaspoons baking powder
¼ teaspoon salt
¾ cup raisins
*¾ cup chopped toasted
    blanched almonds*
½ cup dried currants
4 egg whites, beaten until stiff
*Halved blanched almonds, to
    decorate*

Preheat oven to 325° F.

In a heavy saucepan bring the honey to the boil and stir in the cinnamon, ground ginger, nutmeg and cloves. Add the baking soda and allow the mixture to cool. In a bowl cream together the butter and dark-brown sugar and add the egg yolks, one at a time, and the honey mixture. Into another bowl sift together 2 cups of the flour, baking powder and salt and sift the mixture, half at a time, into the honey mixture. In a small bowl combine the raisins, chopped almonds and currants, toss the mixture with the remaining ¼ cup of flour and add it to the batter. In another bowl beat the egg whites until they hold stiff peaks, fold a quarter of them lightly into the batter, then fold in the remaining egg whites. Line 2 buttered loaf pans, 7½ by 3½ by 2 inches, with buttered sheets of brown paper and pour the batter into the pans. Decorate the tops with halved blanched almonds and bake the loaves in the preheated oven for 1 hour. Turn the loaves out onto a rack and allow them to cool. The loaves will keep for 3 to 4 weeks, tightly wrapped.

†*BLUEBERRY CORN MUFFINS

MAKES 12 MUFFINS

1 cup corn meal　　　　　　　*1 cup milk*
1 cup flour　　　　　　　　　*1 cup blueberries*
⅓ cup superfine granulated sugar　*⅓ cup butter, melted*
2½ teaspoons baking powder　　*1 egg, lightly beaten*
¼ teaspoon salt　　　　　　　*2 teaspoons grated lemon rind*

Preheat oven to 400° F.

In a bowl combine the corn meal, flour, sugar, baking powder and salt, and add the milk, blueberries, melted butter, egg and grated lemon rind. Stir the batter lightly, spoon it into 12 buttered 3-inch muffin tins, and bake the muffins in the preheated oven for 25 to 30 minutes, or until they are golden.

†*BLUEBERRY SCONES

MAKES 18 SCONES

1⅓ cups flour　　　　　　　　*⅓ cup buttermilk*
2½ tablespoons superfine granulated　*1 egg*
　sugar　　　　　　　　　　*1 cup blueberries tossed with 1*
1 tablespoon baking powder　　　*teaspoon flour*
½ teaspoon salt　　　　　　　*1 egg white*
⅓ cup butter, softened and　　　*Sugar, for topping*
　cut into bits

Preheat oven to 350° F.

In a large bowl sift together the flour, sugar, baking powder and salt. Add the softened butter, and blend the ingredients until they are well combined. Add the buttermilk mixed with the egg and toss the mixture until the liquid is well incorporated. Fold in the blueberries tossed with 1 teaspoon of flour, and, on a well-floured surface, form the dough into a ½-inch-thick rectangle. Cut the dough into 18 triangles and transfer the triangles to a baking sheet. Brush the triangles lightly with egg white and sprinkle them with sugar. Bake the scones in the preheated oven for 15 minutes or until they are lightly browned. Serve with butter.

†BACON POPOVERS

MAKES 6 POPOVERS

1 cup sifted flour
½ teaspoon salt
3 eggs, lightly beaten

1 cup milk
2 tablespoons melted butter
4 to 5 slices cooked and crumbled bacon

Preheat oven to 450° F.

Into a large bowl sift the flour with the salt, add the eggs, milk and melted butter and combine. Beat the batter with a rotary beater until it is smooth. Stir in the crumbled bacon. Butter iron popover pans and heat them until they are sizzling. Fill the cups half full with the batter and bake the popovers in the preheated oven for 20 minutes. Reduce the temperature to 350° F. and bake the popovers for about 20 minutes more, or until they are brown and crisp.

†CHEESE AND CARAWAY BISCUITS

MAKES APPROXIMATELY 12 BISCUITS

2 cups flour
1 tablespoon baking powder
1 teaspoon salt
3 tablespoons butter, cut into bits
¼ cup fresh-grated Parmesan cheese

¾ cup light cream
12 teaspoons grated Cheddar cheese
1 egg, lightly beaten with 1 tablespoon heavy cream
Sprinkling of caraway seeds

Preheat oven to 400° F.

Into a bowl sift together the flour, baking powder and salt. Add the butter and combine the mixture until it resembles meal. Add the Parmesan cheese and enough light cream to form a smooth, soft dough. Turn the dough out on a lightly floured board and knead it for 30 seconds. Roll the dough ¼ inch thick, and with a 2-inch biscuit cutter cut out 24 rounds. Put half the rounds on a baking sheet and top each one with 1 teaspoon Cheddar cheese. Brush the edges of the rounds with water, top them with the remaining rounds and press down the edges to seal them. Brush the biscuits with the egg-and-cream mixture and sprinkle the tops with caraway seeds. Bake in the top third of the preheated oven for 15 to 20 minutes, or until they are golden.

†SOUR-CREAM AND CHIVE BISCUITS

MAKES APPROXIMATELY 12 BISCUITS

2 cups flour
2½ teaspoons baking powder
1 teaspoon salt

¾ cup sour cream
⅓ cup chopped chives
⅔ cup milk

Preheat oven to 450° F.

Into a bowl sift together the flour, baking powder and salt. Add the sour cream and chopped chives. Add just enough milk to form a smooth, soft dough. Turn the dough out onto a lightly floured board and knead it for 30 seconds. Roll the dough out ¾ inch thick, and with a 2-inch biscuit cutter cut out rounds. Put the rounds on a baking sheet and bake in the top third of the preheated oven for 15 minutes, or until they are golden.

†*BALTHAZARS

8 ounces semisweet chocolate, grated   2 tablespoons rum
8 ounces shelled walnuts, grated   2 eggs, well beaten
½ cup confectioners' sugar

In a mixing bowl combine all the ingredients, reserving some grated walnuts. Shape the mixture into a long roll, 1 inch in diameter, roll it in the reserved walnuts and wrap the roll in heavy waxed paper. Chill the roll for 3 days and cut it into thin slices before serving.

†*MY MOTHER'S BROWNIE RECIPE

⅔ cup butter   1 tablespoon vanilla extract
1 cup brown sugar   Pinch of salt
3 eggs   1 cup chopped walnuts
8 ounces unsweetened chocolate   2 tablespoons special brownie
½ cup flour   syrup (see page 320)

Preheat oven to 350° F.

Cream the butter and sugar, and gradually add the whole unbeaten eggs. Then add the melted chocolate, flour, vanilla, salt and nuts. Mix together and add the special brownie syrup. Spread the batter in a 12-inch baking pan and bake in the preheated oven for about 20 minutes. Important: Wait until completely cool to cut into squares.

†*SPECIAL SYRUP FOR BROWNIES

---

1 cup superfine granulated sugar   *1 tablespoon cocoa*
½ cup coffee   *1 scant teaspoon cornstarch*

Boil the sugar and coffee together for 5 minutes. Then add the cocoa and cornstarch and boil up once again. Store in a jar in the refrigerator and use when needed for brownie recipe.

†*CINNAMON CRESCENTS

MAKES APPROXIMATELY 12 COOKIES
1 cup sifted flour   *¾ cup ground walnuts*
¼ teaspoon salt   *¼ cup superfine granulated sugar*
¼ pound butter   *1 tablespoon cinnamon*
¼ pound soft cream cheese   *1 teaspoon grated lemon rind*
1 egg white, beaten until stiff

Preheat oven to 375° F.

Sift the flour with the salt into a large bowl. With the hands, work in the butter and cream cheese. Roll the dough out on a lightly floured board, fold into thirds, and chill it overnight, or for at least 2 hours. Roll out the dough to ⅛ inch thick and cut it into 4-inch squares. Combine the egg white with the ground walnuts, sugar, cinnamon and grated lemon rind and spread 1 tablespoon of the mixture on one corner of each square. Roll up the square diagonally from that corner, curving the ends to form a crescent. Bake the crescents on a baking sheet in the preheated oven for 20 minutes, or until they are golden brown.

†*CINNAMON OATMEAL COOKIES

MAKES APPROXIMATELY 12 COOKIES

1 cup flour
3 tablespoons superfine granulated sugar
2 teaspoons baking powder
1 teaspoon cinnamon
½ teaspoon salt
¼ teaspoon ground cloves

½ cup oatmeal
¼ cup butter, cut into bits
1 egg, lightly beaten
¼ cup milk
Melted butter
12 raisins

Preheat oven to 400° F.

Into a bowl sift together the flour, 2 tablespoons of the sugar, the baking powder, ½ teaspoon of the cinnamon, the salt and ground cloves. Add the oatmeal. Add the butter and combine the mixture until it resembles meal. Add just enough of the egg and milk to form a smooth, soft dough. Turn the dough out onto a lightly floured board and knead it for 30 seconds. Roll out to ½ inch thick, and with a 2-inch biscuit cutter cut out rounds. Brush them with melted butter and sprinkle with a mixture of the remaining sugar and cinnamon. Make an indentation in each round and fill it with a raisin. Put the rounds on a buttered baking sheet and bake them in the top third of the preheated oven for 10 to 15 minutes, or until they are golden.

†*CINNAMON RICE CAKES

MAKES APPROXIMATELY 24 COOKIES

½ cup uncooked rice
2 cups boiling milk
3 eggs, well beaten

½ cup superfine granulated sugar
½ teaspoon cinnamon
½ teaspoon nutmeg

Cook the rice in the milk until it is fluffy. Mash with a fork and cool thoroughly. Add the eggs and stir in the sugar, cinnamon and nutmeg thoroughly. Shape the mixture into thin round cakes 2 inches across and fry the cakes on a well-greased griddle or hot plate until they are lightly browned on both sides. Serve with fruit preserves.

†*FLORENTINES

MAKES APPROXIMATELY 24 COOKIES

½ cup superfine granulated sugar
⅓ cup light cream
⅓ cup light corn syrup
3 tablespoons butter
¼ cup flour

1 cup blanched almonds, sliced
⅓ cup slivered glacé orange peel
2 ounces semisweet chocolate
3 tablespoons strong liquid coffee

Preheat oven to 375° F.

In a heavy saucepan combine the sugar, cream, corn syrup and 2 tablespoons of the butter and cook over low heat until the sugar is dissolved. Increase the heat to moderate and boil the mixture until a candy thermometer registers 238° F. Transfer to a bowl and sift in the flour, stirring. Stir in the almonds and glacé orange peel. With a teaspoon, drop the batter in mounds 2½ inches apart on a well-buttered baking sheet. Bake the biscuits in the preheated oven for 8 to 10 minutes, or until they are well browned. Allow to cool for 1 minute, or until the cookies are firm enough to lift, and with a metal spatula transfer them to a rack to cool completely. In another heavy saucepan melt the chocolate with the coffee and the remaining butter over low heat. Form a cone from a doubled sheet of waxed paper and fill it with the chocolate mixture. Snip the tip from the cone and decorate the cookies with chocolate. Let the chocolate set in a cool place.

†MOLASSES COOKIES

MAKES APPROXIMATELY 30 COOKIES

½ cup butter
¾ cup superfine granulated sugar
1 egg
1½ cups flour

¾ teaspoon baking soda
Pinch of salt
⅓ cup molasses
¾ cup coarse-chopped walnuts

Preheat oven to 350° F.

In a bowl cream together the butter and sugar. Beat in the egg and beat the mixture until it is light. Sift together the flour, baking soda and pinch of salt. Add the flour to the butter mixture alternately with the molasses and combine well. Add the chopped walnuts. Drop the batter by heaping teaspoons, spaced 2 inches apart, onto a baking sheet and bake in the preheated oven for 15 minutes.

†POPPY-SEED COOKIES

MAKES APPROXIMATELY 4 DOZEN

1 cup butter, softened
1 cup vanilla sugar
  (see page 348)
1 egg yolk, well beaten
1 cup chopped hazelnuts

1 cup ground poppy seeds
2¼ cups flour
½ teaspoon cinnamon
¼ teaspoon salt
Pinch of ground ginger

Preheat oven to 325° F.

In a large bowl cream together the butter and vanilla sugar. Stir in the egg yolk, hazelnuts and poppy seeds. Sift together the flour, cinnamon, salt and ground ginger, and add gradually to the creamed mixture. Blend well and shape the dough into rolls 2 inches thick. Wrap the rolls in heavy waxed paper and chill for several hours. Cut into slices ¼ inch thick and arrange them on an unbuttered baking sheet. Bake the biscuits in the preheated oven for 10 to 15 minutes, or until they are lightly golden in color.

†*MRS. RALPH F. COLIN'S CHOCOLATE CAKE

1¾ cups sifted flour
3 teaspoons baking powder
¼ teaspoon baking soda
¼ teaspoon salt
½ cup butter
¼ cup superfine granulated sugar

3 egg yolks
8 ounces semisweet chocolate
1¼ cups milk
¼ teaspoon vanilla extract
3 egg whites, beaten stiff
Fudge frosting (see below)

Preheat oven to 350° F.

Sift the flour and baking powder separately and mix. Add the baking soda and salt, and sift together twice more. Cream the butter thoroughly, adding the sugar gradually. Cream until light and fluffy. Beat the egg yolks until light. Add them to the butter and sugar and then add the melted chocolate. Next add the flour mixture, alternating a little at a time, with the milk. Beat until smooth. Add the vanilla extract and fold in the beaten egg whites. Pour the batter into two 8-by-2½-inch cake pans and bake in a preheated oven for 30 minutes. When cool split the layers horizontally to make a 4-layer cake. Spread fudge frosting between each layer and over the top of the cake.

†*FUDGE FROSTING

5½ ounces semisweet chocolate
1¼ cups milk
2½ cups superfine granulated sugar
¼ cup butter

2 teaspoons vanilla extract
Confectioners' sugar for
   decoration

Melt the chocolate, add the milk and sugar. Boil until the mixture forms a ball when dropped into cold water. Add the butter and vanilla extract. Let stand, then beat until cool. If the frosting is too thick to spread easily, add milk until a spreading consistency is obtained. For decorating cakes, add confectioners' sugar until it is sufficiently thick. Freeze the frosting separately and ice after both cake and frosting have been defrosted.

†*FIONA CHARLTON-DEWAR'S MOCHA CAKE

6 ounces semisweet chocolate
3 tablespoons strong liquid
  coffee
1 cup butter

40 whole ladyfingers
⅔ cup very strong liquid
  coffee
½ cup chopped almonds

If you are making this cake for the freezer, take a large piece of aluminum foil, butter the inside and make the cake on top of the foil. If making the cake to eat at once, construct it on the dish on which it will be served.

Make the mocha cream by melting the chocolate with the 3 tablespoons of coffee in the top of a double boiler over warm water. When it has melted allow it to cool completely, then beat in the butter. If the cream is too liquid, place it in the freezing compartment of your refrigerator for 5 to 8 minutes.

Dip 10 lady fingers quickly on both sides in the remaining strong coffee and lay them on the foil or dish side by side. Spread a layer of mocha cream onto the fingers. Then make another layer by dipping 10 more fingers into the coffee and placing them on top of the mocha cream. Spread more mocha cream on top of them. Continue doing this until you reach the height desired, usually 4 layers (40 lady fingers). Coat the whole cake, top and sides, with the remaining mocha cream, and cover with the chopped nuts. If the cake is to be used at once, place it in the refrigerator to harden for 2 hours. If it is to be frozen, wrap it immediately in aluminum foil and place it in the freezer.

†*SWISS CHOCOLATE CAKE

THE CAKE

4 ounces semisweet chocolate, grated
1⅔ cups blanched whole almonds,
pulverized in a blender
7 tablespoons fine dry bread crumbs
1 tablespoon baking powder
½ cup butter

1 cup superfine granulated
sugar
6 egg yolks
2 tablespoons rum
6 egg whites, beaten until
stiff
Ground almonds

THE CHOCOLATE GLAZE

4 ounces semisweet chocolate
¼ cup water

¼ cup butter
¼ cup confectioners' sugar

Preheat oven to 350° F.

Blend the chocolate and almonds in a blender and combine them with 5 tablespoons of the bread crumbs and the baking powder. Cream the butter until soft, add the sugar gradually and beat the mixture until it is light. Add the egg yolks, one at a time, beating hard after each addition. Stir in the chocolate-nut mixture and the rum. Fold the stiff egg whites into the batter, gently but thoroughly. Oil a 9-inch cake pan, line it with waxed paper, and oil the paper. Sprinkle the bottom and sides with remaining bread crumbs. Spoon the batter into the pan and bake the cake in the preheated oven for about 1 hour, or until a skewer inserted in the center comes out clean. Cool the cake for about 10 minutes, remove it from the pan, and put it on a wire rack set on a tray lined with waxed paper.

To make the chocolate glaze, melt the chocolate in the water in the top of a double boiler set over simmering water. Remove the pan from the heat and add the butter, stirring until it is melted. Add the confectioners' sugar and beat the glaze until smooth. Pour the chocolate glaze all at once over the top of the cake and tip the cake back and forth so that some of the glaze runs down and covers the sides. Sprinkle the top and sides with ground almonds.

Both cake and glaze may be made in advance and frozen separately. Do not glaze the cake until both have been defrosted.

†*CHRISTMAS FRUITCAKES

MAKES 2 CAKES

2 cups sultanas	*2 cups sifted flour*
½ cup currants	*1 teaspoon mace*
½ cup Cognac or dark rum	*1 teaspoon cinnamon*
2 cups glacé pineapple	*½ teaspoon baking soda*
1 cup glacé cherries	*¾ cup butter, softened*
½ cup walnut halves	*1 cup light-brown sugar*
½ cup chopped blanched almonds	*1 cup sugar*
¼ cup glacé orange peel	*5 eggs*
¼ cup glacé lemon peel	

Preheat oven to 275° F.

In a large bowl combine the sultanas, currants and Cognac or dark rum, and allow the mixture to macerate overnight. Add the glacé pineapple, cherries, walnut halves, almonds, orange peel and lemon peel, and toss with 4 tablespoons of the flour. Into a bowl sift the rest of the flour together with the mace, cinnamon and baking soda. In another bowl cream together the butter and both sugars. Beat in the eggs, one at a time, beating well after each addition, and blend in the flour mixture, 4 tablespoons at a time. Pour the batter over the fruit mixture and combine well. Line two buttered loaf pans, 9 by 5 by 3 inches, with buttered parchment or buttered brown paper, transfer the batter to the pans, and bake the cakes in the preheated oven for 3 hours. Allow the cakes to cool in the pans for 15 minutes, then turn them out onto racks. Peel off the paper and allow to cool completely.

†*CHRISTMAS HONEY CAKES

MAKES ABOUT 90 CAKES

THE CAKE

1½ cups honey
1¼ cups sugar
7 tablespoons butter
¾ cup lightly toasted almonds
1 tablespoon cocoa
1 teaspoon cinnamon
¼ teaspoon ground cloves

1 egg
2 tablespoons lemon juice
2 tablespoons milk
1 tablespoon kirsch
Grated rind of 1 lemon
4½ cups flour
2 tablespoons baking powder

THE SUGAR ICING

1½ cups confectioners' sugar
2 tablespoons kirsch

Preheat oven to 350° F.

In a saucepan melt the honey, sugar and butter over low heat, stirring 4 or 5 times. Pour the honey mixture into a bowl and allow to cool. Beat in the almonds, cocoa, cinnamon and ground cloves. In a small bowl beat the egg lightly with the lemon juice, milk, kirsch and grated lemon rind. Beat the egg mixture into the honey mixture. Stir in the flour sifted with the baking powder, a little at a time. Butter a baking pan, 17 by 11 inches, and line it with buttered waxed paper. Turn the batter into the pan and spread it evenly with a metal spatula. Bake the cake in the preheated oven for 35 minutes, or until it is golden and a skewer inserted in the center comes out clean. Allow the cake to cool in the pan.

To make the sugar icing, combine the sifted confectioners' sugar with enough kirsch to make a runny mixture. Spread the cake with the icing and allow it to dry. Cut the cake into rectangles, 2 inches long and 1 inch wide, and store in an airtight container for at least 5 days.

†*FRUITCAKE WITH GUINNESS

1 cup butter
1¼ cups soft brown sugar
4 eggs, lightly beaten
1½ cups flour
2 teaspoons commercial
*   mixed spice*

1 to 1½ pounds dried mixed fruit
1 cup chopped glacé cherries
8 to 12 tablespoons Guinness stout, or
*   dark beer*

Preheat oven to 350° F.

Cream the butter and sugar together. Gradually beat in the eggs. Fold in the flour sifted together with the mixed spice; add the fruit and mix well. Stir in 4 tablespoons of the Guinness. Bake in a buttered 7-inch cake pan in the preheated oven for 2 hours. Remove from the oven, turn the cake upside down on cake rack. When cold, spike the bottom of the cake with a skewer and pour in about 6 tablespoons Guinness. Allow the stout to soak in until cake is no longer soggy. Keep in a closed tin for a week before serving.

†*MRS. MARK MAINWARING'S GINGERBREAD

This is the best gingerbread I have ever eaten. When it was made for me by Mrs. Mainwaring, I put half in the freezer, with thoughts of keeping it for guests two weeks later. But it was such a success with my family that the second half appeared the following day and vanished by the evening. In fact, it will freeze very well.

3 cups self-rising cake flour	*¼ cup butter*
Pinch of salt	*¾ cup brown sugar*
1½ teaspoons baking soda	*1 pound black treacle*
1 teaspoon commercial mixed spice	*3 tablespoons milk*
2 tablespoons ground ginger	*4 eggs, beaten*
Handful chopped ginger	*⅔ cup boiling water*
¼ cup vegetable fat	

Preheat oven to 300° F.

Sift together all the dry ingredients except the sugar. Melt the vegetable fat, butter, sugar and treacle in a saucepan, then pour into a well in the dry ingredients. Stir well, add the milk and beaten eggs. Add the boiling water and beat until the mixture bubbles. Bake in a foil-lined 8-by-11-inch pan for 1 hour in the middle of the preheated oven.

†*NUT SPICE CAKE

1 pound raisins
4 cups water
1 cup butter, cut into bits
3½ cups flour
2 cups superfine granulated sugar
2 teaspoons baking soda
2 teaspoons cinnamon

2 teaspoons nutmeg
½ teaspoon salt
¼ teaspoon ground cloves
¼ teaspoon ground allspice
1 pound walnut halves
2 eggs, lightly beaten
4 teaspoons vanilla

Preheat oven to 325° F.

In a large saucepan combine the raisins and water. Bring the water to the boil and simmer the raisins, covered, for 10 minutes. Add the butter, simmer the mixture for 5 minutes more, and allow it to cool for 10 minutes. Into a large bowl sift together the flour, sugar, baking soda, cinnamon, nutmeg, salt, ground cloves and allspice. Pour the raisin mixture over the dry ingredients and combine well. Fold in the walnut halves, eggs and vanilla. Pour the batter into a buttered and floured baking pan, 10 inches in diameter and 4 inches deep, and bake the cake in the preheated oven for 1 hour 20 minutes, or until a cake tester inserted in the center comes out clean. Let the cake cool in the pan on a rack for 1 hour before turning it out.

PICKLING AND PRESERVING

To Sterilize Jars

Wash the jars in hot soapy water and rinse them in very hot water. Place the jars, lids, tops and rubber rings in a large saucepan, cover them with hot water and boil for 5 minutes. Turn off the heat and allow the containers to stand in the hot water. Immediately before using, invert the jars on a rack to dry. The jars must be filled while still hot.

CITRUS AND GINGER MARMALADE

MAKES APPROXIMATELY FIVE I-POUND JARS

3 limes	1 cup fresh ginger root, peeled and minced
2 oranges	Granulated or preserving sugar, to measure
8 cups water	

Cut the limes and oranges lengthwise into the thinnest slices possible. Cut the slices crosswise into julienne strips and remove the seeds and heavy membranes. Slice more fruit in the same manner, if necessary, to measure 4 cups. Put the fruit in a heavy jamming pan with the water and the ginger root and allow the mixture to stand for 12 hours. Bring to the boil and simmer for 20 minutes, then allow it to stand for 12 hours more. Measure the fruits and liquid together and, for each cup, add 1 cup sugar. Bring to the boil over moderate heat, stirring until the sugar has dissolved and skimming the froth as it accumulates. Increase the heat and boil the marmalade, being careful that the fruit does not burn, until it reaches jelly stage or 220° F. on a candy thermometer. Ladle into hot sterilized preserving jars and seal the jars with their lids.

FOUR-FRUIT PRESERVE

MAKES APPROXIMATELY EIGHT 1-POUND JARS

8 cups sugar	1 pound rhubarb, cut into ¾-inch
2 cups water	pieces
1 pound cherries, pitted	1 pound raspberries
1 pound strawberries, halved	

In a jamming pan combine the sugar and water. Bring the mixture to the boil over moderate heat, washing down any undissolved sugar crystals clinging to the sides of the pan with a brush dipped in cold water. Cook the syrup until a candy thermometer registers 240° F. Add the cherries and simmer for 10 minutes. Add the strawberries and simmer for 10 minutes more. Add the rhubarb and raspberries and continue to simmer for another 10 minutes. With a slotted spoon transfer the fruits to hot sterilized jars. Skim the froth from the syrup and allow it to cool for 15 minutes. Pour the syrup slowly over the fruits. Seal the jars with their lids.

GRAPEFRUIT MARMALADE

MAKES APPROXIMATELY FOUR 1-POUND JARS

2 large grapefruit	Approximately 3 cups sugar
1 small lemon	(either superfine granulated
5¾ cups water	or preserving)

Peel the grapefruit and lemon, trim away the inner white part so rind is about ⅜ inch thick, and cut it into fine slivers about ½ inch long. Discard pith and seeds from the fruit, and chop fruit fine, reserving the juice. Measure 1½ cups of the rind to use in the marmalade. Bring the rinds and 4 cups of the water to the boil in a small saucepan, then drain; repeat the boiling and draining process twice. Mix the rind and chopped, seeded grapefruit and lemon sections in a very large, heavy enamel or stainless-steel saucepan or jamming pan, add the remaining 1¾ cups water and simmer, uncovered, for 10 minutes. Cover and allow to stand in a cool place overnight. The next day wash and sterilize four ½-pint jars and tops, stand them on a baking sheet and keep hot in a 250° F. oven until needed. Measure the fruit mixture, and for each cup add 1 cup sugar. Return to the pan, insert a candy thermometer, and slowly heat, uncovered, to boiling, stirring until the sugar dissolves: boil slowly uncovered, stirring now and then, for 30 to 40 minutes or until the thermometer reaches 218 to 220° F. Take a little of the juice in a large metal spoon, cool slightly, then tilt. If the drops slide together in a sheet, the marmalade is done. Remove from the heat, stir for one minute, skim off the froth and ladle into jars, filling to within ⅛ inch of the top. Cool, and store in a cool, dark, dry place. Orange marmalade can be made the same way by substituting oranges for grapefruit.

BLACKBERRY JAM WITH ORANGE

MAKES APPROXIMATELY FIVE 1-POUND JARS

2 pounds blackberries
¾ cup water
1 cup orange juice
3 tablespoons lemon juice

1 tablespoon grated orange peel
4 cups superfine granulated or preserving sugar

In a large saucepan cook the blackberries in ¾ cup of water until heated through. Put half the fruit through a sieve and add the purée to the blackberries remaining in the saucepan. Add the orange and lemon juices and grated orange peel, and stir over high heat until it comes to a rolling boil. Stir in the sugar, bring back to a rolling boil, and boil, stirring constantly, for 1 minute. Remove from the heat and stir for several minutes to prevent the fruit from floating. Pour into sterilized jars and cover with a ⅛-inch layer of melted paraffin or a round of waxed paper and screw on the lids.

MRS. ANTHONY HAMBRO'S CREOLE JAM

MAKES APPROXIMATELY SIX 1-POUND JARS

3 pounds bananas
4 cups superfine granulated or preserving sugar
1 cup water

2 large lemons or limes
1 teaspoon powdered cinnamon
¾ cup rum

Peel the bananas, cut into slices and blanch for 2 minutes in boiling water. Leave to drain thoroughly. Boil the sugar and water together until syrupy. Mix with the bananas and cook for 25 minutes. Meanwhile, peel the lemons or limes carefully, reserving the pith. Cut the zest into thin slices with scissors. Blanch 2 minutes and leave to drain. Squeeze the lemons or limes and add the juice to the bananas with the zest and cinnamon. Leave on the heat to thicken for 15 minutes. Remove from the heat, pour in the rum, mix well and put into jars.

PLUM JAM

MAKES APPROXIMATELY SIX 1-POUND JARS

4 pounds purple or red plums,   ½ cup water
halved, and pits removed   8 cups preserving or superfine
and reserved   granulated sugar

Crack six of the plum pits and remove the kernels. In a large jamming pan combine the plums, water and the kernels. Bring the mixture to the boil and simmer for 40 minutes, or until the plums are tender. Add the sugar and cook over low heat, stirring, until the sugar is dissolved. Increase the heat to high and continue to cook until a candy thermometer registers 222° F. Skim off the froth and spoon the jam into hot, sterilized jars. Seal the jars with their lids.

RHUBARB GINGER JAM

MAKES FOUR TO SIX 1-POUND JARS

4 pounds rhubarb, washed and   ½ cup preserved ginger, drained
cut into ½-inch pieces   and cut into ¼-inch pieces
4 cups soft brown sugar   Juice of 1 lemon
4 cups superfine granulated or   Peel of 1 lemon, cut into julienne
preserving sugar   strips and blanched
½ cup water

In a heavy jamming pan combine the rhubarb, brown and white sugar and water. Bring the mixture to the boil over high heat and simmer, stirring frequently, until the rhubarb is tender. Increase the heat and boil the mixture until it reaches the jelly stage, or a candy thermometer registers 220 to 222° F. Remove the pan from the heat and add the preserved ginger pieces, the lemon juice and lemon peel. Put the jam into heated preserving jars and seal with their lids.

MRS. ANTHONY HAMBRO'S THREE-FRUIT JAM

MAKES SEVEN TO EIGHT 1-POUND JARS

4 big blood oranges   *12 cups water*
2 big grapefruit   *10 cups superfine granulated or preserving*
2 thin-skinned lemons   *sugar*

Cut the fruit into coarse pieces, put in a pan with the water and leave overnight. In the morning cook for 50 minutes, skimming the foam as necessary. Let stand until the following day, then add the sugar and recook for 1¼ hours. Put into jars and seal.

TOMATO GINGER JAM

MAKES FOUR TO SIX 1-POUND JARS

2½ pounds ripe tomatoes, peeled   *1 teaspoon ground ginger*
   and quartered   *¼ teaspoon turmeric*
1½ cups firmly packed brown   *¼ teaspoon pepper*
   sugar   *3 to 4 tablespoons minced*
2 lemons chopped fine   *crystallized ginger, or to*
1 onion, grated   *taste*
1 teaspoon sweet Hungarian
   paprika

In a jamming pan combine the tomatoes, brown sugar, lemons, grated onion, paprika, ground ginger, turmeric and pepper. Cook over moderate heat until slightly reduced and add the crystallized ginger. Simmer, stirring frequently, until the mixture is thick. Spoon the jam into sterilized jars and seal with their lids.

APPLE AND RAISIN CHUTNEY

MAKES APPROXIMATELY TEN 1-POUND JARS

6 pounds cooking apples

6 cups brown sugar

5 cups malt vinegar

½ pound nuts (hazelnuts or almonds)

2 pounds onions, peeled and sliced

2 pounds raisins or sultanas

2 tablespoons ground ginger

1 teaspoon cayenne

Grated rind and juice of 1 lemon

Peel, core and chop the apples. Dissolve the sugar in 2 cups of the vinegar. In a jamming pan, cook the apples, nuts, onions and raisins in the remaining vinegar, until they are all soft and well cooked. Add the ginger, cayenne and lemon juice and rind. Then add the sugar-and-vinegar mixture. Cook in the pan, uncovered, until thick. Spoon the chutney into 1-pound sterilized jars, allow to cool and seal the tops. Allow the chutney to stand for a few weeks, preferably 1 month, before using.

APRICOT AND DATE CHUTNEY

MAKES APPROXIMATELY TWO 1-POUND JARS

1 pound dried apricots

1½ cups sultanas

1½ cups white-wine vinegar

1¼ cups dark-brown sugar

1¼ cups dates, coarse-chopped

1 cup water

5 tablespoons crystallized ginger

1½ tablespoons salt

1½ tablespoons mustard seed

½ teaspoon chili powder

Soak the apricots in water to cover for 30 minutes. Drain the apricots and put in an enamel casserole. Combine all the remaining ingredients and add to the casserole. Simmer over low heat for 2 hours and let cool. Pack the chutney into hot, sterilized jars and seal.

CRANBERRY CHUTNEY

MAKES APPROXIMATELY FOUR I-POUND JARS

4 cups cranberries
2 cooking apples, peeled, cored
  and chopped
2 oranges, unpeeled, sliced
  thin and seeded
1 cup dark-brown sugar
1 cup cider vinegar
8 tablespoons preserved ginger, diced

5 tablespoons crystallized
  fruits
2 cloves garlic, chopped
6 whole cloves
6 whole allspice
1 tablespoon curry powder
1 teaspoon salt
½ teaspoon mustard seed

In a large jamming pan combine all the ingredients and bring the mixture to a fast boil; reduce the heat and boil gently for about 15 minutes, or until it has thickened. Stir frequently. Spoon the chutney into warm, dry, sterilized jars and seal. Allow to stand for more than 1 month before using.

GOOSEBERRY CHUTNEY

MAKES APPROXIMATELY SIX I-POUND JARS

3 pints gooseberries, washed, stems
  removed and chopped
3 medium onions, chopped
3 cups light-brown sugar
1½ cups malt vinegar
1½ cups white-wine vinegar

1 cup sultanas
1 tablespoon salt
2 teaspoons dry mustard
1 teaspoon ground ginger
1 teaspoon ground turmeric
½ teaspoon cayenne

Combine all the ingredients in a large saucepan or jamming pan and cook the mixture over low heat, stirring frequently, for about 2 hours or until it thickens. Spoon into warm, dry, sterilized jars and seal them. Allow to stand for 1 month, if possible, before using.

TOMATO CHUTNEY

MAKES APPROXIMATELY FOUR 1-POUND JARS

2 pounds ripe tomatoes, peeled, seeded and chopped

¾ cup preserving or granulated sugar

½ cup raisins or sultanas

½ cup malt vinegar

2 tablespoons chili powder

2 tablespoons chopped fresh ginger root

1½ teaspoons salt

1 clove garlic, minced

½ pound onions, sliced

3 green peppers, seeded and sliced thin

Combine all the ingredients in a large jamming pan and boil gently for 1 to 2 hours, or until the vegetables are thoroughly cooked and soft, and the mixture becomes thick. Spoon into warm, dry, sterilized jars. Tie or seal the tops with screw lids.

AJVAR

MAKES ONE 1-POUND JAR

2 green peppers, halved and seeded

1 medium-sized eggplant

2 medium-sized tomatoes, peeled and seeded

2 cloves garlic, chopped

1 to 2 fresh hot chilis, seeded

⅓ cup olive oil

2 tablespoons wine vinegar

Salt and pepper to taste

Bake the peppers and eggplant on a rack in a 400° F. oven for 5 to 10 minutes or until the skin is charred and the pulp soft. Allow the vegetables to cool until they can be handled and peel them. Put the tomatoes in the container of a blender. Add the eggplant, peppers, garlic and chilis and blend until they are a thick purée. Stir in the olive oil, vinegar and salt and pepper to taste. Seal in sterilized jars.

PICKLED BEAN RELISH

MAKES APPROXIMATELY TWO I-POUND JARS

2 pounds fresh or canned kidney beans	1 clove garlic, crushed
	Pepper to taste
¾ cup vegetable oil	1 medium onion, sliced thin
¼ cup white-wine vinegar	½ teaspoon salt

If using fresh beans, soak them overnight. Drain and simmer for 1 to 2 hours, or until tender. Combine all ingredients except the beans in a bowl. Pour mixture over cooked, drained beans and toss to mix well. Put relish in jars and chill overnight.

BLACKBERRY RELISH

MAKES APPROXIMATELY NINE I-POUND JARS

5 pounds blackberries	1 tablespoon ground cinnamon
7½ cups light-brown sugar	1 teaspoon ground cloves
1 cup malt vinegar	1 teaspoon ground allspice

Put the blackberries in a heavy jamming pan with all the rest of the ingredients. Bring to the boil over moderate heat, lower the heat and simmer until the berries are soft. Pack the relish into preserving jars and seal them with their lids.

CUCUMBER AND ONION PICKLE

MAKES FOUR TO FIVE 1-POUND JARS

*12 medium cucumbers, cut
into ¼-inch-thick slices
1 pound medium white onions,
cut into ¼-inch-thick slices
⅓ cup salt*

*3 cups cider vinegar
¾ cup sugar
3 tablespoons mustard seed
2 teaspoons celery seed
1 teaspoon turmeric*

In a large ceramic or glass bowl, combine the cucumbers and onion slices and the salt. Allow the mixture to stand, covered, overnight and then drain it through a colander. Rinse the vegetables under running water to remove any remaining salt. In a jamming pan combine the cider vinegar, sugar, mustard seed, celery seed and turmeric and bring to the boil. Add the cucumber and onion slices and cook, covered, for 3 minutes. Spoon the cucumbers and onions into hot sterilized jars and pour the liquid over them. Seal the jars with their lids.

OLIVES WITH ROSEMARY AND GARLIC

MAKES 1 CUP

*1 cup green olives with pits
½ lemon, sliced thin
4 to 5 sprigs fresh rosemary,
coarse-chopped*

*2 cloves garlic, peeled and bruised
½ teaspoon peppercorns, bruised
Fruity olive oil, to cover*

Wash the olives under cold running water. With a meat pounder, rolling pin or mallet, hit the olives gently on one side so that they crack slightly but the pits remain inside. Pack them in a sterilized preserving jar alternately with the slices of lemon, the rosemary, garlic cloves and peppercorns. Fill the jar with the olive oil, seal and let olives stand at room temperature for 2 to 3 days.

PICKLED WALNUTS

MAKES APPROXIMATELY TEN 1-POUND JARS

100 green walnuts	*Whole black peppercorns*
Salted water, to cover	*Allspice*
Malt vinegar	*2 fresh ginger roots*

Prick the walnuts well with a fork. Put in a large pan and cover with salted water, using 1 pound of salt for each gallon of water. Let the walnuts stand in the brine for 9 days, changing the liquid every 3 days, or until they are black. Pack into jars three-quarters full. In a large saucepan combine enough malt vinegar to cover the walnuts with 1½ ounces whole black peppercorns, 2 tablespoons allspice and a 2-inch piece of ginger root, bruised, for each 2 pints of vinegar. Boil the mixture for 10 minutes, immediately pour over the walnuts and seal the jars. Store in a cool place for 1 month before using. The nuts will keep for 2 to 3 years.

POTTED KIPPERS

3 boned kippers	*¼ cup clarified butter (see page 275)*
2 tablespoons lemon juice	*¼ teaspoon cayenne*
½ cup butter, softened	

Cover the kippers with boiling water and allow them to stand for 5 minutes. Drain and pat dry with paper towels. Flake the fish. In the container of a blender, combine one half of the fish with the lemon juice. Blend, adding the softened butter, a piece at a time, alternately with small portions of the remaining fish and clarified butter until the mixture forms a smooth paste. Stir in the cayenne. Pack in small crocks, filling them to within ½ inch of the top, and chill. The kippers will keep for 2 weeks in the refrigerator.

CHEDDAR CHEESE WITH SAUTERNES

MAKES APPROXIMATELY 2¼ POUNDS

*1½ pounds Cheddar cheese, grated
  and rubbed through a sieve
⅔ cup sour cream
½ cup butter, softened
½ teaspoon Dijon mustard*

*½ teaspoon mace
Salt and pepper to taste
½ cup Sauternes
¼ pound clarified butter (see
  page 275)*

In a bowl combine the Cheddar cheese, sour cream, butter, mustard, mace, salt and pepper. Add the Sauternes, a little at a time, beating well. Pack the cheese into crocks, pour a layer of clarified butter on top, and store them in the refrigerator. Keeps indefinitely, sealed.

DUXELLES

MAKES APPROXIMATELY 2 POUNDS

This will keep stored in a tightly covered jar in the refrigerator for several weeks. Used as a seasoning agent, it can be added to egg dishes, to many sauces, to stuffings or dressings for fish, poultry or meat and as a filling for crêpes and sandwiches.

*2 pounds button mushrooms
4 shallots, chopped fine
1 teaspoon each of oregano, salt,
  fresh-ground pepper*

*1 cup butter
2 teaspoons meat glaze‡
⅔ cup white wine*

‡ Meat glaze can be bought at most specialty food shops or ordered from Maison Glass, 52 East 58 Street, New York, New York 10022.

Wipe the mushrooms, chop fine and cook with the shallots and seasonings in the butter, over very low heat, until most of the liquid has been absorbed and the mushrooms are dark. Stir in the meat glaze dissolved in the white wine and cook the mixture until it forms a paste.

GINGERED PEAR BUTTER

MAKES APPROXIMATELY 1½ POUNDS

3 pounds pears, peeled, cored
   and sliced thin
2 cups superfine granulated sugar
2 teaspoons crystallized ginger

2 tablespoons lemon juice
1 teaspoon grated lemon peel
¼ teaspoon grated nutmeg
½ teaspoon ground cloves

In a bowl combine the pears with the sugar and ginger. Allow the mixture to stand, covered, for 2 hours. Transfer to a saucepan and add the lemon juice, grated lemon peel, nutmeg and cloves. Simmer until the pears are soft and the mixture becomes thick. Put through the fine disk of a food mill and pour into hot, sterilized jars and seal.

SHERRY PEPPERS

MAKES APPROXIMATELY 2 CUPS
To add to Bloody Marys along with lemon juice.

5 to 6 fresh hot chili peppers, 2½ inches long
2 cups dry sherry

Wash the peppers under cold running water (wearing gloves to protect your hands from the burning oil of the peppers) and pat them dry. Put them in a saucepan with the sherry and bring the wine just to the boil. Allow the mixture to cool. Put the peppers and wine into a bottle, cover it tightly and let the mixture stand for at least 1 week before using.

INDIAN SPICE

MAKES APPROXIMATELY ¾ CUP

One 2-inch piece stick cinnamon   2 tablespoons whole
¼ cup cardamom pods   peppercorns
2 tablespoons cloves   1 tablespoon whole coriander
2 tablespoons cumin seed

Preheat oven to 250° F.

Combine all the ingredients in a heavy frying pan. Heat over very low flame, stirring occasionally, for 15 minutes, or in the preheated oven for 15 minutes. Remove the cardamom seeds from the pods and combine them with the other spices. Break the cinnamon into smaller pieces and pulverize the mixture in a blender. Store the spice in an airtight container and use to flavor curries.

ONION SPICE

MAKES ½ CUP

Use to season lamb.

¼ cup dried onion flakes   1 tablespoon pepper
1 tablespoon ground cumin seed   1 tablespoon basil
1 tablespoon garlic powder

Combine all the ingredients in a bowl and store in an airtight container.

SPICED PEPPER

MAKES ½ CUP
Use for roasts and steaks.

¼ cup mixed black and
   white peppercorns
2 tablespoons thyme
1 tablespoon ground caraway seed

1 tablespoon sweet Hungarian
   paprika
1 teaspoon garlic powder

Combine all the ingredients in a bowl and store in an airtight container.

SWEET SPICE

MAKES APPROXIMATELY ¼ CUP
Use to flavor gingerbread and other sweet things.

1 tablespoon cinnamon
1 tablespoon ground ginger
1½ teaspoons allspice

1½ teaspoons nutmeg
1 teaspoon ground cloves

Combine all the ingredients in a bowl. Store the spice in an airtight container.

MEXICAN CINNAMON SUGAR

MAKES 1 CUP

Use to sprinkle over warm puddings and custards.

> *1 cup superfine granulated sugar*
> *1 tablespoon cinnamon*
> *1 tablespoon cocoa*

Sift all the ingredients together into a bowl. Store the sugar in an airtight container.

VANILLA SUGAR

MAKES 1 CUP

In a blender blend 2 vanilla beans for 1 minute or until they are pulverized. Add 1 cup superfine granulated sugar and blend the mixture for 1 minute more, or until it is well combined. Transfer to a glass jar and seal with its lid. Sift the sugar before using it. Keeps indefinitely, sealed. Sift over cakes and cookies and use to flavor sweet batters.

COCKTAIL SAUCE

MAKES APPROXIMATELY 6 QUARTS

26 pounds ripe tomatoes,
  peeled, seeded and chopped
4 onions, grated
2 large cloves garlic, mashed
  to a paste with ½ teaspoon salt
2 cups cider vinegar
1½ teaspoons sugar
2 tablespoons salt
4 teaspoons English dry mustard
4 teaspoons pepper
½ teaspoon ground allspice

½ teaspoon cayenne
¼ teaspoon ground cloves
Spice bag containing 5
  tablespoons mustard seeds
  and 3 tablespoons celery seeds
Juice and rind of 1 lemon
¼ to ½ cup grated fresh horseradish, or to taste
¼ cup lemon juice
Tabasco sauce to taste

Put the tomatoes into a jamming pan. Add the onions and garlic paste and cook over moderate heat until the tomatoes are reduced to a thin purée. Add the cider vinegar, sugar, salt, mustard, pepper, allspice, cayenne, ground cloves and the spice bag. Add the lemon juice and rind and bring the sauce to the boil. Simmer it, stirring occasionally, for 1 to 3 hours or until it has thickened. The cooking time depends on the amount of water in the tomatoes. Remove the spice bag and the lemon rind and discard them. Stir in the grated horseradish, the ¼ cup lemon juice and Tabasco sauce to taste. Pour into sterilized preserving jars and seal with their lids.

CRANBERRY KETCHUP

MAKES APPROXIMATELY 2 QUARTS

1 pound cranberries
2 cups water
1½ cups cider vinegar
5 cups granulated sugar
5 cups soft brown sugar

2 teaspoons cinnamon
1 teaspoon salt
¾ teaspoon ground cloves
¾ teaspoon ground allspice

In a large saucepan combine the cranberries, water and cider vinegar. Bring the liquid to the boil and simmer for 5 to 7 minutes, or until the cranberries have popped and are soft. Force the mixture through a sieve into a bowl, pressing the pulp through the sieve with the back of a spoon. Discard the skins. Stir the white and brown sugar, cinnamon, salt, ground cloves and ground allspice into the purée. Transfer to a saucepan and bring it to the boil, stirring, over moderately high heat. Boil the mixture for 10 to 15 minutes, or until it has thickened slightly. Pour the ketchup into sterilized preserving jars and seal them.

FRESH TOMATO JUICE

MAKES APPROXIMATELY 4 QUARTS

18 pounds tomatoes, peeled
and coarse-chopped
1 large bunch celery,
including leafy tops, chopped
6 onions

3 green peppers, seeded
3 cups water
2 tablespoons soft brown sugar
1½ tablespoons salt

Put the tomatoes in a large jamming pan and cook them over moderately high heat, stirring occasionally, until they are soft. Force the pulp through a sieve into a bowl, discarding the seeds. Put the celery, onions and green peppers in a large saucepan and cook them in the water over moderate heat until they are soft. Purée the vegetables through the fine disk of a food mill or in a blender. In the jamming pan combine the tomato pulp, the vegetable purée, brown sugar and salt. Bring to the boil and cook over high heat for 5 minutes. Pour the hot juice into sterilized preserving jars and seal the jars with their lids.

MRS. ANTHONY HAMBRO'S LIQUEUR À L'ORANGE

2 pounds juicy oranges with thin skins
5 cups Cognac
1 stick cinnamon

1 pound superfine granulated sugar
5 quarts very fruity white wine

Preheat oven to 450° F.

Put the oranges in the preheated oven until brown. Allow to cool for 10 minutes, slice and leave to macerate for 3 weeks in the Cognac and cinnamon. Combine the sugar with a glass of water and boil until syrupy. Add to the wine. Add the oranges and Cognac, pressing the oranges with a wooden spoon to extract the juice. Keep in a cool place for 3 days, then press through a sieve and bottle the liquid.

SPICED CIDER VINEGAR

MAKES 3 PINTS
8 cups cider vinegar
½ cup peppercorns
¼ cup whole allspice

6 shallots, chopped
4 bay leaves
One 1-inch piece fresh ginger root

Combine all the ingredients in a bowl and allow the mixture to stand, covered, overnight or longer. Transfer to an enamel saucepan and simmer for 1 hour. Strain the vinegar and let it cool. Bottle it.

DISHES
PARTICULARLY
GOOD FOR
LARGE GROUPS

SOUPS

Artichoke Soup
Avocado Soup
Castilian Mussel Soup
Cold Borsch
Cold Curried Chicken and Apple Soup
Cold Curried Mushroom Soup
Cold Curried Vegetable Soup
Cold Orange and Carrot Soup
Cold Sorrel Soup

Cold Summer Soup
Crab Soup
Creamed Game Soup
Curried Pea and Avocado Soup
Dublin Mussel Soup
Garlic Soup
Gazpacho Soup
Green-Bean Soup
Green-Pepper Soup
Jellied Cucumber Soup
Lemon Ale Soup
Lentil Soup
Shrimp and Corn Chowder
Thin Chestnut Soup
Tomato and Dill Soup
Tomato Soup with Basil
Vegetable Soup with Garlic

FIRST COURSES

Avocado and Caviar Mousse
Avocado Ramekin
Cheese Puffs with Herbed Tomato Sauce
Chicken Liver and Caper Pâté
Cream Cheese and Ham Ramekin
Curried Melon and Shrimp
Deviled Sardines
Egg Mousse
Eggplant with Ginger and Sesame Seeds
Gingered Tuna Puffs
Kipper Pâté
Marinated Mussels
Pâté with Olives, Pine Nuts and Prosciutto
Potted Cheese
Scallops and Mushrooms in Lemon Dressing
Spinach Quiche
Taramasalata

FISH

Cold Salmon with Piquant Mayonnaise
Crab Cakes
Kedgeree
Salmon and Sole Paupiettes
Smelts Provençale

GAME AND POULTRY

Baked Cinnamon Chicken
Chicken Hashed in Cream
Chicken Livers in Devil Sauce
Chicken Rouxinol
Circassian Chicken with Kasha
Roast Stuffed Turkey
Viennese Fried Chicken with Sweet and Sour Sauce

MEAT

Baked Spareribs
Baked Virginia Ham
Barbecued Steak
Beef Ragoût with Bread Dumplings
Cranberry Beef Stew
Derek Hart's Stew
Gingered Lamb Stew
Honey-Glazed Spareribs
Lamb in Peach Sauce
Spiced Beef
Veal Goulash
Yugoslavian Beef Stew

VEGETABLES

Almond Wild Rice Pilaf
Brussels Sprouts with Chestnuts
Curried Corn and Onions
Deviled Parsnips
Etuvée de Céleri Rave
Fennel, Mushroom and Tomato
Fried Snow Peas
Gingered Carrots
Herbed Rice
Honey-Glazed Carrots and Onions
Hungarian Mixed Peppers
Lima Beans with Garlic
Lima Beans with Salami and Ham
Lima Beans with Sour Cream
Moroccan Rice
Mushroom Rice
Parsleyed Rice
Parsnips in Rosemary
Peas with Mushrooms and Celery
Peas with Prosciutto
Pesto with Rice
Red Cabbage with Chestnuts
Rice and Peas
Spiced Rice
Spinach with Rosemary and Pine Nuts
Spinach with Sorrel
Stuffed Potatoes with Duxelles and Chicken Livers
Sweet and Sour Parsnips
Vegetables with Aïoli Sauce

DESSERTS

Blackberry Sorbet
Blueberry Sour-Cream Pie
Burnt Ice Cream

Coeur à la Crème with Raspberries
Fresh Strawberry Sorbet
Frozen Lime Soufflé
Frozen Orange Mousse
Gingersnap Pudding
Green Grapes in Cognac
Hazelnut Crêpes with Strawberry Butter
Iced Cranberry Soufflé
Lemon Crêpes
Lime Sorbet
Mousse au Chocolat
Old English Plum Pudding
Peaches with Raspberry Syrup
Peach Ice Cream
Peach or Nectarine Sorbet
Pineapple and Blueberry Trifle
Pistachio Soufflé
Raspberries and Honey Cream
Red-Currant Mousse
Strawberries à l'Orange

LUNCHEON OR SUPPER DISHES

Brown Beans and Bacon
Fettucine with Pesto
Ham Jambalaya
Paella
Sausages with Lima Beans and Dill
Scrapple
Vegetable Curry
Wild Rice with Mushrooms in Cream

SALADS

Bean-sprout Salad
Chickpea Salad

Cucumber and Yogurt Salad
Lentil and Sausage Salad
Marinated Sweet Red Peppers and Mushroom Salad
Mushroom Salad with Green Sauce
Rice Salad
Spinach and Mushroom Salad with Bacon Dressing
Yogurt and Spinach Salad

DISHES COOKED
IN UNDER
ONE HOUR

SOUPS

Apple and Wine Soup
Avocado Soup (plus chilling time)
Cold Curried Chicken and Apple Soup (plus chilling time)
Cold Curried Vegetable Soup (plus chilling time)
Cold Orange and Carrot Soup (plus chilling time)
Cold Sorrel Soup (plus chilling time)
Cold Summer Soup (plus chilling time)
Creamed Game Soup
Curried Pea and Avocado Soup (plus chilling time)
Garlic Soup (plus chilling time)
Gazpacho Andaluz (plus chilling time)
Green-Bean Soup

Green-Pepper Soup (plus chilling time)
Gruyère Soup
Lemon Ale Soup
Mushroom Consommé (plus soaking time)
Onion Soup
Quick Greek Lemon Soup
Shrimp and Corn Chowder
Shrimp Soup
Spinach Soup
Tomato and Dill Soup (plus chilling time)
Tomato Soup with Basil (plus chilling time)

FIRST COURSES

Avocado and Caviar Mousse (plus chilling time)
Avocados with Hot Sauce
Chicken Liver and Caper Pâté (plus chilling time)
Curried Cream Cheese and Ham Ramekin (plus chilling time)
Curried Melon and Shrimp
Deviled Sardines
Egg Mousse (plus chilling time)
Herbed Eggs Mornay
Kipper Pâté (plus chilling time)
Mushroom Caviar (plus chilling time)
Oeufs Chimay
Oeufs en Cocotte with Duck Jelly
Oeufs en Cocotte with Sour Cream
Oeufs en Cocotte with Truffles
Polish Baked Mushrooms
Potted Cheese
Scallops and Mushrooms in Lemon Dressing (plus chilling time)
Taramasalata (plus chilling time)

FISH

Baked Trout with Garlic Butter
Baked Trout with Hazelnuts

Baked Trout with Tarragon
Broiled Herring Roe
Broiled Marinated Mackerel (plus marinating time)
Crab Cakes
Crab Mousseline in Scallop Shells
Fresh Herring Baked in Beer
Kedgeree
Salmon and Cucumber en Brochette
Salmon Steaks in Caper Sauce
Shrimp Fondue
Smelts Provençale (plus chilling time)
Spiced Shrimp en Brochette (plus marinating time)
Stir-Fried Shrimp and Peas

GAME AND POULTRY

Broiled Duck with Molasses Marinade (plus marinating time)
Chicken Hashed in Cream
Chicken in Yogurt Marinade (plus marinating time)
Chicken Livers in Devil Sauce
Chicken Livers in Madeira Sauce
Ginger Chicken (plus marinating time)
Roast Wild Duck
Quail Flambé
Viennese Fried Chicken with Sweet and Sour Sauce

MEAT

Filets Mignons with Mustard Sauce (plus marinating time)
Fondue Bourguignonne
Herbed Rack of Lamb
Kidneys in Cream and Calvados
Lamb and Veal Kebabs (plus marinating time)
Lamb Chops en Papillote
Marinated Calves' Liver (plus marinating time)
Marinated Lamb Chops (plus marinating time)

Pork Medallions with Mustard-Cream Sauce
Steak au Poivre (plus marinating and chilling time)
Veal Kidneys in Port

VEGETABLES

Baked Tomatoes with Sesame Seeds
Beet Greens Vinaigrette
Broccoli with Pine Nuts and Capers
Broiled Deviled Tomatoes
Buttered Beets with Tarragon
Cabbage and Bacon
Caraway Potatoes
Cauliflower with Herbs
Chopped Cabbage in Egg and Lemon Sauce
Curried Corn and Onions
Deviled Parsnips
Étuvée de Céleri Rave
Fried Parsley
Fried Snow Peas
Gingered Carrots
Glazed Onions
Herbed Rice
Honey-Glazed Carrots and Onions
Hungarian Baked Sprouts
Hungarian Mixed Peppers
Leeks
Lima Beans with Garlic
Lima Beans with Sour Cream
Moroccan Carrots
Moroccan Rice
Mushroom Rice
Orange-Glazed Beets
Parsleyed Rice
Parsnips in Rosemary
Peas with Mushrooms and Celery
Peas with Prosciutto

Pesto with Rice
Potatoes with Truffles
Rice and Peas
Salsify Buttered with Garlic and Herbs
Soufflé Potatoes
Spiced Mushrooms
Spinach with Rosemary and Pine Nuts
Spinach with Sorrel
String Beans Amandine
String Beans in Sour-Cream Sauce
Sweet and Sour Parsnips
Tomatoes with Choron Sauce
Turnips with Mushrooms
Wild Rice

DESSERTS

Baked Bananas in Orange
Blackberry Sorbet (plus chilling time)
Chilled Zabaglione (plus chilling time)
Crêpes Copacabana (if crêpes and ice cream are already made)
Fresh Strawberry Sorbet (plus chilling time)
Fruit-Stuffed Cantaloupe (plus chilling time)
Gingersnap Pudding (plus chilling time)
Ginger Soufflé
Green Grapes in Cognac (plus chilling time)
Iced Brie (plus chilling time)
Iced Cranberry Soufflé (plus chilling time)
Lemon Crêpes (if crêpes are already made)
Lime Sorbet (plus chilling time)
Mocha Parfait
Mocha Pots à la Crème (plus chilling time)
Mousse au Chocolat (plus chilling time)
Peaches with Raspberry Syrup
Peach Ice Cream (plus chilling time)
Peach or Nectarine Sorbet (plus chilling time)
Pistachio Soufflé (plus chilling time)

Raspberries and Honey Cream (plus chilling time)
Red-Currant Mousse (plus chilling time)
Strawberries à l'Orange
Wild Strawberries Carcassonne

LUNCHEON OR SUPPER DISHES

Cheese Soufflé
Eggplant with Crab Meat
Fettuccine with Pesto
Spinach Omelette
Swiss Cheese Fondue
Vegetable Curry
Welsh Rarebit
Wild Rice with Mushrooms in Cream

DISHES COOKED IN ONE TO TWO HOURS

SOUPS

Almond and Watercress Soup
Artichoke Soup
Castilian Mussel Soup
Chickpea and Spinach Soup (plus 24 hours' soaking)
Cold Borsch (plus chilling time)
Cold Curried Mushroom Soup (plus chilling time)
Crab Soup
Dublin Mussel Soup
Fennel, Egg and Lemon Soup
Hot Beer Soup (plus standing time)
Jellied Cucumber Soup (plus chilling time)

Oyster Stew
Vegetable Soup with Garlic

FIRST COURSES

Baked Stuffed Mushrooms
Cheddar Corn Soufflé
Cheese Puffs with Herbed Tomato Sauce
Crab Soufflé
Creamed Spinach
Dilled Crêpes with Smoked Salmon
Eggplant with Ginger and Sesame Seeds
Eggs in Tomatoes Florentine
Gingered Tuna Puffs
Marinated Mussels (plus chilling time)
Mushroom Soufflé
Pâté with Olives, Pine Nuts and Prosciutto (plus chilling time)
Peas with Eggs and Tomato Sauce
Spinach Quiche

FISH

Baked Salmon with Lemon Mustard Sauce
Cold Salmon with Piquant Mayonnaise (plus chilling time)
Creamed Halibut with Caviar
Fillets of Sole with Curry Sauce
Mackerel with Fennel
Mussels in White Wine
Poached Sea Bass
Salmon and Sole Paupiettes
Scallops and Bacon en Brochette
Herbed Shrimp in Garlic Butter

GAME AND POULTRY

Anthony West's Good Chicken Recipe
Baked Cinnamon Chicken (plus marinating time)

Broiled Pheasant with Deviled Butter Sauce
Casseroled Partridge with Port Wine Sauce
Chicken Rouxinol
Chicken with Chickpeas
Chicken with Lemon (plus marinating time)
Circassian Chicken and Kasha
Deviled Pheasant
Georgian-Style Pheasant
Lemon Chicken with Tarragon Sauce
Moorish Chicken and Rice
Pheasant in Boursin
Roast Duckling with Peaches
Roast Duck with Honey Butter (plus marinating time)
Saddle of Venison (plus soaking time)
Stuffed Squab

MEAT

Baked Spareribs
Baked Virginia Ham
Barbecued Steak
Cold Fillet of Beef with Sour-Cream Filling
Ham Croquettes
Honey-Glazed Spareribs
Honey-Marinated Roast Lamb (plus marinating time)
Lamb in Peach Sauce
Lamb with Cumberland Sauce
Osso Buco
Paupiettes of Veal on Pea Purée
Sautéed Veal Kidneys with Curried Rice and Peaches
Spareribs in Beer Marinade (plus marinating time)
Veal Goulash
Veal Roast

VEGETABLES

Almond Wild Rice Pilaf
Artichokes with Herbs

Baked Potatoes with Eggs
Brussels Sprouts with Chestnuts
Eggplant with Herbed Tomato Sauce
Fennel, Mushroom and Tomato
Lentils
Lima Beans with Salami and Ham
Mushrooms in Madeira and Cognac
Mushrooms with Grape Leaves
Parsnips with Madeira
Red Cabbage with Chestnuts
Stuffed Potatoes with Duxelles and Chicken Livers
Vegetables with Aïoli Sauce

DESSERTS

Burnt Ice Cream (plus chilling time)
Chestnut Soufflé
Frozen Lime Soufflé (plus chilling time)
Frozen Orange Mousse (plus chilling time)
Grand Marnier Soufflé
Hazelnut Crêpes with Strawberry Butter
Lemon and Parsley Ice (plus chilling time)
Lemon Crêpes (if crêpes are not already made)
Lemon Meringue Pie
Melon and Blackberries (plus chilling time)
Pineapple and Blueberry Trifle
Walnut Crêpes with Chocolate Sauce

LUNCHEON OR SUPPER DISHES

Brown Beans and Bacon (plus soaking time)
Crêpes Stuffed with Spinach
Ham Jambalaya
Paella
Sausages with Lima Beans and Dill
Vegetable Stew

DISHES COOKED
IN OVER
TWO HOURS

SOUPS

Lentil Soup
Pheasant Soup
Thin Chestnut Soup

FIRST COURSES

Avocado Ramekin
Eggplant Soufflé

FISH

Catalan Frogs' Legs with Piquant Sauce

GAME AND POULTRY

Broiled Gingered Squab
Jellied Pheasant Pie
Jugged Hare
Normandy Quail
Roast Pheasant with Chestnut Stuffing
Roast Stuffed Turkey
Truffled Turkey with Two Stuffings

MEAT

Baked Pork Chops
Beef Ragoût with Bread Dumplings
Carbonnade à la Flamande
Cranberry Beef Stew
Curried Leg of Lamb
Derek Hart's Stew
Gingered Lamb Stew
Orange-Marinated Pork
Spiced Beef
Stuffed Shoulder of Lamb
Stuffed Shoulder of Pork
Yugoslavian Beef Stew

VEGETABLES

Cabbage and Chestnut Purée
Onions Stuffed with Peas
Spiced Rice

DESSERTS

Apricot and Almond Soufflé
Blueberry Sour-Cream Pie
Bread Pudding with Bourbon Sauce
Coeur à la Crème with Raspberries
Crêpes Copacabana (if making crêpes and ice cream)
Date and Nut Pudding
Old English Plum Pudding

LUNCHEON OR SUPPER DISHES

Cheese Pudding
Scrapple

SUGGESTED
MENUS

Avocado and Caviar Mousse§

Ham Jambalaya
Mixed Green Salad

Cheese and Fruit

Egg Mousse§

Baked Cinnamon Chicken§
Broiled Deviled Tomatoes
Buttered Beets with Tarragon

§ Dishes that may be made in advance.

Bread Pudding with Bourbon Sauce

Polish Baked Mushrooms

Anthony West's Chicken
Onions Stuffed with Peas

Blueberry Sour-Cream Pie§

Avocados with Hot Sauce

Veal Goulash§
Herbed Rice§

Lime Sorbet§

Dublin Mussel Soup§

Veal Roast
Spiced Mushrooms

Hazelnut Crêpes with Strawberry Butter§

Scallops and Mushrooms in Lemon Dressing§

Lamb Chops en Papillote
Tomatoes with Choron Sauce
Gingered Carrots

Red-Currant Mousse§

Artichoke Soup§

Honey-Marinated Roast Lamb
Broccoli with Pine Nuts and Capers
Honey-Glazed Carrots and Onions

Green Grapes in Cognac§

Dilled Crêpes with Smoked Salmon§

Herbed Rack of Lamb
Moroccan Carrots, String Beans Amandine

Mocha Pots à la Crème with Praline Powder§

Mushroom Consommé§

Broiled Pheasant with Devil Butter Sauce
Red Cabbage with Chestnuts
Spinach with Rosemary and Pine Nuts

Crêpes Copacabana§

Mr. Brigg's Avocado Ramekin§

Salmon Steaks in Caper Sauce
Fried Parsley
New Potatoes

Lemon Crêpes§

Curried Melon and Shrimp§

Roast Duck with Honey Butter
Peas with Mushroom and Celery
Roast Potatoes

Ginger Soufflé

Cold Green-Pepper Soup§

Baked Virginia Ham
Red-Currant Sauce
Soufflé Potatoes
Spinach with Rosemary and Pine Nuts

Frozen Orange Mousse§

Baked Stuffed Mushrooms

Kedgeree§
Green Salad

Lemon Meringue Pie§

Tomato and Dill Soup§ (hot or cold)

Orange-Marinated Pork
Spiced Mushrooms
Spinach with Sorrel

Blackberry Sorbet§

Spinach Soup§

Chicken with Lemon
Mushroom Rice

Gingersnap Pudding§

INDEX

PAMELA HARLECH

Pamela Harlech was born in New York City and has worked for both American and British Vogue. Currently, she is a Contributing Editor writing a regular food column for British Vogue.

She is married to Lord Harlech, former British Ambassador to the United States.